PEOPLE OF THE
OLD MISSURY
Years of Conflict

PEOPLE OF THE OLD MISSURY

Years of Conflict

Nancy Mayborn Peterson

Illustrations by Asa Battles

RENAISSANCE HOUSE PUBLISHERS

A Division of Jende-Hagan, Inc.
541 Oak Street • P.O. Box 177
Frederick, CO 80530

Other books by Nancy M. Peterson

PEOPLE OF THE TROUBLED WATER
A Missouri River Journal

PEOPLE OF THE MOONSHELL
A Western River Journal

Copyright ©1989 by Nancy M. Peterson. Printed in the United States of America. All rights reserved. This book or any parts thereof, may not be reproduced in any manner whatsoever without the written permission of the publisher:

Renaissance House Publishers
A Division of Jende-Hagan, Inc.
541 Oak Street ~ P.O. Box 177
Frederick, CO 80530

First Printing September, 1989

Library of Congress Cataloging in Publication Data

Peterson, Nancy M., 1934-
    People of the Old Missury : years of conflict / Nancy Mayborn Peterson ; illustrations by Asa Battles.
        p. cm.
    Includes bibliographical references
    ISBN 1-55838-105-8 -- ISBN 1-55838-106-6 (pbk.)
    1. Missouri River Valley--History. 2. Indians of North America-Missouri River Valley--History. I. Title.
F589.P43 1989
978--dc20

89-10723
CIP

For Stephanie and Jamie,
who are the future.

Foreword

Historian Frederick Jackson Turner insisted that a period of American history had ended with the disappearance of the line of the frontier from the official maps of the nation in the early 1890s. The open country of the West, he pointed out in his "frontier hypothesis," had been a place of hope, of new opportunities, of second chances -- a laboratory of democracy where new ideas could be tried, such as Woman Suffrage, then in vogue only in the distant territory of Wyoming.

As the years rolled on, scholars modified the views of Frederick Jackson Turner. But the image of the frontier still lifted one's spirits. And even if after a century, the frontier no longer lured so many people physically toward the setting sun, still one could re-create the spirit of the old times by reading the tales of the people who crossed the wide plains, ascended the "Old Missury," crested hills that gave one a view "over the world," and breathed the invigorating air beneath pinnacles that pointed like white arrows into the blue sky.

The stories of the wide plains and distant mountains, of hunters and Scandinavian homesteaders, appeal today as do stories of no other section of our country or period of our history. Countless volumes responded to this interest. Some of these books stemmed from the research of scholars who uncovered new material or offered new interpretations in carefully documented treatises. Some were fictional re-creations solidly anchored in historic events and places.

Nancy Peterson offers her readers something different in her *People of the Old Missury*. She gives in her own words the story of a section of the West through the eyes of individuals who left their record. She tells of well-known people such as Sioux warrior Sitting Bull on the high plains and abolitionist John "Osawatomie" Brown in "Bleeding Kansas." We also see scarcely-known citizens such as Susan McCausland, a Virginia-born southern sympathizer who witnessed the first Civil War battle along the Missouri River at Lexington, Missouri in 1861; and Union Captain Henry E. Palmer, who did his best to stop the last major raid of Missouri Confederates at Westport in 1864, bringing the Civil War in the Missouri River region to a close. Through the eyes of these two the reader has a look at the conflict from an unexpected vantage far from Gettysburg or Shiloh.

The first two selections, that on artist Rudolph Kurz and surveyor Isaac Stevens, speak of the great missionary, Father De Smet, perhaps the most significant person of the Upper Missouri at the time. The reader presumes he will read more of De Smet, perhaps a sketch. Some readers might look for an account of one of the French mountain men, so important in the opening of the West. These stories and others pertaining to the earlier history of the Missouri are to be found in Peterson's preceding book, *People of the Troubled Water: A Missouri River Journal*, which covers the period from the late 1600's through 1850.

Academic historians might point to some more recent research on a given point or question an interpretation. Nancy Peterson's type of presentation avoids areas of controversy among professional historians, and sometimes simplifies complex matters. But that detracts little from the fascinating accounts of colorful and interesting people who went up the danger-filled Missouri over a century ago. Their story intrigues and fascinates. In reading Nancy Peterson's book the reader lives again the heroic days of the frontier. One can enjoy the book in continuous reading or, even more, in choosing an appropriate sketch for a given time.

William Barnaby Faherty, S.J.
Archivist, Missouri Province

Preface

In the early years of Missouri River history, the conflicts were elemental ones -- men struggled against the inconceivable power of the river itself, violent weather and a land which did not forgive mistakes. They filled their journals with epic stories of survival -- dodged logs flung like battering rams by the current, gasped to clear their lungs of its opaque water, strained to heave their loaded pirogues and keelboats another dogged step upstream, wept in exhaustion and despair when their strength failed the task.

They wrote of wild creatures which challenged their intrusion; grizzlies that roared through their nightmares, then materialized in broad daylight with a rage more fearsome than their dreams. They endured cold that struck to the bone marrow, wind that tore their breath away, distances so vast they overwhelmed the imagination and the will. Many left names that stalk through history larger than life: John Colter, Meriwether Lewis and William Clark, Hugh Glass, Daniel Boone; a testament to the lives they lived.

By the middle of the 19th century, the huge Missouri watershed had been in American hands for nearly 50 years, and time was beginning to work its changes. Not that the troubled waters of the river itself were transformed. They continued to sweep where and when they pleased, regularly denuding its shores and using the kindling produced to scour out its valley. Travelers still remarked on "a terror in its manner which is sensibly felt the moment we enter its muddy waters from the Mississippi." Most of them would have appreciated the irony, conscious or unconscious, in Daniel Boone's reference to the river as "the Old Missury." It was no kinder to steamers than to keelboats, and one roustabout, exasperated at efforts to find and follow its channel, declared that God had created the world in seven days, but he had not yet made up his mind *where* he wanted the Missouri River.

Nevertheless, change had come. By 1850 enough voyagers had braved its waters and planted themselves on its shores, probed the valleys it drained and sampled the mountains which gave it life, that the nicks in the wilderness were becoming clearings, the trading posts towns and the gardens fields. The small Siouian tribe which gave the river its name was already just a footnote in history, and the other river tribes no longer contemplated resistance.

But not all tribes were as malleable as those who farmed the river bottom. And the people who pushed up and across the Missouri from the east had very divergent goals and dreams. When Swiss artist Rudolph Kurz sojourned in the Missouri country from 1848 to 1852 he caught it on the cusp of change. He saw the beginnings of problems which would swell into bloodshed and color the history of the river for most of the next 50 years. These conflicts had a sharper edge, and the hurt they inflicted was keener and more lasting; for these conflicts were between man and man.

One would affect the life of farmer Jason Brown, glory-seeker Henry Palmer, Lexington belle Susan McCausland and body servant James Milton Turner. Another would catch gold seeker Fanny Kelly, teacher Helen Clarke, pilot Grant Marsh, Sitting Bull and Chief Joseph, the Ponca chief Standing Bear, reporter John Finerty and poet Elaine Goodman. Thrown against each other like cottonwood trees caught in the violence of the raging river, some people of the Old Missury splintered and disintegrated; others, though battered and torn, rode through the flood. Their stories, as individual as their faces, remind us how the currents of history can catch us all and sweep us irresistibly in directions never contemplated.

Table of Contents

Iron Eyes' Search for his Ideal 1
    Rudolph Kurz, 1848-52; Artist, adventurer to Fort Union
At War With Life 10
    Isaac Stevens, 1853; Survey of Northern Pacific railroad route
What Manner of Work it Was 19
    John Brown, Jr. and Jason Brown, 1856; Kansas Border Wars
A Name and a Brother 29
    Sitting Bull, 1856-57; Early life of Sioux chief
The Girl with the Flag 36
    Susan McCausland, 1861; The Battle of Lexington from Southern viewpoint
To the Golden Hills 43
    Fanny Kelly, 1864; Indian captive
The Winter of the White Woman 50
    Sitting Bull and Fanny Kelly, 1864; Continuation Sitting Bull, Conclusion Kelly
Deprived of Glory 58
    Henry E. Palmer, 1864; Battle of Westport from Northern viewpoint
Up the Rainwater Creek 65
    Grant Marsh, 1866; Steamboat captain up the Missouri
A Humble Niche 71
    James Milton Turner, 1866; Black educator in post-war Missouri
Of Neither World 78
    Helen P. Clarke, 1869; "Half-breed" school teacher in Montana
Goodbird's Mother 84
    Waheenee, Hidatsa woman, 1870; Continuation of Waheenee's story
Die Auswanderer 92
    Paul Tschetter, 1873-5; Hutterite immigrant in South Dakota
A Sad and Terrible Blunder 100
    Grant Marsh, 1876; Marsh's part in Custer battle
The Whence, the Why and the Whither 109
    Edward Drinker Cope, 1876; Paleontologist in Montana
The Great Spirit Looks Some Other Way 118
    Chief Joseph, 1877; Capture of Nez Perce band in Montana
Even an Indian 128
    Bright Eyes and Standing Bear, 1879; Case that declared Indians were people
Beyond the Stone Heaps 138
    John Finerty, 1879; Correspondent, Sitting Bull in Canada
Abode of Iron 146
    Teddy Roosevelt, 1880s; Ranching in North Dakota
A Conqueror with a Coupling Pin 156
    James J. Hill, 1887; Great Northern Railway
Chasing Crane's Story 164
    Elaine Goodale, 1889; Teacher involved in Wounded Knee
Traveling the New Way 175
    Goodbird, 1890s; Hidatsa Indian learns to farm
Epilogue 182
Bibliography 184
Index 190

Iron Eyes' Search for his Ideal

Jostled by the other passengers, Swiss citizen Rudolph Friedrich Kurz leaned eagerly against the rail of the steamer that carried him up the Mississippi River the morning of January 17, 1847. The air was cold, but clear enough that even his spectacled eyes had no trouble picking out the dome of the courthouse and the old stone tower which had marked St. Louis for nearly 70 years. Soon smoke from his boat's stacks was mingling with that of others as the pilot worked his way through the river traffic to the levee. Kurz, tense with expectation, waited impatiently to debark and find his future.

Where it lay he wasn't sure. Perhaps he would take the Santa Fe Trail to Mexico. He might cross the prairies to Fort Laramie and California. He might decide to boat on up the Mississippi. Or perhaps he would travel to the upper reaches of the Missouri. He was 29 years old and he had already spent 12 years preparing for this trip. But unlike his fellow Germans who crowded ashore with him, he was not looking for a corner to set up shop or a hill to hold a vineyard. He was an artist, and he was seeking the primeval forest and her inhabitants.

As he trudged up the cobblestoned slope from the levee, he was immediately taken with St. Louis. He was surprised at her size, nearly 75,000 people, and delighted with her energy and diversity. On February 15 he watched the parade that celebrated her 83rd birthday. Ancient Pierre Chouteau, five years older than the city, rode proudly in his carriage, escorted by four of the Indians whose trade had produced the family fortune. Mountain men, school children, Free Masons, Odd Fellows and militia men marched by. Bands played, bells clanged on spotless fire engines and sailors paraded with a model of the first steamboat to tie up at the levy just 30 years before.

That night, with bonfires and sky rockets lighting the streets, the surviving city father spoke of the early days when his half-brother, Auguste, and stepfather, Pierre LaClede, had founded the settlement on the Mississippi bluffs just below the Missouri's mouth. His speech had to be translated, for few of the newcomers spoke French anymore, and only a handful still made their living in the fur trade, but he was cheered roundly just the same.

Kurz made friends easily. Nearly one-third of the population had German roots and the old Spanish governor's house was now a German brewery. However, a job seemed out of the question unless he consented to paint houses. His heart set on more artistic subjects for his brushes, he headed up the Missouri in 1848.

The river was everything he'd expected. Its churning brown waters, swollen with spring rains, hid every kind of obstacle. The pilot, he knew, standing high above in the pilot house, was fiercely studying the water, watching for whirling tree trunks, embedded snags, sawyers that swung wickedly from banks and shallows -- hoping by a combination of skill and luck to get to his destination before his craft was impaled or his paddle wheel reduced to kindling.

This wild river colored the Mississippi, Kurz had noticed, contributing the silt and debris it had scoured from 2,500 miles of river bed in its rampage toward the sea. Had it been up to him, he'd have ended the Mississippi at the Missouri's mouth and given the lower river its name all the way to the gulf.

They passed the old French settlement of St. Charles, the hills supporting the vineyards of Hermann, the imposing state capitol building that reared on a cliff at Jefferson City, towns like Boonville that had bustled, then subsided, as the wagon outfitters moved on up the river to form their trains. He stood on the hurricane deck of the steamer, enjoying the richly wooded banks, broken now and again with bare cliff faces of streaked gray limestone. Gargantuan cottonwoods towered over clumps of willows, and sycamores, oaks, walnuts, and maples marched in a tangle of vines up the slopes. He'd not been disappointed in the primeval woods along the Mississippi and Missouri. Now he would see the Missouri's animals and people.

As long as he could remember, he'd been drawn to the primitive. The books he'd poured over as a child had been filled with virgin woods and stags, wild boars and unicorns, chamois and dragons. He'd determined early to devote his talents to portraying the aboriginal forests, their wild animals and people. For 12 years he'd willed himself to be patient as he worked both to support himself and perfect his technique of painting landscapes, animals and human beings. After consideration he'd decided on the North American Indian as the perfect subject to illustrate the beauty of primitive life.

"The dreams of my youth are to be realized. My life purpose in art is to be accomplished," he wrote in his journal as he docked at St. Joseph.

The settlement which had grown up around old Joe Robidoux's fur trading post was just six years old, but it already boasted substantial buildings. Red-brick businesses and homes lined the narrow streets which climbed the Black Snake hills above Robidoux's riverside rowhouses. The streets thronged with fur traders and immigrants, for this was now the jumping off place for Indian country, for Santa Fe, and for Oregon and California.

Kurz watched mountain men in their fringed and grease-stained buckskins unload bales of buffalo hides from up on the Platte or the Missouri. He sought them out, in the taverns and on the street, and peppered them with questions. Disarmed by his earnestness and open admiration, they were soon teaching him Indian sign language and coaching him on Indian customs.

He needed instruction, for there were Indians all around. He frequented the ferryboat landing, where Potawatomi, Fox, Kickapoo, Iowa and Oto gathered to cross to and from Indian Territory on the west side of the Missouri. Most of them, like the Americans, were emigrants, moved from their homes east of the Missouri by the government in order to open land for settlement. Many were pitching tipis now across the Missouri from St. Joseph so they could collect their share of the annual payment promised in treaties for their land.

Kurz was entranced. Though he knew these were no longer true savages -- they wrapped themselves in blankets now instead of buffalo robes, and passed the whiskey bottle while they waited for the ferry -- he found their forms and dress as superb as any Greek statue at the Parthenon.

"Forms more beautiful than those I found among the Iowa Indians I cannot imagine," he declared in his journal. He began crossing the river to visit their camp and before long he was a welcome guest in the lodge of a chief.

Toward the end of January 1849 the first two gold seekers appeared in town. Residents of St. Joseph had heard rumors of a strike in California months before, but most had not taken it seriously. These two men had no doubts. They'd driven a sleigh all the way from New York, intending to be the first to California.

Others were not far behind. After the river opened to navigation in the the middle of February the town was swamped with thousands of hopefuls. Kurz watched the wild scene on the waterfront as boat after boat unloaded horses, cattle, mules, wagons, carts and supplies. Soon every room was full, tents enough for an army surrounded the settlement, and any fenced lot became a stable.

The air dripped with their golden dreams. They might have nothing now, might have rumbling bellies and horses they couldn't afford to feed -- but when they came back they'd each have $50,000, at least! Gold could be scratched out of El Dorado with the fingernails. The inns rang with their songs of Californy as they waited with cheerful impatience for the grass to green so they could travel on. They brought life and excitement the village had never known.

They also brought cholera. One night Kurz woke to the shaking of his bed. His young roommate was racked with convulsions. In a few nightmarish hours he was dead.

Many of the townspeople fell to cholera -- in St. Louis they were sending wagons around to collect the dead -- but Kurz stayed healthy until June. Then he felt chilled in spite of the muggy heat and by night he was down with fever. For several days, without food or care, he sank in and out of delirium. Finally he awoke on the floor, clinging to the fireplace, unable to believe, at first, that his visions of the house falling in on him had been only a bad dream.

Gradually the fever passed, but his legs swelled with dropsy. He could scarcely walk or stand. As he watched his legs grow more gross, watched the fluid rise, he thought he couldn't bear to wait for death, to come so close to accomplishing his aims without achieving them. He contemplated suicide.

At last the fluid began to subside and

after three long months he was well again. He resumed his painting and cemented his friendship with the Iowa chief by marrying his daughter. For a few weeks he was happy in his house in St. Joseph with his graceful young wife. But the girl grew more and more homesick for her family and finally one night she disappeared. St. Joseph had lost its charm. Lonely and disillusioned, he cast about for a way to continue his work. In May 1851, he started up the Missouri again.

Once underway his spirits lifted. He would wait at Council Bluffs for the American Fur Company steamboat, he decided, and hope to buy passage north. They passed the spreading mouth of the Platte, threading in from the west among the numerous islands created by its sand-filled waters. The vegetation was sparser, now; the bluffs lower and more yellow. The land stretching away to the west was a monochrome of spring-green grass.

At Bellevue, just above the Platte, he went ashore to study a different type of Indian housing. The Omaha, like the Missouri tribe which gave the river its name, and the Pawnee farther west on the Platte, built sturdy, rounded earth lodges large enough to house extended families. They'd been in the area for some 200 years, tending their fields of corn and melons, leaving only a few months of the year to chase the buffalo.

White men had been visitors for more than 50 years; residents for nearly 40. Fur trade pioneer Manuel Lisa was said to have named the settlement for the view Kurz now enjoyed. As he left Peter Sarpy's Indian Agency and the missionaries' cabins and climbed the bluffs, he could see from the Platte's mouth on the south to the roofs of Kanesville across the river.

The sign language he'd learned stood him in good stead when he first approached the Omaha, but soon he discovered a woman who spoke both English and French, making communication easier. He also made friends with an intelligent young man named Joseph La Flesch. Son of a French trader and an Omaha woman, La Flesch had lived in St. Louis for a time. Now he worked for Sarpy, but he was much involved with the lives of his mother's people and had the honored seat next to Chief Big Elk in the Omaha councils.

While Kurz waited for the fur company steamer, he spent as much time as he could sketching the Omaha. He was much happier there than in Kanesville, which choked with gold-seekers just like St. Joseph. Kanesville had been founded in desperate times by the Mormons after intolerant mobs killed their prophet and burned their holy city of Nauvoo, Illinois in 1846. Now it was a gathering place for the Saints as they awaited the time they could follow Brigham Young on west to Zion. Their large camp called Winter Quarters, on the Omaha side of the river, was now marked only by the staring doors of deserted dugouts, a few crumbling chimneys and a sizeable graveyard.

Finally, on June 16, Kurz was focusing his telescope on the fur company's steamboat, and as soon as he could manage he was aboard. However, he discovered with horror that the boat he'd boarded was more a hospital than a cargo carrier. Cholera was here, too. Kurz' cabin was piled with the effects of those already dead.

As there was no doctor on board he found himself pressed into nursing duty for the blue-lipped, sunken-eyed, cramp-wracked victims. He administered the only remedy available, meal soaked with whiskey, while a Jesuit missionary, Father Van Hocken, offered the comfort of the church's rites.

They'd been underway for only two days when a torrential rain forced them to tie up under the bluff he was told held the grave of the infamous Omaha chief, Black Bird. Surrounded by the sick and dying, while rain hammered on the cabin, the lightning crackled, and the wind swept cargo from the decks, Kurz offered what care he could. It was as if the malevolent spirit of the sly, murderous chief yet held sway.

Two days later Father Van Hocken was dead. "He died as a Christian," Kurz wrote in his journal. "Had been sick only two hours. It was about four o'clock in the morning when I was awakened by his calling me. I found him, half-dressed, on his bed in violent convulsions. I called Father DeSmet. We anchored in the evening and buried him by torchlight... I had not sketched his portrait for Father DeSmet."

Though he could take no pleasure in the fact, the disease did Kurz some good. The clerk of the fur company succumbed, and the Swiss was asked to take his job. Now he could work for his passage and some badly needed funds.

They stopped to "wood" continually, and the able members of the crew spilled out to cut and load the countless cords necessary to fire the boilers each day. One stop was at the Niobrara, which cut in from the west through cedar-covered bluffs to deliver its swift, clear waters to the Missouri's murk.

The 4th of July they celebrated at Fort Pierre, lifting a toast -- or several -- to its founder, Pierre Chouteau, Jr., son of the patriarch Kurz had seen in St. Louis. On July 7, 1851 the artist ate his first buffalo steak. "One hundred and eighty years ago they were still to be found in the State of Ohio!" he noted. "Good-by buffaloes, Indians and fur companies."

The next day they were at Fort Clark, where Mandan lodges had sheltered a famous culture until the tribe was destroyed by a plague-spreading steamboat 14 years before. That boat had carried smallpox, and by the time the disease had run its course, there were scarcely enough Mandan left to count. Kurz entertained himself by using his glass to spy on a group of women bathing in the Missouri. The telescope his brothers had presented him as a going-away gift had never brought him more pleasure. The women were of the Arikara tribe, which had confiscated the village the weakened Mandan could no longer defend.

On July 9, he was considerably discomfited to learn he was to be left at Fort Berthold above the mouth of the Knife River while the steamer went on upriver. The small post had been established to trade with the remnants of the Mandan and their relatives, the Hidatsa. He stood on the barren bluff, watching the steamer depart for the country he wished to visit, then turned toward the inauspicious log post. He needed the job, he reminded himself. He could not be choosy.

The room he was assigned was lit only by one tiny, dirt-streaked window. The plank bed crawled with bedbugs. The mosquitoes were so insistent he could not hope to sleep until he had smoked his room by burning sagebrush.

But there were Indians! The handful of Mandan and the more numerous Hidatsa, offered him subjects he longed to paint. In a week he had mounted the dirt roof of the fort to study a Mandan funeral procession, and a few days later he witnessed the fervor of a scalp dance.

However, he had to be careful. The traders had told him the Mandan and Hidatsa were superstitious about paintings. They'd been visited by artists before, and nearly every time sickness followed the painter. The fur men warned him he might pay for any indiscretion with his life, so he observed them covertly and retired to his cabin to sketch.

To his consternation the Indians crowded into his cabin, admiring, in spite of their fears, his sketches of white men from the steamer. He could not hide the fact that he was an artist. But the fact that the steamer which brought him also carried cholera lent credence to their beliefs. When the Indians began to develop coughs and fever, and when everyone in the trading post except Kurz fell ill, they were sure he was to blame. Luckily that epidemic did not prove fatal. Kurz decided the sickness had been only colds or flu. He continued to keep a low profile, but he sketched in his room while cheerful, young faces crowded his small window to plea for sugar.

He liked the Hidatsa; thought them a magnificent people. "These Indians have a noble mien that is classic -- all around me are living models of the antique," he gloated to his journal. He listened to the little girls singing in the cornfields and watched the boys stalk frogs with grass-stem arrows. He hoped his studies would eventually enable him to accomplish his ideal -- "to create the human form in its highest perfection," complete with "high intelligence, a noble mind and ardent feeling." This ideal human must necessarily be primitive and be presented nude, with unself-conscious innocence, he believed. He'd found such innocence in the Indians.

Then suddenly on July 16 the wife of a chief was dead from cholera. Kurz knew her vomiting and spasms could come from no other cause; just a few days before they'd found time to unpack the bales from the steamer. Two days later others were dead; the artist was confined to his quarters and told to hide his sketches. The village talked of nothing else, the traders told him, and his life -- all their lives -- were in danger.

Confined, Kurz paced, frustrated at the loss of time and his subjects. Unable to do nothing, he finally blockaded the door to his room with the water tub while he sketched the interior of the fort.

As the days went by and the epidemic spread, all the Indians able to travel fled the plague. The old Indians, and those too sick to go, began to camp in the courtyard of the fort. Their dogs, and the flies and mosquitoes which followed them, made sleeping through the hot August nights impossible. Kurz watched one young squaw, blinded by the illness, beat her abdomen with her fists in hope of driving off the pain. Others writhed in agony. He could do nothing for them. With most of the Indians absent, and not knowing how long he'd be allowed to stay, he dared a visit to the village to sketch a burial scaffold and the Sun Dance pole.

On September 1, after learning the Hidatsa above them had lost 50 people and the Arikara below them were falling like flies at first frost, the bourgeois of Fort Berthold got rid of his bad luck charm by packing him off for Fort Union. With one companion and a poor horse, the artist started on the risky journey.

His soul stirred by the romance of the situation, Kurz was not overly concerned. He was going farther west, where he wanted to go, and he intended to wring the best from every moment. "Constant danger from lurking enemies, the vast prairie, bounded only by sky and sea; buffaloes and bears in prospect, perhaps a violent storm by way of variety; fine health and tense anticipation -- what more could I desire?" he asked his journal.

Wearing his innocence like a shield, he thrilled at the herds of buffalo and survived an enigmatic encounter with his "lurking enemies." At length safely within the huge log bastion of Fort Union, just above the mouth of the Yellowstone, he discovered some of the trappings of civilization still held appeal. The fur post had been famous for its civilized hospitality since the early 1830s and when he was ushered to the table of trader Edwin Denig, Kurz could see why. Milk, butter, omelets, fresh meat, hot bread and chocolate were spread before him. He nearly shed tears of joy; his meals at Fort Berthold had often consisted of dry meat and a piece of hardtack. He dug in with a will.

Established in a private room so spacious it actually held two chairs and a table, he thought with wry amusement about the first job Denig had assigned him. He was to paint the bourgeois' house. He didn't really mind. He was also to paint Denig's portrait, and he found the trader a mother lode of information about the Indians.

He knew he would see different Indians here -- Crow, Assiniboin, Cree and probably Blackfoot. "If I can spend my later life in the painting of pictures that portray the American Indian, if time and strength remain to me until I have realized my ideal, then my cherished aims will have been fulfilled," he wrote. Looking back on the long way he had come and the hardships he had survived so far, he began to feel he was fated to paint the American Indians.

He also began to play with the idea of staying permanently in the West. He felt so healthy, so contented. He rode out with the fort's hunter and envied his life -- the rides through clear streams and across the plains, the dreams beside a crackling fire. But he knew he lacked one important qualification for the job: good eyes. He needed his spectacles at all times and didn't venture onto the prairie without his telescope.

While the Indians who frequented Fort Union viewed his work without fear, they were astonished that he could produce paintings so like the persons who sat for him. They ascribed his talent to his magic spectacles. None of the other Whites wore spectacles, and none of them could paint. They called him Iron Eyes or Four Eyes. One brave wanted to buy the glasses, sure he would then own the magic skill. Unable to convince him otherwise, Kurz let him try on the glasses. When the landscape turned into a fuzzy blur the brave was even more astounded at the artist's medicine.

The artist would gladly have exchanged places. "What I would not give for a pair of Indian eyes," he wrote. Still, he reasoned, it was just as well the way it was. Given keen eyesight he might give up his artwork and remain in the wilderness.

For some weeks Denig kept Kurz' brushes busy. He decorated banners for the Indians with life-size eagles, and, da Vinci-like, spent an uncomfortable day on a scaffold to portray fur company owner Pierre Chouteau, Jr. on the gable above the gallery.

Then one painting brought trouble. Denig stopped in one day when the artist was working on his ideal feminine form and expressed his appreciation of the work. He wanted it for his reception room. Kurz found the bourgeois' comments and reaction to the painting obscene. "I know that I must accustom myself to this conclusion: There will always be ordinary people who see in the nude only physical attraction, not spirit," he fumed. When he refused the trader's request they had sharp words.

He also earned a sharp reprimand for wandering the prairie alone looking for animals to paint. He couldn't resist going, although it was usually fruitless. His thoughts were generally concentrated on artistic or philosophical concepts rather than tracks, and before his eyes could determine if the yellow spot in the distance was an antelope or a rock, the animal was alerted and gone.

As November advanced he had little time for wandering. He was no longer a visitor, but a clerk again, and the Indians were bringing in furs. He had charge of the gate keys, the press room where 20-some varieties of pelts were stored, the distribution of food, tools, vehicles and horses. He spent long, cold hours in the skiff, carrying Indians and hunters back and forth across the river. He was constantly struggling to respond to questions in Assiniboin, Crow, Hidatsa, Cree, Mandan, Blackfoot, English, French, Spanish and German. His head whirled as he tried to answer the demands. Denig, he thought, could happily work 100,000 men. He expected him to know the location of every "rope, every nail, tool, implement, stock, ring, saddle, nay, even every mouse in the fort," the artist complained bitterly to his journal.

Still, the trade goods he dealt out raised a certain nostalgia. There were bells and mirrors from Leipsig, pipes from Cologne, beads from Italy, calicos from France, and wool blankets and guns from England. With the sugar and coffee from New Orleans, knives from New York and powder from St. Louis, it was a cosmopolitan assortment.

Yet even on the upper Missouri, politics intruded. They had long discussions about the slavery question. Kurz believed such bondage was morally wrong, but he thought emancipation was not the answer.

"To declare them free men and yet refuse to treat them as such, to find them unendurable in personal contact, even to sit beside in the Church of God is damned hypocrisy!" he reasoned. He thought the best solution was to purchase their freedom and send them back to Africa. Where the money would come from, he didn't know, but he was convinced the issue was a menace to the Union. The only other solution he could imagine was a black revolution.

Kurz knew how ugly hate could be. His house in St. Joseph had been stoned by boys who'd been told he was too friendly with Indians and Negroes. And he'd been forced to fight several times when local toughs decided a bespectacled Dutchman was fair game.

There were heated discussions, too, about the Indians and the treaty recently completed at Fort Laramie. Thousands of Sioux, Cheyenne, Arapaho, Shoshone, Blackfoot, Crow, Assiniboin, Hidatsa and Arikara had gathered to listen to the government's agents and sign their paper. As recompense for the scar the hordes of gold-hungry emigrants had burned across Indian lands, they were promised annual payments as long as they stayed within the borders the white men set and kept the peace.

Kurz thought futility was written on every page. Even if the government kept its promises, which he doubted, he believed that "without war an Indian is no longer an Indian." War was his education, his only means of winning distinction; to renounce war would be to change his whole existence. Kurz could find few values in white society worth such a sacrifice.

As winter set in and the cold clamped down, tempers began to fray. Kurz reorganized the chaotic storehouses to suit his orderly nature, but he made mistakes out of ignorance and disinterest. "My day's work should engross my attention," he admitted to his diary. "Unfortunately, that is not true; art always occupies my best thoughts. Wherever I am, wherever I go, my eyes instinctively seek beauty of form and color..."

He loved the prairie in winter. "How soft, how harmoniously blended are the colors on the wide prairie, under a light covering of snow. Yellows and browns, black and rose, among the grasses and weeds with their gray seed pods, blended with the snow, give every variety of hue and shade."

But it was so cold the keys froze to his fingers. His watercolors, warmed before the fire, froze as he tried to apply them to the paper. His pigments crystallized on his porcelain palette. One of the men froze his feet and Kurz had to dress them, steeling himself to peel the blackened flesh from his toes.

They were out of sugar, and he was almost out of paper. Worse yet, there was not one whole pencil in the fort. One day the number of things he had yet to sketch boggled his mind; the next he was bored. By the end of February he was writing, "There remain yet four months to live through before the steamer arrives." Yet he knew he'd stay another year if given the chance. He had not yet had much opportunity to hunt.

On March 6, 1852, he wrote ecstatically that he was to go to the horse camp, 12 miles up the Missouri from Fort Union. With a Scottish hunter named Morgan, five yapping dogs and a gleeful heart, he set out.

He was sure he'd found an artist's paradise. Camped in the woods along the Missouri lowlands with three hunters and their Indian families, snug in a snow-banked tipi, he was at first too excited to sleep. "How tall the dark tree trunks seem in the gloom of the forest!" he wrote. "How glorious to smoke my pipe in that romantic place!" What hunts he would follow, what studies he would make, what pictures he would paint! For two weeks he happily followed the hunters on their quests, his only worry his diminishing supply of paper for his sketches.

But by March 18 he was learning the unromantic side of winter life on the prairie. Everything was clamped in ice. They could no longer hack their way down to running water in the river. All their drinking water had to be melted, either in a kettle over the fire or in their mouths. They were out of coffee and had nothing to eat but dried elk. Kurz, cold to the marrow of his bones, had never suffered such thirst. His paints were prisoners of the thermometer.

Then, almost overnight, everything melted. The river ice cracked and popped and the world was suddenly liquid. They sloshed through slush to a higher campsite but they underestimated the Missouri's reach. That night Kurz was awakened with the shout, "Water! Water!" By the time they had grabbed up their bedding and guns, they were waist deep in icy water. Tents and meat were forgotten as they half-swam to safety. On a windy hilltop the artist wrapped his valued sketches, journal and art supplies in the calfskin pouch he used as a pillow, stripped off his wet clothes and huddled on a buffalo robe with Morgan. The five dogs, called close for the warmth they could offer, provided a scratching, quarrelsome, noisy blanket.

They tried to find a campsite between the flooded bottom and the wind-scoured hilltops, but Kurz's shoes were not yet dry when the Yellowstone let loose its waters on top of the Missouri's ice. In two hours the water rose 20 feet. The trench of the river was now filled bank to bank. Chunks of ice, tree trunks, branches and brush tossed on roaring, foaming currents now 30 feet above their level of the day before.

Yet winter returned on the first of April with a violent north wind. The water froze just enough to provide an unreliable, pain-dealing crust which made walking all but impossible. Kurz woke to find everything inside the tent buried in snow. For the first time he began to long for the good food and warm apartment he'd left in Europe. Was anything worth this, he wondered? He reminded himself he'd come in search of just such experiences, but a blizzard on April 13 made him wonder again. In wind so fierce they could neither stand nor hear each other speak, the men struggled to weight down the skins of their tipi. They had crawled back inside and were just biting into a coveted roast goose when the gale snatched the tent from over their heads and whirled it away. Sparks and embers from the fire flew in all directions and their laps, robes, and cloaks were suddenly on fire. They scrambled over the prairie, stomping out the flames, grabbing for their possessions, beating out the sparks in the buffalo robes. Then they crowded into the one remaining tent and sat through the night, grateful for even this uncertain shelter.

As Kurz plucked his gray felt hat from a distant bush the next morning, he knew he had accomplished all he could on the Missouri. His research was done. His head was crammed with what he'd witnessed. Could he turn his rich cache of knowledge into paintings? Would anyone buy them if he did? Would the battle to support himself sap his strength and dim his enthusiasm for his great ideal? "Not that," he wrote. "I would rather die."

On April 19 he grasped an oar on the company keelboat and began the pull for St. Louis. Even though the boat rode the floodcrest, his hands were soon blistered and stiff with pain. He stopped for his possessions and quick good-byes at Fort Berthold and at Bellevue, where his old boarding house hung precariously over the eroded riverbank, and at St. Joseph, once more crowded with gold-seekers. On May 25 he was again in St. Louis.

He spent the summer fighting twin devils of dropsy and unemployment and, with deep regret, sold part of his Indian collection to finance a return to Europe. On September 22 he landed at Le Havre, his health further damaged by ague he suffered on the voyage; two days later he was home and closed his journal. "To earn my livelihood as an artist in Berne," he wrote. "Alas! What a prospect."

His forebodings were well-taken. Four years of effort produced voluminous sketches from his research but few paintings and fewer buyers. No one in Switzerland was interested in the gallery of Indian artifacts he'd envisioned. The critics thought his work untrue to life. In 1856 he took a job as a drawing master in a school, still confident that his trip up the Missouri had not been made in vain and hopeful that somehow, someway, he would finish the great work he envisioned.

Kurz met death before artistic success, dying at age 53 in 1871. But the engrossing journal he left of his Missouri years paints for each new reader a living portrait of the river's Indians, trappers, travelers and settlers he had longed to portray.

At War With Life

While men like Kurz admired all that was primeval in the Missouri country and longed to preserve it, others had entirely different values and ambitions. They looked at buffalo and saw hides, looked at prairie grass and saw cribs of grain, looked at tipis and saw courthouses and church steeples. Their packs were filled with barometers, odometers, compasses and sextants, their daily journal entries with longitudes and latitudes.

The small man surveying the chaos of his camp at Lake Amelia, Minnesota on May 29, 1855 was first moved to explosive anger. He had no tolerance for inefficiency, no patience with wasted time. The scene before him was born of the first and promised the second, but as he watched the picket line explode into a jumble of 200 braying, bucking, kicking mules, and saw man after man sail from his mount to go splat in the mud, even he had to laugh.

Whether the army quartermaster at St. Louis had furnished his expedition with untrained mules out of ignorance, indifference, or malevolence made no difference now. Isaac I. Stevens, mathematical child prodigy, valedictorian of his West Point class, veteran of the Mexican War, chief of the Northern Pacific Railroad Survey, Superintendent of Indian Affairs of Washington Territory and soon-to-be Governor of Washington Territory would surmount the difficulty. It took him only a little pondering to decide how. His decision broke precedents and would stamp on feelings, but he was used to that.

Many of his 111 men had seen him for the first time the morning before, when, just arrived in camp, he'd rousted them out of bed at 4:30 a.m. and given them a taste of how things were going to be on this survey for the northern railroad. His second morning in camp they'd gotten the word about the mules. Each man would handle his own mount. It did not matter if they were army or civilian, if they were trained riders or unschooled, if they were scientists or artists or doctors or clerks. They would catch, saddle, feed and care for their own mounts every day from now on.

The man who gave these orders, to civilians and soldiers alike, was no longer a soldier and did not have a military look. He was more than a head shorter than most of them, his muscular torso supported on legs left stumpy by childhood illness. When he walked his stride was further hampered by a foot damaged at Chapultapec, a war souvenir that still made him limp in spite of a built-up boot. He wore a red flannel shirt and clapped a slouch hat on a head that looked too large for his small body. But his voice and manner were unmistakably commanding.

Only the mules were unimpressed.

Brought 20 at a time into the corral, they dragged erstwhile riders through the muck and fought the lariats until they were exhausted enough to be saddled. The relative quiet was shattered when 20 bottoms met their backs and each mule set about clearing the saddle as he thought best. They whirled, jumped, kicked, climbed on each other, and tangled themselves and their neighbors in lariats and picket ropes until every creature in the moving mass was lathered with Minnesota mud. Some threw their riders immediately. Others took off across the meadow to brush off the annoying weight against a branch of a scrub oak. Still others lay down on the offending presence. After an hour or two, 20 riders took their cuts and bruises to the doctor's tent; another 20 tried their luck in the saddle. Surprisingly the only serious injury was a shoulder so out of place it took three men to slip the bone back into the socket.

Stevens put up with the chaos for a week while he waited for replacements for barometers that had been broken in shipment. Then they were on their way, ready or not.

If there were some questions about the men and the mules, there was no question about Stevens. He had always been ready. He leapt for a challenge like a trout for a fly. If there were no challenges he created his own, setting himself to learn to run three looms in his uncle's Massachusetts mill when he was 10, deciding at 17 he must be first in every subject in his West Point class.

"Surely 12 hours of study per day ought to injure no one of a sound constitution," he had assured his worried sister. Then he'd added an independent reading program, a mathematics assistantship, debate society and school newspaper publishing to his activities.

Characteristically, he was now taking on three jobs at once. He was giving up the brevet major rank he'd earned in the Mexican War and his work with the Corps of Engineers to choose and survey a 2,000-mile railroad route from the Mississippi to Puget Sound.

Once across the Rockies he would become, at age 34, the first governor of the newly created Washington Territory and superintendent of Indian affairs in that undeveloped corner of the West.

For the survey, he had designed a three-pronged attack. One small group, including fur trade veteran Alexander Culbertson, whom Stevens had hired to help him deal with the Blackfoot, was steaming up the Missouri and would rendezvous at Fort Union with his own party moving overland from St. Paul. A third group was working its way inland from Puget Sound to meet the combined eastern forces between the Cascade Range and the Rocky Mountains.

However the survey was to do more than run a continuous compass and odometer line. Small parties were to explore widely within 250 miles of the line. The survey was to examine the mountain passes in both ranges between the 49th parallel and the source of the Missouri, determine the navigability of the Missouri and the Columbia, and collect all possible information on the geology, climate, topography, flora and fauna. They were also to gather information on the culture of the Indians along the route and cultivate their friendship. And they were to be finished in one season.

Stevens had not only volunteered for the job, he had drawn up the specifications. He believed a proper survey would allow the government to plan orderly growth in the Northwest; that choosing the right routes for railroads and roads would foster sensible patterns of settlement and intelligent Indian policy. He'd searched out books about the Russian steppes. Then he'd hired a meteorologist, two astronomers, a naturalist, two civil engineers, a topographer and artist John Mix Stanley, who would record the sights both in sketches and with a daguerreotype camera. True to his nature, he'd designed a survey that would produce a grand treatise on the whole region.

Now all his ambitious plans were threatened by some balky Missouri mules. He would not have it. Evidently the mules were getting the message. They provided an eye-opening start to every day, but as the corps moved west across rain-soaked Minnesota meadows, they became less a hindrance than the weather.

On June 12 Stevens announced another unprecedented decision. Faced with mile upon mile of bottomless trail, he eliminated the division of labor. Soldiers would do more than escort, he informed them. Scientists would do more than collect. Each man would do his part in the labor of the trail; there would be no privileged class. The soldiers would bend their backs with the teamsters. All would go armed, and the scientists would stand guard with the soldiers. All would put their shoulders to the wheel to push the wagons through the muck. And he wanted the men to know that ahead lay not only 180 more miles of bog and marsh before they reached higher ground, but rivers to be forded and bridged, mountains and valleys to be crossed. They'd soon be in Indian country, where they'd have to guard their property. Then came Blackfoot country, where they'd have to guard their lives. Then the mountains and their snow. He would not ask them to do anything he would not do, but he expected obedience. All would be given rank so that orders could be carried out with dispatch and without question. Did anyone want to turn back? He waited, but no voice broke the silence.

Replacements for the indispensable barometers had finally caught up with them and now Stevens needed only one more element to complete his train. That afternoon they heard it coming. A chorus of unearthly, hair-raising squeals grew louder and more unbearable until finally five Pembina carts pulled into camp. The men stared and went into fits of laughter. Before them stood the poorest excuse for a wagon they could imagine. A rickety box was balanced between two spoked wooden wheels. An ox was yoked on each side of the protruding axle. The driver walked alongside. That was all there was, once the hellish noise of the unlubricated wheels was silenced.

Even Stevens had to wonder. The carts looked as if they were made to collapse the moment you got to your destination. If you got there. It seemed incredible the shrieking wheels could last any time at all. But he knew the mixed-blood fur trappers from the Red River Valley near the Canadian border trekked regularly to St. Paul with their catch. If Pembina carts worked for them, they would work for him.

Work they did. The army wagons bogged down continually the next few days, forcing them to unload, push out and load again. They spent hours scything grass and cutting willows to pad the trail, sometimes needing a rope and the combined strength of the mules and every available man to work across a slough. Meanwhile the carts squealed along without aid, their wheels kept on the surface of the mire by buffalo skins wrapped around the rims.

Even the hard-driving Stevens admired the voyageurs he'd hired to transport the expedition. "They are just the men for prairie life," he wrote in his journal, "going into water as pleasantly as a spaniel and remaining there as long as needed...no slough or bog deters them."

Some of his own men were a different matter. By the time they'd reached Lightning Lake on June 22 he'd sent three army men back to the settlements for failure to perform their duties satisfactorily, and he'd faced a strike by the teamsters for dismissing a half-dozen of their number.

He was conscious of the need to tighten his organization, for the country and the obstacles were changing. Flat marsh and frequent streams were falling behind them. They were beginning to climb. Ahead the ground rose in grassy, stone-topped hills and plunged into valleys. Ahead were the buffalo. And the Sioux. He tightened the guard, reassigned his men, issued new regulations. Cook fires would be lighted at 2 a.m. The cooks and teamsters up at three o'clock and the animals set to graze. Reveille would be at 4:00 and tents would be struck at 4:30. They would move out by 5 a.m. Sentinels would fire on any prowling Indians.

The next day the camp roused at 4:00, as ordered. He was at breakfast in his tent when a young lieutenant stuck his head in the door and informed him he had four minutes to finish breakfast. He was still eating at 4:30 when the tent came down on his head. The train moved at 5 a.m. He was delighted.

For once his urgency was not self-imposed. They were already low on food. The carts held only half what they needed to reach Fort Union. He'd already ordered rations reduced and the men had nearly rebelled. He'd tempered their anger by assuring them the game country that lay ahead would supply them with plenty. While he was confident it would, he took stock of the flour supply as they camped below the buttes of the Sheyenne River on July 9. It had shrunk alarmingly. He cut the men to one-half cup a day.

Then, on July 10, pushing ahead of the train as he often did, he topped a rise in the prairie and looked out on an ocean of buffalo. He was awe-struck. There had to be 200,000 in view -- some of the men thought as many as half a million. However many, Stevens wrote in wonder, "they surpassed anything I could have imagined."

He had issued orders there would be no firing from the line of march, so the dragoons could only drool. The professional hunters he employed had a wagonload of meat for them in an hour. A couple of the troopers couldn't resist a brief foot chase after a nearby straggler. They were quickly outdistanced, but their dog had a heyday, racing hysterically after the retreating herd. However, they found out there could be too many buffalo. That night a herd moved on the camp and it was all the men could do to keep their animals from stampeding. The next day several head ran into the herd and proved impossible to recover.

The day's march was almost over on the 12th when Stevens met disaster. A herd of buffalo took fright, whether from the train or some other cause he never knew. In seconds they were a thunderous, rolling mass that threatened extinction to everything in their path. They headed directly toward the expedition. Stevens threw himself into position to begin a deflecting fire. As he hit the ground he felt something tear in his groin. Denying the pain, refusing to acknowledge what he knew had happened, he kept firing until his shots and those of the other men had turned the herd.

He knew, as he was helped back into camp, that his old rupture had torn again. It had first given way in the family hayfield when he was 12 and determined to prove to his stern father that he could outwork any man. It put him in a truss for life, but he'd not allowed it to restrict his activities. The rupture had reopened in the Mexican War six years before and he'd promised himself he'd be less impetuous and headstrong, demand less of his body. Now he was disabled again, with his expedition barely into Dakota. It was unspeakably frustrating. He would have to ride in the ambulance.

The weather that night matched his mood. The expedition was deluged with rain. Twice cook fires were lit only to be drowned before the meal was done. The endless supply of buffalo chips they now depended on lay soggy and useless. He couldn't sleep for the pain. He was facing more than 1,500 miles of travel over plains and mountains, much of it in a jolting wagon, but the thought of turning back never entered his mind. "We have duties to perform, trials to encounter, victories to achieve," he had written his wife two years before. "Life is a warfare. We must contend with evil. We must accomplish good."

His evil now was pain. He would not yield to it.

Morning brought a surprising fog and a new worry. He'd sent civil engineer Tinkham off on a side exploration and he and his two men had not returned. Stevens had known Tinkham for 10 years and had recruited him for this expedition. That night in camp on the James River, he ordered rushes collected for a huge signal fire, but they heard nothing from the missing men.

At dawn he had the howitzer fire three rounds and delayed the start. No one appeared.

He could feel unease invade the camp. Many of the men were convinced the Indians had got the three men and they'd not be returning. But they could have lost their animals, lost the trail, been slowed by injury. How could he be sure? He decided to leave 10 men and the howitzer to keep signaling while the main party moved on up the James 20 miles. He spent another sleepless night, his groin throbbing, while mosquitoes impacted the tent sides like rain and thrummed relentlessly in his ears.

On July 15 he delayed again, hoping Tinkham might be found. Though he was too ill to be up and about, he saw the time was put to use shoeing the animals and rearranging the wagonloads. It was near noon when scouts returned, but they had no news of Tinkham.

Instead, they reported excitedly that a thousand lodges of Sioux were less than nine miles away. Expecting the Indians might be Red River half-breeds or friendly Sioux looking for gifts, Stevens prepared to visit their camp.

No, the scout insisted. They were hostiles. They were surely responsible for Tinkham's absence, and now they were moving to surround the train. Stevens ordered ammunition distributed and the train made ready to move to a more defensible position. Before they could get underway, another scout rode in shouting that Indians were already approaching. White with pain, Stevens forced himself onto his horse and rode to meet them.

It was a false alarm. They were Red River hunters, after all. The peaceable 1,300 mixed bloods from near Pembina penetrated the Missouri plains twice a year to hunt buffalo. There would be feasting, not fighting. Later in the day, when news came in that Tinkham was safe after all, tensions were released in heartfelt cheers.

The expedition moved on, through miles that stunk of the carcasses from the Red River hunt, to cross the headwaters of the Sheyenne River and enter the drainage basin of the Souris. One straight ridge they traveled for several miles reminded Stevens of nothing so much as a railroad embankment. He thought it beautiful.

On July 22 the Coteau du Missouri was in sight. The gullies were wooded now and deep, measuring at 54, 82, 108 feet below the prairie. On July 27 Stevens was welcomed into camp by a delegation of Assiniboin, a plains people who claimed the territory north of the Missouri into Canada. Twelve hundred of their number were camped nearby, and he and his staff walked over for a talk that evening.

It was the first wild tribe the new Superintendent of Indian Affairs for Washington Territory had ever seen. He had read omnivorously -- Lewis and Clark, Washington Irving, Father DeSmet, Nicollet and every other source he could find. He had interviewed everyone he could who knew the plains. Now he would have to put his book learning to the test.

As he entered the encampment, the engineer's first impression was of barking dogs. They came from in or around every lodge, jostling each other and brushing against the poles of the drying racks. Scores of women and children appeared in their wake, their faces curious. Stevens at first thought the camp prosperous, with numerous horses and racks full of drying skins and meat. But when he studied the people's meager and worn clothing he changed his mind and judged them all "filthy and miserable."

Later, seated on a pile of skins in the back of a great lodge erected for his visit, he managed to restrain his impatient habit of saying whatever he had to say as fast as possible. Knowing the Indians would conduct no business before the proper ceremonies had been observed, he watched as they lit a braid of grass, passed the pipe through its sacred smoke, then lit the pipe. Following the interpreter's lead, he took his turn in smoking the elaborate pipe as it was passed around the circle to more than 60 leaders of the tribe.

Then it was time for food. The Indians gladly treated their guests to a rich buffalo and turnip stew. Only after the meal, with the customs of hospitality observed, did the chief rise to speak. He shook hands with each visitor and began to tell the white men what was on his mind. He knew why the white men were there, he told Stevens, and he was worried. His people were observing the Fort Laramie treaty, he said, but the Sioux were not respecting either the Assiniboin hunting grounds or the peace.

The Great Father of Life had given his people this land to live upon and the buffalo to provide their food and clothing. But the Indians could see the buffalo were disappearing. As the white man came closer, things could only get worse.

"We hear that a great road is to be made through our country," he said. "We do not know what this is for, we do not understand it, but we think it will drive away the buffalo."

Stevens, impressed with the chief's dignity, noted his eloquent gestures and his apparent facility with language. He listened intently to the interpreter.

"We like to see our white brothers," the chief was saying, "we like to give them the hand of friendship; but we know that, as they come, our game goes back. What are we to do?" He shook hands around the circle and returned to his seat. Then, after a considerate pause, he asked for Steven's reply.

Stevens tried to reassure him. The road to the Pacific would not injure the Indians in any way, he told them. The whites who would settle along the line would drive off the buffalo, it was true, but they would bring other goods the Assiniboin could use in place of the buffalo. The President would send them tools for farming. They would learn to till the soil and get food with less labor than the hunt required. More than that, he was about to travel through the land of the Blackfoot and other western tribes, and he was going to insist on peace among all the Indians so the whites who came would be secure.

He listened as each part of his message was interpreted. The Indians responded, he thought, with words of approval. After an exchange of gifts, the expedition moved on. Stevens, propped in the wagon, was satisfied his first council had been a success. He liked the Assiniboin. The people he had first assessed to be filthy and miserable now impressed him as disciplined, honest and sincere in their desire for peace. He thought of them as friends.

Five days later the men broke into a spontaneous cheer as the bluffs of the Missouri came into view. It had taken 55 days, but they'd covered 700 miles. Their first objective, Fort Union at the mouth of the Yellowstone, was in reach. They paused to make their corps' banners so their entrance to the fort could be a grand one.

Stevens, too proud to approach the impressive stockade in a wagon, mounted for the first time since the Sioux scare and rode in under the engineers' banner -- a locomotive "rampant" on a field of grass, bearing down on a retreating buffalo. The motto read, "Westward Ho!"

Their rifle volley was answered by the guns of the fort and they were greeted warmly and given every assistance by Culbertson and the other fur traders. Stevens spent 10 days compiling and writing reports, sending parties out to explore the badlands to the south, the Missouri on west, and the source of the Souris to the north -- ignoring the nicety that his probe into Canada was unauthorized and illegal. While artist Stanley sketched the fort and intrigued the Indians with images he produced with his black box and mysterious bottles, Stevens set the men to making more Pembina carts, which they no longer laughed at, bought more mules and oxen and consulted Culbertson, who had a Blackfoot wife, about the temper of the Indians west of Fort Union.

He had already met with 60 Blood and Piegan representatives at the fort and although Culbertson warned the Blackfoot were increasingly restless, Stevens was hopeful his negotiations would bear fruit. When the corps, now trail-hardened and confident, struck out west on August 10, he invited the delegations along so that he could get to know them better and persuade them to attend a peace council the next year at Fort Benton.

He also quizzed them on the route across the Rockies. Yes, the Blackfoot told him, he could take his wagons across the mountains to the Flathead country. He was buoyed by the news, but he was forced to face an unsettling fact. His injury gave him constant pain, and his daily schedule of rising before most of the men and doing paper work until midnight was driving him to exhaustion. If he hoped to get through the mountains -- even last long enough to reach them -- he had to slow down. Difficult though it was, he relinquished daily command of the expedition and tried to recoup his health.

By August 15, following the route Culbertson had pioneered between Fort Union and Fort Benton two years before, they had crossed Big Muddy Creek and the Poplar River and were making good time through dwarf sage scattered over the flat Missouri flood plain. The river was smaller now, making its way along the north edge of a range of gray buttes. Stevens, knowing the health of the animals was at least as important as the men's, now issued another unpopular order: from now on the men were to walk a portion of every day to spare their mounts.

It worked for a few days, as they moved on to the Milk River and Stevens began to realize his maps were wrong -- the river flowed more from the west than from the north. Although it would require bridges, it would provide a good route for the railroad.

He almost had time to enjoy the cool cottonwood groves, the throngs of antelope and buffalo, the prairie dog towns and the beaver. One of the side parties reported seeing wild horses, and someone shot a fine eagle for the doctor's collection. But as the hot August days wore on and the fissured bluffs of the Bear Paw Mountains moved across the horizon to the south, he faced a mutiny. The army men didn't like taking orders -- especially these orders -- from a civilian. The doctor thought he was too important to walk with the rest.

Stevens didn't blink. He felt no need to persuade. Orders were orders and they would be obeyed. The men grumbled. But they walked on.

On August 24 he had a new worry. Visiting Gros Ventre told him about a feud between the Blackfoot and their tribe. They had been wronged and they planned revenge. Feeling stronger, he pushed up the Milk River ahead of the train the next day to the Gros Ventre camp to see if he could head off disaster.

The 2,000 Indians greeted them with hospitality equal to the Assiniboin, but these Indians did not impress him; they seemed dirty, improvident and sexually loose. Yet he knew if he were to achieve his goal of peace among the tribes he had to reach them. He sat in council with them, "determined to put an end" to inter-tribal warfare that had existed for hundreds of years.

War was folly, he told them. They would

suffer much and gain little. The Great Father wanted peace between his children. War would make the country dangerous for Whites and he would not permit that. "It is my duty to demand that you not endanger the life of a single man of my party, or of any white man who shall later travel through this region," he told them. "I must insist on the safe conduct of every white man through this country."

At least that's what he thought he told them. The experienced Culbertson's eyes must have bulged as he struggled for a diplomatic way to convey Stevens' ultimatum. The fur men had trod lightly with the Indians west of Fort Union for 40 years. Only in the last 20 had they dared to set up shop in their territory and two of these pioneer posts had gone up in smoke.

Perhaps the Gros Ventre were impressed with the little man's nerve. Perhaps the expedition's 40 wagons, 100 men and mountain howitzer seemed a formidable opponent. Probably the gifts he promised them for keeping the peace seemed more desirable than the scalp of one Blackfoot brave. The Gros Ventre agreed to let Stevens mediate the difficulty at Fort Benton when he reached there in a few weeks, or failing that, to wait for satisfaction at the grand council he promised the next year. Stevens distributed the blankets, shirts, calico, knives, paint, powder and tobacco the Indians craved. Then he fired the howitzer for their entertainment and edification and was on his way.

The Gros Ventre were not wrong about Steven's courage. On August 30, determined he would no longer ride in the ambulance, he mounted his horse. He endured the pain for six miles. Then he walked another six. That was no better; his wounded foot had never entirely healed. He allowed himself a two-hour rest where they crossed the Milk and turned south toward Fort Benton. Then he mounted again and rode 18 miles to camp. Thirty miles. It was one of their best days. The next day they put 33 miles behind them and could see the Missouri again, Citadel Rock on its far side and the dark mound of the Belt Mountains to the south. At 3:30 p.m. on September 1 they rode into Fort Benton.

All along the way, almost as if to mock Steven's goal of a pacified native population, the landmarks reminded Culbertson and the accompanying Indians of battles between the tribes. Here the Gros Ventre had fought the Cree, there the Blackfoot had battled the Assiniboin, here the Gros Ventre had annihilated some Crow. He recorded the stories in his journal without comment.

Fort Benton, the most recent of several trading posts that had tried to maintain a position in the Blackfoot country, was not the impressive edifice Fort Union was. Within log palisades, the American Fur Company was converting this newest post on the west bank of the river (present Fort Benton, Montana) from its original log structure to adobe. This white man's version of an earth lodge had originally been called Fort Lewis, but it had been christened Fort Benton on Christmas night three years before in honor of the West's champion, Sen. Thomas Hart Benton. It housed about a dozen traders with their Indian wives and families. A few tipis were pitched nearby and the headquarters of a rival trader sat within sight upriver, but the cliffs across the river and the bluffs beyond easily dominated the view.

Stevens immediately quizzed everyone knowledgeable about the best route west and sent out small parties to reconnoiter the Bitterroot Mountains, hoping he could find a pass that would accommodate wagons. The locals seemed to think it was possible, and he ordered 12 wagons made ready. Then he faced the political end of his job. He was out of funds. It was nearing winter. Some of his most strenuous exploration still lay ahead. He would need $80,000 and almost two more years to complete the survey, he decided. He wrote the government for permission, but in the meantime he authorized purchases and requisitioned supplies.

On September 9 he started the train out towards Cadotte's Pass (near Rogers Pass on Highway 200) while he headed north with a few men to make one last try to contact the Piegan, reported to be 110 miles north of the fort. Halfway there, he received news that was both gratifying and immensely disappointing. The men in the Bitterroots had met the party from the Pacific, as planned. He knew now, what his odds against that success had been, and he was thrilled. But they also reported it was impossible for wagons to make the trip on west. He must turn back to Fort Benton to reorganize his train.

That took another week, and he delayed a few more days to meet with 30 Piegan chiefs who had come to him after all. The meeting was a success; the Piegan chiefs accepted his arguments against war and promised to attend the grand council. Stevens dispatched Culbertson to Washington to plead for funds to finance the council and finish his task.

The engineer-turned-diplomat left Fort Benton on September 22 with a happy heart. Up the Teton, the Sun and the Dearborn he pushed, until "with great gratification...we...left the plains of the Missouri to enter upon the country watered by the Columbia."

Not one to miss a chance for drama, he halted the men at the summit of the pass on September 24, 1853. They stood in the mists of a passing storm to hear him declare that the civil territorial government was hereby extended and inaugurated over the new Territory of Washington. Then he welcomed "the gentlemen of the party" to his future home.

Only one factor grated on his glory. He was sure the men were wrong. He could have gotten wagons through.

Stevens arrived in the village of Olympia on Puget Sound in late November 1853. It was 1855 before he got back to Fort Benton and the Blackfoot. But when he finally met with the Blood, Piegan, Gros Ventre, Blackfoot, Nez Perce, Koot, Pend d'Oreille, Flathead, Cree and Snake at the Judith River in October that year, he received their promise to give up inter-tribal warfare and keep the peace.

After four constructive but combative years as Washington's governor, he returned east to serve in Congress. While there he completed a 1,500 page, three-volume account of his northwest explorations so accurate and detailed it remained the primary resource on the area for decades. Highlighted with Stanley's softly tinted lithographs, the report also gave the Northwest a new positive image. Where others had seen only desert, Stevens envisioned golden wheat fields, green crop land, and rich pasture for cattle, horses and sheep.

When hostilities broke out between the states he volunteered to serve the Union and was promoted to major general within a year. On September 1, 1862, leading his men in a charge across a rain-wet cornfield near Chintilly, Virginia, he raced to pick up the unit's fallen flag. He succeeded in rallying his men, but as he ran again toward the enemy a bullet pierced his temple. He fell dead, the water-soaked and mud-splattered colors still clutched in his hand. He was 44 years old.

Not quite two years later, Pres. Abraham Lincoln signed an act authorizing the construction of the Northern Pacific Railroad over the route Isaac Stevens recommended.

What Manner of Work It Was

The railroad route Isaac Stevens mapped in 1853 had ramifications far south of his survey line. Northwest boosters, determined to see the route he surveyed become a reality, supported the organization of two new territories in 1854. They believed organizing the great open stretches west of the Missouri would promote travel in the north and ensure their coveted line would be built. Southerners, wanting a southern route for the railroad, thought if properly conceived the new territories could further their own, very different goals. In concert with a man who was a twin to Stevens in stature, Stephen A. Douglas, both forces worked for passage of the Kansas-Nebraska Bill.

When they had finished, the Missouri Compromise had been repealed and settlers in the huge new territories -- which stretched from the Missouri to the Rockies and from the 37th Parallel to the Canadian border -- were free to sanction or forbid slavery as they saw fit. Some saw the bill as a sensible, democratic solution to a problem that had divided the nation for decades. Others feared that what had been a rift would become a chasm through the core of the nation.

 In late April 1855, two auburn-haired brothers gathered up their plow and their corn grinder and ushered their wives and small sons onto a steamboat at the St. Louis levee. Like many of the passengers who crowded aboard with them, they were burning with fever. However, the fever that warmed their brows was not the usual spring ague; they had caught the fever for Kansas.

They came from Ohio where, the summer before, blazing sun and parching winds had sucked all the juices from the land. They'd never been tied to one place too long, and Kansas sounded ripe with promise -- a good place to begin again. Their missionary uncle was already there and he sent word that Kansas needed good men.

They had talked of little else for months. They could stake out new farms, plant an orchard, perhaps develop a herd of livestock. A new territory should be ripe for many types of business enterprises. Jason Brown, the slim, sensitive, impractical brother, had dug his treasured experimental grape vines and the fruit trees which were his pride, and he worried now that they would sprout in their crate on deck before he could get them planted. John, who had his father's square chin and at least some of his aggressive, outspoken nature, watched over his wife, Wealthy, and their young son, Jonny, and wondered about the future of his obviously backward son.

But it was Jason's son, Austin, who brought them grief. They were only a few days up the Missouri when they discovered there was cholera aboard the boat. The four-year-old came down with the sickness and before they reached Waverly he was dead. With Jason and his wife, Ellen, nearly prostrate at the loss of their only child, the two young families debarked at the small river town, while the steamer paused for repairs, and trudged up the bank to find a place to bury him.

Perhaps the thunderstorm caused them to delay too long, or perhaps the captain had never intended to wait. By the time they got back to the landing the boat was gone. They had to spend money from their shrinking nest egg to buy stage passage on to the City of Kansas at the mouth of the Kansas River.

John was furious. He was convinced there was a darker cause for their predicament. The boat was filled with southerners, revolvers and Bowie knives in prominent display, bound to Kansas to help make it a slave state. He'd made no effort to hide the fact that he and Jason were free staters. He'd been warned by a Virginian that he was heading for trouble -- that the slave staters were organized and ready to scare away the free staters.

John had flashed with anger at that idea. He'd fight slavery with whatever it took -- a cartridge box if the ballot box failed; a sword if necessary.

His whole family was against slavery. His father was adamant about it. As long as John could remember, his parent had fought openly against it, working in the Underground Railroad, earning expulsion from his church by seating black members in his pew, raging against the Fugitive Slave Law and organizing groups to fight it.

In fact, that was much of the attraction of Kansas. Emigrant societies from both north and south were packing the state with settlers who would vote the right way when the issue was decided.

John and his brothers (Owen, Salmon and Frederick were already there with the livestock) were convinced that if Kansas went slave the whole West was lost. The boys had tried to convince their father this cause should supersede all others -- that other plans could be postponed. But their intense parent was seldom open to suggestion. He remained in the East, trying to decide where he could do the cause more good.

Finally in a tent on their brothers' claims about 50 miles southwest of Kansas City on North Middle Creek, John sat down to write his father a long letter. The hills and ravines were beautiful, he told him, or would be if the rain ever stopped. The creek was lined with good stands of cottonwood, sycamore, oak and black walnut, the prairie grass was high and green.

However he had seen and heard much since he'd arrived. They'd all had a closer look at what slavery meant and were newly resolved to fight it. There was imminent danger of an armed invasion from Missouri. Hundreds of thousands of armed proslavers were poised across the border for attack.

Missourians, heavy with weapons, had already demanded to know the family's loyalties. The neighbors on Pottawatomie Creek were mostly for slavery, and the free staters who were already there did not have the courage to defend their rights.

Those opposing slavery desperately needed to arm and organize in military companies, he told his father. He and his brothers could supply leadership, but they had only two squirrel rifles and one revolver between them. Could his father get them some Colt revolvers, Minnie rifles and Bowie knives? They needed these more than bread. He addressed the letter to John Brown at the free-Negro community of North Elba, New York and set about to organize his neighbors.

In North Elba the letter ended months of indecision. The elder Brown decided he belonged in Kansas.

By the end of June, John, Jr. had been to Lawrence, 30 miles north on the Kansas River, settled by the New England Emigrant Aid Society the year before. He was a college man, a teacher, an accomplished speaker, and soon he had helped chair a meeting to organize resistance. He again wrote his father. "The storm every day thickens, its near approach is hourly more clearly seen by all," he wrote. "...the great drama will open here...Give us arms and we are ready for the contest."

Jason, who roused himself from his grief long enough to add a note, had different things on his mind. It was wonderful country, but Ellen was so depressed and lonely that he might have to take her back east. It didn't help that she had no stove to cook on. Could his father bring them out a stove?

It was more and more clear there would be a contest. In July the legislature, elected three months before when proslavery forces flooded over the border to pack the ballot boxes, convened at the Shawnee Mission to adopt Missouri's laws for Kansas.

Abolitionists could not hold office, sit on juries or voice antislavery views without risking imprisonment.

Seeing they could not hope for help from the proslave governor, the free staters called meetings of their own. In mid-August John, Jr. helped draw up a call for a convention to be held in Topeka to write another constitution -- one which would demand Kansas be admitted to the Union as a free state. A free-state party was organized and elections for a free-state legislature were set for October 9.

John, incensed at the unfairness of territory laws and unable to wait for organized resistance, decided to challenge the law restricting his freedom of speech. Meeting a slavery advocate in the settlement on Pottawatomie Creek, he declared no man had a right to hold a slave in Kansas and no one was going to stop him from saying so. He would declare against slavery wherever he was. Any officer of the so-called law who tried to arrest him risked death.

The settlers on the creek were not men to ignore a challenge. There was giant Dutch Henry Sherman and his brother William, bachelor squatters who, it was whispered, enriched their tavern profits by stealing livestock from passing emigrants. Tennessean Allen Wilkinson, a violent man who was said to release his anger by beating his wife. The Doyles, father James and two grown sons, who'd brought nothing from the hills of Tennessee except a loyalty to the southern way. Yet in spite of Wealthy's expectation that "we shall probably get shot for disobeying their beautiful laws," John rode the seven miles back to their tents on North Middle Creek without incident.

The weather did not show the same forbearance. The next three weeks were so cold and miserable the family could do little more than try to keep warm. One after another they fell ill with fever. The crops were ungathered, the stock untended, the cabins not yet begun. And the father of the clan was due any day.

John and Jason had complicated feelings about their wiry, sharp-faced father. Both had vivid memories of his fierce blue eyes and his lash, applied with vigor for any childhood transgression. He was stern and strict and never satisfied with what they did. At times it had been like living with an avenging angel who could call down the wrath of God at will, an unapproachable tyrant who ruled them all with an indomitable will.

Yet they had other memories, too. Of a father who shed tears while he whipped them, who held them on his knee while he sang hymns and who sat up through the night when they were sick. Who hated injustice with an enduring passion and did whatever he had to to fight it. A man who grieved over the plight of the slaves and risked his family's well-being to help them. A man who had wanted to be a minister, who prayed constantly for guidance, and who accepted without question what he thought was God's will for his life.

John, Jr. and Jason had both finally rejected the religion that ruled their father's life. They had tried to break away and live their own lives. In spite of his father's distress, John, Jr. investigated phrenology, spiritualism and mesmerism. He bought his own farm in Ohio and served his community as justice of the peace.

But their father's teachings were still part of them. The namesake nurtured the same aggressive hatred of slavery. Jason could not deny the family ties.

Now they needed his prodigious energy, and when he arrived on October 7 with their brother-in-law, Henry Thompson, and their teenaged brother, Oliver, he was as usual their tower of strength.

He was 55 years old, a stovepipe of a man in his black frock coat, his short bristly hair streaked with gray. But he nursed them, gathered the crops, chased down the livestock and began cutting logs for cabins to house Jason and John and their families. Jason and Ellen were especially touched when, in addition to crates of revolvers, rifles, knives and broadswords, he unloaded the casket containing young Austin's body. He'd unearthed his grandson and brought him from Waverly so the boy could be buried in free Kansas soil.

The election of October 9 went peacefully enough, but in early December the family learned a mob of Missourians and the Kansas militia were threatening to burn Lawrence. As the chill landscape darkened December 6, with bullets run, swords sharpened and bayonets mounted on poles, five Browns marched for Lawrence -- John, Sr. on the wagon seat, his namesake, Owen, Salmon and Frederick walking alongside.

Lawrence, which looked as if it had been picked up in a piece from a New England valley and transplanted to the Kansas plain, was thronged with excited people. They learned that a second free stater had been murdered and that proslavery forces were massed on the Wakarusa River. The elder Brown, introduced by his son to free-state leaders Charles Robinson and James Henry Lane, advocated immediate attack. Instead the leaders negotiated a peace treaty with the governor and in a week the Browns were home without firing a shot.

On December 15 Kansas voters ratified the constitution free staters had drawn up at Topeka. Although a clause the Browns considered reprehensible excluded free Negroes from the territory, it looked as if Kansas were on the way to being free. In January the family forced its way through a countryside clamped in ice to political meetings in Osawatomie. John, Jr. was easily elected a delegate to the Topeka legislature. They nursed their frostbitten toes, tried to quiet their hunger with johnnycakes and began to believe the struggle was almost over.

However, by February 1 somber news had made its way south through the snowdrifts. The elections in Leavenworth had not been so peaceful. Four were wounded. One killed. A free stater had later been hacked to death with a hatchet, and the proslave press was screaming for war. The Missourians were not about to accept defeat and they were recruiting other southerners to help them.

Then mail from the east splashed through the February thaw. President Franklin Pierce, true to the southern cause, had rejected the Topeka legislature as spurious and offered U.S. troops to the proslave Kansas governor. Resisting proslavery laws was now treason. The free staters began to sleep with their guns.

John, Jr. spent much of March in Topeka as the Pottawatomie delegate to the free-state legislature. He signed a memorial to Congress asking that Kansas be admitted as a free state under the Topeka constitution, but when the rest voted their government should not take effect until Kansas was admitted to the Union, he declared the document too conservative and stood alone against the resolution. Returning to Brown's Station he voiced his frustration to his family and began writing friends in Ohio that they should come thoroughly armed for the impending struggle.

He saw still greater ramifications of the Kansas struggle. "The war cry heard upon our plains will reverberate not only through the hemp and tobacco fields of Missouri but through the 'Rice Swamps,' the cotton and sugar plantations of the Sunny South," he warned. If "the first act in the Drama of insane Despotism is to be performed here, you may look elsewhere for the theatre of other acts."

In Osawatomie, a proslave judge picked proslave jurors and prepared to enforce the law from Dutch Henry's tavern. Facing probable arrest, 30-some free staters in the Pottawatomie area organized a home-defense company of rifles. They elected John, Jr. captain. Jason, who had never so much as engaged in a fistfight, signed on with his brother. The elder Brown did not join. Nor did his unmarried sons or son-in-law.

Tired of the threat hanging over their heads, the family decided to challenge the grand jury as it met April 21. John, Jr. gathered the Pottawatomie Rifles and marched to the tavern.

They left their arms at a nearby cabin, but the judge could not mistake their manner when the delegation crowded into the barroom and tried their hands at intimidation. They repudiated the laws under which the jury met, they announced; any official who tried to enforce those laws did so at his peril.

They were desperate words of desperate men, for they could now see in action the government which meant to destroy their cause. Local law, state government and federal troops were now aligned against them, and they listened daily to insults and threats from those who'd never needed a law to hide behind. They'd be more fun to kill than snakes. They were to be hounded out, burned out of the valley. If they were alive to go.

John, Jr. and his father argued about the validity of the threats. The son listened to Wilkinson, the Sherman brothers and the Doyles brag that they would exterminate the abolitionists and sweep the valley clean, but he thought it was mostly bluff -- the whiskey talk of illiterate trash.

His father thought otherwise.

Still the more immediate threat seemed to lie in Missouri.

When the proslave sheriff was wounded near Lawrence the proslave press screamed for revenge for the "murder." Two free staters were murdered in turn, and the Missouri militia began to mobilize to invade Kansas. On May 2 the Browns discovered a company of Georgians camped not far from Pottawatomie. John, Sr. went to investigate and came home convinced they were intent on wiping out all free staters -- especially the Browns.

Now the territorial government felt strong enough to move on the free staters. A jury indicted the free-state leaders for treason and charged the free-state press with sedition. On May 21 the Browns got urgent word: a proslavery army is camped outside Lawrence. Send help!

John, Jr. rode from farm to farm, calling up the Pottawatomie Rifles. By afternoon 34 had grabbed their guns and come. John, Jr. mounted and led his men north on the road toward Lawrence. Jason turned his back on his orchard and marched in the rank behind him.

John, Sr., who preferred to command his own small company, called Owen, Salmon, Oliver, Frederick and son-in-law Henry to his side and marched with -- but apart from -- his son's command.

The next morning as they neared the crossing of the Marais des Cygnes River a messenger galloped up with incredible news. The people in Lawrence had decided not to fight. They were standing by while proslavers sacked the town. The mob was looting stores and smashing the printing presses. The Free-State Hotel was on fire.

Stunned, they paused for breakfast while they mulled over the problem. Should they try to save people who would not save themselves?

Before they could decide, a third messenger rode into camp. U.S. troops had moved in and taken control of Lawrence. The proslavers were leaving the smoking town. The crisis was all over and they should go back home.

Should they? Or should they go on to Lawrence and do what they could? They argued among themselves. John's father, frustrated and furious at the cowardly behavior of Lawrence citizens, urged them to go forward and strike a blow for freedom. By the time John, Jr. called for a vote, the compelling voice of the old abolitionist had swung the others to his side.

A few miles down the road toward Lawrence they learned what that might cost. Proslave forces held the bridge over the Wakarusa River which lay between them and the town. They reconsidered and voted to move back to Ottawa Creek until a company of Osawatomie volunteers arrived to reinforce them.

The elder Brown was beside himself. What was wrong with everybody? He'd rather be ground into the earth than meekly submit to usurpation and wrong. He shouted at them and waved his arms, his fury seeming to grow instead of cool. When the others bedded down for the night, the old man brooded by the fire. Late that night he called his personal squad to him.

The Rifles were moving around in the chilly gray dawn to fix breakfast on May 23 when yet another message arrived from Lawrence. Again the abolitionist cause had been humiliated. South Carolinian Preston Brooks had beaten Massachusetts Sen. Charles Sumner to bloody unconsciousness with a heavy cane. Unbelievably the attack had taken place on the floor of the U.S. Senate! When they heard the news, the free-state camp was loud with incredulous and angry exclamations, but the elder Brown had already moved beyond rhetoric. It was time to retaliate, he told them. Time to deliver a blow even barbarians could not ignore; time for *them* to be afraid instead of us. He called for volunteers for a secret mission.

John, Jr. objected. The enemy was only a few miles away. He needed his men; this was no time to divide their forces. For a few moments the two stood toe to toe. Then the father wheeled on his heel and strode off. John, Jr., his voice tight with apprehension, called after him, "Father, be careful. Commit no rash act."

That afternoon he stood with Jason and the Rifles and watched a wagon creak out of camp and head south toward Pottawatomie. The wagon -- the only one in camp -- belonged to settler James Townsley and he drove the team. Their father, his face steely below his straw hat and a pistol in his belt, sat beside him.

Hulking settler Theodore Weiner, who never could be kept from any fight, rode his horse alongside. Inside the wagon box, along with pots, provisions and several freshly honed broadswords, rode their brothers Owen, 31, Frederick, 25, their sister Ruth's husband, Henry, and their half brothers, 19-year-old Salmon and 17-year-old Oliver.

That evening the Rifles were reinforced by a company from Osawatomie and they moved on north to camp near the Santa Fe Trail. John decided to ride the 15 miles into Lawrence and assess conditions there for himself.

The damage was not as bad as he'd pictured it. Shelves in the stores that fronted the wooden sidewalks were empty or in disarray. The type from the newspapers had been dumped in the river and their files and libraries thrown to the wind. The free-state cannon were gone. The three-story hotel, which had resisted cannon fire and two kegs of gun powder, had finally been gutted when print stock from the papers had been piled inside and set fire. Governor Robinson's house was a pile of charred timber.

But the proslave forces were gone. He rode back to his men the next day and they argued whether there was any point in staying longer.

John, Jr. was reluctant to go home.

They'd accomplished nothing; the proslavers had never even been challenged. Chafing under the feeling of impotence, he looked for a way to vent his frustration. A nearby farm caught his eye. It was not only proslave, it housed slaves. He recruited some men and liberated the slaves.

The companions he'd expected to cheer his return, reacted with shock. They did not approve of "stealing" slaves. The Rifles took the Blacks from him and and returned them to their owner.

His leadership had never been so publicly repudiated, and he felt betrayed. What did these people want? In the last four days he'd gone from a pitch of excitement to confusion and uncertainty. Nothing seemed reliable anymore. He'd fought with his father, watched his brothers take another road, and now his command was rejecting him. He felt exhausted and terribly drained. What should he do?

The U.S. Army made the decision for him. Meeting the Pottawatomie company on the trail, they ordered Brown to disband the Rifles. Totally dejected, he told his men to go home.

Before they could depart, a messenger rode in on a sweat-lathered horse. There'd been a massacre on Pottawatomie Creek! Five proslavers had been dragged from their cabins in the night and cut to pieces with swords. Terror now reigned on the creek and the person responsible was Old John Brown.

Full of fear for their families, the Rifles threw the rest of their belongings together and hurried down the road toward home. As they marched they damned the old man and his shocking deed. It was not unexpected; most of them had heard at least hints of his intent. But the barbarous reality appalled them all.

John, Jr. and Jason took the brunt of their anger. John tried to cling to a belief that his father had had reason -- some excuse -- to do what he did. Jason stumbled along in a fog, wanting to believe it wasn't true. Calm, philosophical Owen? Level-headed Salmon? Young Oliver, the bookworm? Ruth's husband, Henry, one of the family for six years now? How could it be?

The next morning they had the proof they dreaded. The old man had ridden into camp during the night. The horses he brought belonged to the proslavers who died on the Pottawatomie. When John, Jr. saw the horses he fell apart and resigned his command.

As they straggled on home, the tormented Jason finally approached his father. The son who could not bear to eat game if he had watched its death throes asked, "Did you have a hand in the killing?"

The old man met his gaze. "I did not do it, but I approved of it," he said.

"Whoever did it, it was a wicked thing!" Jason blurted.

"God is my judge," his father answered. "We were justified under the circumstances."

What circumstances? Jason turned to Frederick, whom they all knew could be stout and reliable one day and, crazed by the pain of terrible headaches, driven to weird, impulsive behavior the next. Did he know who'd done the killing?

"Yes," he said, "I do, but I can't tell you."

Jason forced himself to ask the next question. "Did you kill any of them with your own hands?"

At that Frederick broke down. "No," he sobbed, "when I came to see what manner of work it was I could not do it."

They were near North Middle Creek by now and the five raiders turned toward home and hiding. Jason and John, Jr. moved on toward Osawatomie, where Ellen, Wealthy and Jonny had taken refuge with their missionary uncle.

They'd been able to escape notice on the road, although the country was alive with men gunning for the Browns, but in Osawatomie everyone knew them. They were immediately surrounded by angry free staters who thought they'd had a part in the murders.

John, Jr. heard people he thought were his friends curse him and label him the lowest kind of animal. Trying to convince them of his innocence, he grew hysterical and incoherent. Jason, for once the stronger, had to lead him away to the uncle's cabin.

The uncle refused to open the door to them.

Even their own family. It was almost too much. With John babbling and useless, it was up to Jason to convince Uncle Adair of their innocence. Only then did he unbar the door so they could be reunited with their wives.

Before long they had another visitor. Their tawny-haired brother Owen arrived to tell them their father had set up camp in the brush. He wanted them to come. Owen was the closest to them of any brother (the three had been born in the space of four years), the one who could make them laugh. But he had ridden along on the bloody night and he spoke for the father they could no longer support. They sent him back alone.

However, Jason knew their very presence could endanger their uncle's home. Innocent or not they bore the stain of the Brown name. He decided to try to make contact with U.S. troops, explain his innocence and ask protection. He tried to convince John, Jr. to go with him.

He could not. His older brother, seeing threat in every face and guns behind every tree, fled into the brush behind Adair's cabin to hide like the animal he was accused of being.

On Tuesday, May 27, the free staters of the area, afraid they would all be annihilated, met to repudiate the murders. They knew now how unspeakable a crime could be. How Tennessean Doyle and his sons, 20-year-old Drury and 23-year-old William, had been pulled from their cabin and butchered with broadswords, in spite of the pleas of Mrs. Doyle and the cries of his younger children. How next Allen Wilkinson had been ordered from his sick wife's side and walked stocking-footed to his slaughter. How finally William Sherman had been left with the waters of the Pottawatomie washing away his brain.

Yet some in the crowd could find justification for the deed. Six free staters had died at the hands of proslavery men that spring. These local proslavers were all violent men. They had made threats of their own. The Doyles had just given a free-state storekeeper a week to clear out or be killed. Maybe Brown had just gotten to them first. It was possible he'd saved all their lives.

The proslave press, the governor and the militia, handed the excuse they had longed for, were not about to respond with moderation. Warrants were issued for John, Sr. and Jr. and others and troops began combing the state. Missourians found Jason on Ottawa Creek and were about to kill him when cooler heads prevailed and turned him over to authorities. Even then he came near being lynched by a mob.

John, Jr., wild-eyed and disheveled, was run down in a ravine near Adair's cabin. He was turned over to U.S. troops but found them no more merciful than Missourians. Believing he was one of the murderers, the soldiers dragged him to a tent pole, chained him up and let all comers have at him with fists and rifle butts until he lost whatever hold he'd had on sanity.

In mid-June he and Jason were reunited when, chained two by two with four other captives, they were marched more than 50 miles to Tecumseh in the space of two days. On June 20 Jason was released after a preliminary hearing. John, Jr., still in his own strange world, was bound over for trial. The charge was treason.

Jason made his way home, but he found only charred ruins where his house and John Jr.'s had stood. Weeds were already creeping into the garden.

For it was war now in southeast Kansas. Guerilla bands of both persuasions ranged the country, burning homes, stealing livestock, driving settlers to whatever protection they could find. Ellen and Wealthy had sought uncertain refuge in Osawatomie. Sick and defeated, Jason sought the only security he knew of, his father and brothers in the brush.

He found his father unrepentant and convinced that whatever he did he did in God's cause. He'd been busy during Jason's confinement. He'd conducted several raids to get supplies and won a battle at Black Jack, "the first regular battle fought between Free State and pro Slavery men in Kansas," he said proudly. "May God still gird our loins & hold our right hand, & to him may we give the glory."

But Henry had been wounded in the battle, and Brown had lost to Federal troops the prisoners he'd hoped to exchange for Jason and John, Jr. Salmon had accidentally shot himself later. Owen was sick and frail. They all were tired of life in the brush. In the middle of July the old man decided to leave Kansas.

Jason, hoping someday he'd be able to raise his orchard in peace, decided to return to Ellen in Osawatomie. John, Jr., contacted in prison in Lecompton and evidently beginning to recover his balance, urged his father to go where he could "be of more use." The old man started north, but when he reached Nebraska City he changed his mind. He sent the other boys on east while he returned to Kansas with Frederick. Perhaps he could rescue John, Jr. before he left.

The imprisoned son asked him not to try. He was not guilty of murder. The state was full of free men who were as treasonous as he. He was hopeful the grand jury might release him. If not, he would ask to be sent to the states for trial. Whatever happened, he was convinced he could not remain in Kansas and keep his sanity.

However, the father was not ready to go in peace. Free-state forces were now on the offensive and he recruited a band to fight. Late in August he was back in Osawatomie planning raids on proslavery homesteads and helping set the town's defenses for expected Missouri retaliation. Jason was drawn into the struggle once more.

On August 30 Missouri raiders threatened both Lawrence and Osawatomie. Frederick, carrying messages between the two towns, was shot dead near his uncle's cabin. Jason and his father rode with a force of Iowa volunteers to help defend their town.

They were 30-some against 250 and a cannon. The odds were impossible, but the elder Brown held his men at the river ford until the last instant. As grapeshot crackled through trees overhead he urged them to pick their targets carefully and fire low.

When they finally had to break, and run or swim for their lives, Jason saw the old man stagger. He'd been hit in the back by a load of grapeshot, but luckily its force was nearly spent and he was not badly wounded. As friends crumpled around them, the two Browns made their way to shelter in the timber.

A short while later, as they tried to find a way to Adair's cabin and Frederick's body, Jason looked up to see smoke billowing above the trees. The proslavers had torched Osawatomie. "God sees it," his father said with tear-filled eyes. "I have only a short time to live -- only one death to die. I will die fighting for this cause. There will be no more peace in this land until slavery is done for."

A week later he rode through Lawrence to the cheers of the citizens and began recruiting men to serve his cause. But on September 9 a new governor arrived in Lecompton and pledged to end all guerila warfare. He showed his good faith by disbanding the proslave Kansas militia and ordered all the other units to lay down their arms. The next day he released the free state leaders, who returned to Lawrence in triumph.

John, Jr., freed on $1,000 bail, came, too. The Browns spent another uneasy month hiding from arrest as the guns were gradually silenced. Then, the war over that had cost 200 lives, and Kansas apparently safe from slavery, they turned their faces back east. Wealthy, Jonny and Ellen were put on a steamer for Ohio, while Jason, John, Jr. and Owen traveled with their feverish father north to Nebraska, across Iowa and on east.

They had nothing material to show for their 18 months in Kansas. One brother was dead. Three of them had been wounded physically. One was damaged mentally. They had learned much about each other, and family loyalties had been strained past mending.

Still, the first blow had been struck for freedom, and the father of the clan was convinced the issue could only be resolved with blood. He was no longer just John Brown. He was John Brown of Osawatomie, and the stories he'd sent east to newspapers and prominent citizens, the letters of praise from Kansas abolitionists he carried in his pockets, would open many doors.

He needed the testimonials, for he planned nothing less than an invasion of the south, an insurrection of the slaves and a new government that would wipe the stain of slavery from the face of the nation.

As soon as he was able, the elder Brown began raising funds and recruiting supporters for his obsession. Jason had sworn off fighting forever, and John, Jr., settled again in Ohio, managed to stay removed from his father's scheme for more than a year. But in 1858 his father asked him to travel the east and help raise funds, and he could not refuse.

In December that year Osawatomie Brown was back in Kansas where the southeast still festered as the territory waited for a final political decision on its future. Just before Christmas he led a raid into Missouri and liberated 11 slaves from border plantations. He escorted them north with much hoopla and sent them on to new lives in Canada.

However, his focus was no longer on Kansas. His family knew by now that he had decided to begin his revolution at the federal arsenal at Harpers Ferry, Virginia. John, Jr., suffering from a melancholy so deep that he felt scarcely able to function, dutifully spent the summer of 1859 traveling from city to city to recruit supporters.

Some of the brothers refused to be part of the mad plan. Jason, Henry and Salmon all refused to go. Nevertheless on October 18 Brown led his 21 men against the arsenal on the bank of the Potomac River. With him were sons Owen, Oliver and Watson.

When the fighting and the ensuing trial were over, Oliver and Watson were added to the list of family dead and old Brown was scheduled for execution.

On December 2, while southerners cheered, northern church bells tolled and northern Blacks prayed, the abolitionist was hanged. John, Jr., Jason and their brothers were left with the memory of their remarkable father and his final admonition to them to love and serve God, to abhor slavery and to "build up again the broken walls" of his shattered family.

A Name and a Brother

Far to the north on the Missouri in the mid-1850s, just below the route surveyed for the railroad by Isaac Stevens, there were other men in conflict. Their hatreds were as deep and their grievances of longer standing. They, too, crossed each other's borders to rob and plunder, and their young men had to test their worth on the field of battle.

The Hunkpapa Sioux had been hunting for the Crow camp for several days. Winter was on them, but the weather was open enough that they'd left their women and children in their snug camp between the Chalk Buttes and the Powder River to try the fortunes of war. They needed horses. It was a constant, elemental need, and one they knew the Crow could supply, however unwillingly. They'd probably have to earn their spoils, but they'd never shrunk from that.

The Sioux braves numbered nearly a hundred and most of them were on foot as they pushed north along the Powder to the Yellowstone River and Crow hunting grounds. This was their country and they knew every landmark. One could see for miles from the crest of the pine-topped hills to the east and some of them were always seeking the high ground to keep watch. The undulating grassland between the hills and the river could support any number of ponies, summer or winter. They left the flat-topped pillar of Fighting Butte behind and rode past the striated points of Medicine Rocks with mounting excitement. Some of them, especially the teen-aged boys, were thirsting for a fight, longing for the chance to prove their bravery by touching an enemy, and so claim their first coup.

Sitting Bull could understand the hot ambition of the boys. A man without coups to relate at councils was not a man. He had no voice in tribal affairs, no right to take part in ceremonies, not even status enough to name his own children. He might as well be a woman. Many warriors of long standing could recite long strings of examples of their valor, naming the time and place of each deed and swelling with pride at the murmur of appreciation from their peers: in this fight he had been the first to touch a dead enemy; in another skirmish he had been the second; another time -- highest of all honors -- he had ridden into the enemy force unarmed, touched a live opponent and ridden away to safety.

Only a dozen winters before Sitting Bull had stolen along in the wake of a Hunkpapa war party, dared to join their council uninvited, and announced with confidence he did not feel that he was going, too. He'd been 14 winters and of only average size, except for his broad shoulders. A sometimes awkward child who seemed to consider every move, he was known as Slow. He did not yet own a man's weapons, only blunt-tipped arrows for hunting birds.

Gratified by his initiative, his father, Sitting Bull, had let him join the party and had handed him a slender, peeled stick to use for counting coups. For the first time, then, he'd stripped for battle, painting his nearly naked body with yellow and daubing his gray pony with red. He'd fastened a black-tipped eagle feather to the tip of the coup stick and gripped it as they lay in ambush in an eroded coulee.

The enemy was barely within range when Slow could wait no longer. He jabbed his heels into his horse's flanks and charged into the open. As the coulee disgorged more screaming Hunkpapa, the startled enemy turned to flee. But they were not fast enough.

One, aware the pounding hooves behind him were too close to lose, yanked his mount to a stop and leaped down to face the Sioux. Slapping an arrow on his bowstring, he took aim on the foremost Sioux. But Slow's coup stick was faster. He lashed the outstretched arm, knocked the arrow away and whirled his pony into the brave's body, sending him sprawling. He had struck the first blow! Slow had counted a coup and left the enemy disarmed for others to kill.

For the first time, then, he'd charged with the warriors into the home camp, all of them loud with triumph, singing their victory songs, yelling their deeds, parading to the shrill din of the women's praise. Slow, coated with the black paint of victory, knew the heady thrill of hearing his father proclaim his bravery to the world, the fiery satisfaction of stamping to the rhythm of the victory drums, the swelling pride of joining the warriors to act out his brave deed.

After that he'd been Slow no longer. His father had given him a gift beyond value -- his own name. It was a name he'd received from the mouth of the buffalo bull, himself, the first of four names he'd heard the great animal mutter -- a gift from the Buffalo God who showed them strength and stamina and heedless courage. The father had used it for his own and brought it honor.

But now Sitting Bull the elder became

Jumping Bull, and the son bore the honored name of Tatanka Iyotake, the Buffalo Bull that Resides Among Us. He'd lived up to his name in the past years. With only 25 winters behind him, he was already one of two sash wearers of the premier warriors, the Strong Hearts.

Angling west, the Hunkpapa party crossed the ice-shrouded waters of the Yellowstone and moved into the prairie spreading north. It was antelope country, and the fleet animals seemed to have taken their colors from the tawny winter grass, spotted here and there with patches of snow. It was also Crow country and the war party paused to ask the shaman what luck they could expect.

Sun-Dreamer smoked the pipe, sang his songs and told them his suddenly blackened palm meant they would meet enemies within a day. Sure enough, as they neared Porcupine Creek, the scouts spotted the smoke of the Crow camp. At the news, Sitting Bull prepared himself for battle.

Unhurriedly he stripped to breechclout and moccasins and took his Strong Heart headpiece from its pouch. The black feathered cap fitted close to his head, and its two buffalo horns flanked the black horn of his own hair, which he'd gathered into a knot on his forehead. Ribbons of ermine edging the cap spilled down his bare back. He slipped his shoulder through one end of the long red sash. The feathers on the other end trailed on the ground behind him as he strode to his horse. A man who wore the sash must be willing to stake himself to the ground in the face of the enemy and fight until death or a comrade freed him.

The horse, too, had his badges of honor. He was a black, so fast that his white-stockinged legs seemed to disappear as he ran. He'd carried Sitting Bull safely through a charge at an enemy and run down his foe without flinching. For this he'd earned the right to sport a red and black horse tail on his bridle, and the warrior methodically fastened it in place.

Then it was time for his shield and his gun. The gun was new, just purchased from a trader, and he hefted the weight of the muzzle-loader proudly. His blue shield, a sacred circle painted with an open-beaked black bird and edged with four eagle feathers, had kept him safe through many conflicts. Satisfied with his preparations, he joined the others to wait for darkness.

It came quickly, as if the dark and cold had suddenly combined to overwhelm the day. The Sioux watched as the Crow camp gradually quieted in the chill night. Tipis which had glowed with light dimmed as fires were allowed to die to embers. When even the dogs curled against the tipis and sank into sleep, it was time to move.

Quickly, silently, Sitting Bull and the other chosen warriors crept from their hiding places and worked into the horse herd at the edge of the camp. The herd stirred, a horse snorted and was silenced by a practiced hand, a dog gave a tentative bark, but the tipis remained quiet. They edged the horses to the far side of the meadow. Then suddenly they were all thundering away down the valley.

There was need for speed, for it was a large camp and they'd had to leave many horses behind. Quickly they divided the horses among those without mounts and pointed the herd south. Sitting Bull and most of the warriors rode at the rear of the herd, ready to fight off the Crow they knew would come after them. The Hunkpapa pushed the herd as fast and as far as they could through the dark hours, but when the sun gave light again they looked back to see the furious Crow charging in their wake. Hurriedly the raid leaders ordered the young men to group the herd and raced to the rear to defend it.

The screaming Crow, expecting to harry a retreating enemy, galloped over a rise to face a determined line of Sioux. Most of them pulled to a halt. Only three leaders came on, riding alone toward the Sioux line, contemptuous of the odds, reckless of the danger. One counted two coups on startled Hunkpapa and raced away to safety, leaving only the tail of his war bonnet in Loud Bear's hands. Another killed Paints Brown. Sitting Bull charged out to meet the third. There in the no man's land between the two tribes he threw himself from his horse and challenged the Crow to personal combat. "Comrades," he sang as he ran to close with the warrior, "whoever runs away, he is a woman, they say; Therefore, through many trials, my life is short." It was a Strong Heart song and not every man had the right or the courage to sing it.

The Crow had a rifle, too, he could see as they pounded closer over the frozen ground. He could see the man's breath, white on the frosty air, his red shirt, its ermine trim bouncing crazily, and knew he faced a chief. Closer. He must get closer. Now they were almost within arm's reach. The Crow was swinging his barrel up to shoot. Sitting Bull dropped to his knee and took aim.

The Crow's finger was just a little faster. His gun spit fire and the Sioux felt his shield jerk in his hand and a ball tear into his left foot. In the next instant he fired his own gun. His enemy, thrown to the ground by a hit in the belly, writhed before him. Sitting Bull did not hesitate. Limping to the prostrate warrior, he pulled out his knife and plunged it into the Crow's heart.

The action seemed to bring the rest of the Sioux to life. With a wild yell they charged the disheartened Crow party, counting coup after coup on them as they retreated down the valley. Sitting Bull, his left moccasin streaming blood, watched with satisfaction. Then he bound up his wound, caught his horse and turned toward home. After two or three days he was glad to see the Chalk Buttes glaring in the distance.

Four days later, after a proper period of mourning for Paints Brown, the Hunkpapa held their victory dance. Sitting Bull, no longer just a rising young warrior, could not dance on his wounded foot, but he could relate a coup that would be told around camp fires for years to come. His killing of the Crow chief was more than *sha*, it was *sha-sha*, very red, the best of the best. Soon he had a new title, leader of the Midnight Strong Hearts, the elite of the warrior corps.

The foot was a problem. The bullet had entered beneath his toes and plowed the length of his sole. Though the most knowledgeable of the tribe treated it as best they knew how, the sole of his foot contracted as it healed and he would never again walk without a limp. However, the wound did not keep him restricted for long. As head of the Strong Hearts, and soon thereafter a husband, he was responsible for the hunts which fed his family and the tribe.

In the past two generations his people, the Teton Sioux, had carved a hunting ground from the territory of the Missouri River tribes, a sweep of grassy hills and eroded valleys that centered on the Moreau River as it flowed into the Missouri from the west.

In the days before his grandfather's time, the Sioux had been a people of the woods and lakes to the east. They'd been pushed west of the Missouri by pressure from other tribes who had obtained guns from white traders. It was a different land -- dry, nearly treeless, with limitless sky and endless grass, with constant winds that hurled rain and snow and sand in turn, with dazzling sun and mountains of clouds and air that flowed to the last cell of the lungs; a land of distances, sometime rivers and an ocean of game. In time, the Sioux had taken the plains, and the horses they needed to exist there, as their own. They soon excelled in the skills of wandering hunting life.

In the 1850s the Hunkpapa did not feel much pressure from the *wasicun*, the bearded white skins who came up the rivers. They knew the trail which the gold seekers had carved up the Platte River was cutting through the lands of the Oglala and Brule Sioux to the south. They heard of these troubles, but they suffered no forts with marching soldiers, no squabbles over treaty papers, no chastisement with rolling guns. They wandered west far beyond the headwaters of the Moreau to challenge the Crow near the Yellowstone, kept the river tribes prisoners in their villages, and regularly pushed north of the Missouri to pillage the Assiniboin, free to do whatever their strength allowed. Few could challenge them, and their children grew up knowing the Sioux owned the world.

When the Winter When the War Bonnet was Torn (1856) was over, the Hunkpapa began the new year with a successful spring hunt. The hunts were a joy and a celebration to Sitting Bull and the other men -- the game of stalking a herd, moving upwind and stripping as if for battle; it was a battle, and the enemy was both honored and formidable.

Then it was a leap onto the bare back of his buffalo pony and the mad race into the herd just as it broke into a gallop. The horse, trained for months to be almost an extension of his body, answered the slightest pressure of his knees as he sought out his kill. Tearing through the panicked beasts he'd draw alongside a huge animal, with dust and clods flying, so close he could nearly touch the dark fur. Too close and one lunge, one quick twist of the massive head, would disembowel his horse; he'd be beneath those churning hooves. Too far, and the arrow would lose its power. Pounding along, he'd aim an arrow just behind the left shoulder and let it fly -- to bury itself up to the feather and pierce the buffalo's heart, if his aim was true.

Later, as his horse blew and the dust settled, he'd drop to the prairie beside the warm carcass, cut out the liver, season it with gall and gulp it down, the blood warm and rich in his throat.

He'd dropped his first bison calf when he was 10, and the thrill of the hunt did not change, although he was more conscious now of the needs of his people, more discriminating in his choice of kill. The Big Females were best for meat; the Four-Teeth, who'd seen four winters, were best for robes; the aged Cracked Horn bulls were of use only if you needed glue. Sitting Bull was a deadly adversary of game; few animals escaped after he had them in his sights. Yet he was always conscious that he took the life of other creatures who were not so different from himself. He always asked their forgiveness before he shot and offered thanks to Wakan Tanka afterward. Bones of bison, lying scattered in the grass where there had been a surround, could bring him down from his horse. Facing the white skulls toward the sun, he'd remind the younger men to treat them with honor. "These are the bones of those who gave their flesh to keep us alive last winter," he'd say.

He revered all wildlife, but he felt especially close to birds. He'd spent hours studying them and listening to their calls, until he was sure he could understand their messages. Once a small yellow bird had saved him from a grizzly, and he'd written a song in its honor. He wrote many songs and knew many more; he could call the right one to mind whatever happened. Whether it was a feast or a funeral, a homecoming or a leave-taking, his rich voice could be counted on to provide the proper song, and he was a popular guest around the fire.

Scarlet Woman, the wife he had bought to lie with him in his tipi, brought warmth and comfort to his days. It was a pleasure to hear her praise when he brought home game, to watch her bend over the cooking fire, to accept the bowl from her hand, to pull on a pair of moccasins she had cut and shaped to his feet. It was satisfying to see her stand stiff with pride while he danced his coups, to have someone besides mother and sisters to tan the hides from his kills, to weave colorful quills into his leggings and bead his war shirt. Satisfaction turned to joy when she presented him with a son.

He looked forward to the day he would make the boy his first bow and arrows and begin teaching him all the lore of the hunt. He'd learn to throw the lance, catch butterflies to develop agility, and run and swim to develop endurance. He'd have to be taught to see, hear, smell, feel and understand every nuance of the prairie and its creatures, and adopt their skills to his own use. Any pebble, any twig could hold a message. He'd know that the leaves of cottonwood trees were darkest over the water hole, that a swallow flying with an empty mouth was going toward water, that a tumblebug's horns could point the way to buffalo, that one who lay on his belly and sighted along the top of the grass when the sun was low could track any animal -- or man -- by the broken webs of tiny spiders. When he'd learned to ride, he would care for the family horses and become wise in their ways. Soon after that, if he was a good learner, he would be invited to carry the moccasins for a party out for horses or coups -- then rise to horse tender, if he showed good sense and courage. He'd have to know how to make fire, read tracks, predict weather, find his way across the plains.

Most important of all, he must learn to respect the gods and listen to their voices, to obey the laws, provide for his family and take pride in himself and his people. Through it all he'd be learning the skills and the joy and the glory of the game of war. It took much to become a man, even more to become a leader. Sitting Bull hoped he could be as good a father to his son as Jumping Bull had been to him.

However that summer the warrior's songs became those of mourning. His lodge was visited by a sickness and in spite of the healer's herbs and songs, he lost both Scarlet Woman and his baby son. The women of his family did not leave his needs untended, but his lodge was empty as it had never been before.

After the fall hunt, with the drying racks hung with strips of meat, the women busy curing robes and the camp well supplied for the coming cold, the Hunkpapa warriors craved some action before the long, dark days locked them in their tipis. One brave passed the war pipe, suggesting a foray against the Assiniboin. Sitting Bull, brooding over the death of the wife and son he'd had for so short a time, was grateful for a distraction. He gladly smoked the war pipe. Bundling up in his white blanket capote, leggings and winter moccasins, he headed north with the handful of others who made up the party.

They were scarcely on their way when the wind whipped down from the north and turned the landscape hard as iron. By the time they reached the Missouri it was frozen solid and a skiff of grainy snow swirled over the ice. There on the far bank stood a lone Assiniboin lodge. The Hunkpapa could see they were alone, a father and mother with a baby, a small boy and a son just approaching his teens.

Immediately the Sioux loosed their war cries and galloped over the ice. The Assiniboin father turned to cover his family as they tried to run to safety. His older son grabbed for his small bow and stood with him to face the closing Sioux.

Sitting Bull's horse, as always one of the fastest, lost his footing on the ice. By the time he reached the far shore the deed was nearly done. Father, mother, babe and small boy lay in bloody heaps on the snow. The older boy, still standing fiercely defiant, was firing his last arrows.

The Hunkpapa braves rode at him to count coup. He did not run and he did not cry out. But as he looked into the fierce faces surrounding him, the tall, thin youngster chose one for a last appeal. "Big Brother!" he called to Sitting Bull.

He touched a cord. The warrior had no full brother. He'd just sent his own small son to live with the spirits. Acting on impulse, he jumped from his horse and shielded the boy with his body. "Don't shoot him!" he cried. "Don't shoot! This boy is too brave to die. I have no brother. I take this one for my brother. Let him live."

His companions milled in confusion. They had a right to the boy's life, some grumbled. He'd shot at them like a man. He was an enemy. Why spare him? They respected Sitting Bull too much to challenge him physically, and after some hot words they agreed to settle the matter when they got home. Sitting Bull hoisted the boy up behind him and the group headed back across the Missouri.

In camp, the argument continued. The boy had seemed brave, but could he ever be taught to be a Sioux warrior? Perhaps he'd never forget that he was Assiniboin. Perhaps he would turn on them later and take vengeance for his family. However, Sitting Bull had much influence for his age. His kind heart had won him friends before, and championing this helpless orphan was a thing to be much admired. He was not only strong in battle, he was versed in the ways of the spirits and careful always to respect their laws. When the council was over his wishes had prevailed. The young Assiniboin was to live and become one of the Hunkpapa tribe.

Sitting Bull took the boy to his tipi, dressed him in new clothes, painted the young face that was as light and narrow as his was dark and broad, and called in the holy men to perform an adoption ceremony.

The public declaration as they walked through the village to the special lodge, the symbolic tying together of their bodies, reminded the warrior this was not a responsibility to be taken lightly. Brother-friends, as one of the old ones reminded them, must be one in thought and action. They must give preference to each other before all mankind. They must be willing to give anything to, or do anything for, the other. They must both pray and try to please the gods.

If they succeeded in keeping these vows, the gods would give them success and the women would sing them praise songs. The Great Spirit would harden their shields, direct their arrows and put breath into their war horses. The buffalo would provide them with plenty of robes and moccasins, and they would have places of honor in the tents of their people. When they went south for the afterlife their spirits would be found worthy and they'd not be compelled to wander homeless over the world. When the rites were complete, the medicine man painted a red stripe on the boy's face and declared him a *hunka*, an adopted brother. Then, the serious business over, the feasting began.

Cheerfully the warrior dispersed food and horses until most of his wealth was gone. It was the work of a great man. The careful, deliberate brave now had an unknown boy, the son of enemies, for his brother. Whether the two of them could please the gods in the life to come, only time would tell.

The Girl With the Flag

On the lower Missouri events were stirring which would destroy brothers, not create them. While John Brown's scheme had been ill-planned and premature, his sentiments swept a widening portion of the population toward action. Kansas was finally admitted to the Union as a free state in January 1861, and that March Abraham Lincoln took the oath of office as President. Within a month Fort Sumter had felt the impact of Confederate shells. The sound of those shells, reverberating across the country, would strike the state of Missouri with unexpected violence. She was the gateway to the West, and as such a funnel that caught and mixed citizens whose attitudes were shaped in every state from Maine to Florida, and immigrants from every part of Europe. She was neither South nor North, yet she could control the Mississippi and its vital traffic and help or hinder the movement of supplies and men from the West.

The Federal government was desperate to cement the state to its cause, but the governor of Missouri, asked to supply men for the Union, vowed not one son of Missouri would bear arms against the South. Instead, he asked the Confederacy to ship him guns to attack the U.S. Arsenal at St. Louis. A proslavery militia began gathering at Camp Jackson nearby.

One May morning Union forces confronted the camp and forced its surrender, but hostile Missouri citizens lined the street to pelt the successful federal forces with rocks. Shots rang out, and before the morning was over 28 people were dead, including a baby. Many more were wounded.

The citizens of Missouri were shocked. They'd been thinking of war, talking of war, playing soldier at Sunday drills without paying much attention to their compatriots' politics. But now Missouri had real war casualties in her largest city -- casualties caused when St. Louis citizens fired upon each other. Some were convinced the federal troops had been justified in defending themselves and keeping order. Others were just as sure they had committed an atrocity. All across the state, people began to realize that in a war, one must choose sides. Their choices inked a line that would turn fence lines into walls, separate worshipers in church pews, split business partnerships, slice through communities and lie between brothers and friends, black and uncrossable.

Susan Arnold McCausland, belle of Lexington, Missouri and recent bride of successful merchant William McCausland, had posted her colors early. The day she learned of Virginia's secession she floated a small Confederate flag from the pole in the spreading lawn of the father's home on the corner of Broadway and Third streets.

Her father, E. G. Arnold, was a doctor in the prosperous town on the south bank of the Missouri, but he was also a graduate of the Virginia Military Institute, and Susan was Virginia-born. Although William's prominent family had pioneered near Lexington nearly 20 years before, he also had Virginia roots. She had no doubts about where her loyalty lay.

Still, the war had at first meant little to her but something new to watch on long afternoons, as her father and an ex-U.S. Army officer drilled the town's young men on the campus of the Masonic College. But she'd been horrified at the unprovoked attack U.S. troops had made while taking Camp Jackson, and she was gratified to see many Southern colors join hers, not only on Lexington's lawns and houses but on every public building. Many of them were homemade, but that didn't matter. Even the white-pillared Lafayette County Court House sported the Stars and Bars. She'd listened with delight to the news that the legislature in Jefferson City had formed a state army and commissioned Gen. Sterling Price to defend the state government and its sovereignty.

In June, while the state army alternately skirmished with and retreated from Federal forces to buy time, Price and Gov. Claibourne F. Jackson arrived in Lexington to recruit troops. It was a thrilling time. The citizens of the country polished up their deer rifles, cleaned their bird guns and hunted up their pistols. Companies and regiments were organized. The women got out their sewing baskets. Susan watched "Old Sacramento," a 12-pound brass cannon that had seen action in the Mexican War, made ready for battle. The old relic had signaled the Fourth of July as long as she could remember. Now it had more serious business.

Their purpose accomplished, Price and his new forces marched out of Lexington near the end of June, heading south to join the rest of the state forces and unite with the Confederate Army of Arkansas. The girls pressed beautifully tailored uniforms on their men, complete with gold braid, bright gold buttons and colorful sashes, and waved fond good-byes. The town sat quiet, with only the homemade flags drooping in the heavy air to remind them this summer was different.

Then, on July 9, the stacks of the steamboat *White Cloud* appeared along Gratz Bluff. Ordinarily the whistle of a steamer at the levee meant an excuse for a party. The town's young people often donned their finest and flocked down to board the vessel for dinner and a dance. Sometimes they persuaded the captain to tie up for the night and the fiddle played in the salon until dawn. Other times their ballroom continued down river until daybreak and they caught the stage, or the next boat, back home.

This boat promised no such festivities. It was a transport full of Federal troops come to occupy their town. In the sudden commotion of their arrival, one after another of the Confederate flags were snatched down and hidden away. Only Susan's remained, flying as it had for months.

It was her right, she thought, to show loyalty to whom she pleased on her own property. Besides, she was a woman. Her wishes would be respected for that reason if for no other. She and her friends gathered on the lawn to watch the troops march up from the levy, their spreading skirts like bright butterflies hovering over the green grass.

As the soldiers disembarked from the steamer, jeers and taunts filled the air. They were foreigners, the townspeople whispered, Germans from St. Louis, with a commander named Stifel. Some of them couldn't even speak English. How could they tell Missouri citizens what they could or could not do?

To Susan's astonishment the commander brought his troops to a halt at the Arnold home. Before she knew it she and her friends were surrounded. The officer pointed to her flag and demanded she surrender it. She was incredulous. These men -- armed men -- were threatening a woman -- demanding the flag of her native state. She indignantly refused to lower it.

A soldier moved to the staff and began to

lower it for her. She ran to snatch it from him and whirled to face the troops with an angry speech demanding her rights as a woman and a citizen of a free country and state to defend her convictions on her own property.

The officer was not moved. As she gasped in disbelief he reached to wrest the flag from her and she struggled to hold it.

Then, to her horror, Susan saw her young husband running toward them with his shotgun. He'd seen the squabble from his dry goods store and had grabbed the only weapon handy, his old bird gun, and come to her rescue. Conscious all at once of the bayonets and muzzles surrounding them, she cried out and dropped the flag as she reached to push William's gun barrel toward the ground.

The next thing she knew the officer was riding away with both the flag and William -- a prisoner of war. He was marched back down Broadway and onto the *White Cloud*.

As her fury cooled to fear -- and a new understanding of what war meant -- Susan tried to take comfort that the soldier had had to stoop to pick up the fallen flag. He could not say he had captured it, she told herself.

Susan was beside herself as days went by and William failed to return. Several other outspoken young gentlemen were likewise escorted into captivity. When she heard that William's fellow prisoner James Lightner had been killed trying to escape, her heart dropped like a stone. But William didn't try anything so foolhardy, and by late July he'd been paroled.

Before the end of August she had another reason to hate the Federal troops. Stifel had established his headquarters at the Masonic College on the hill just north of town. The brick class building, graced with the usual portico and white columns, commanded acres of open lawns. Stifel had been joined by five companies of militia and two battalions of Illinois Cavalry. Some of the militia were from Fort Leavenworth, but at least 100 volunteers were Germans from the town. They'd promised Lexington citizens in a ceremony the year before always to defend the U.S. flag, and now they marched in to do so. One of the first things Stifle did was to order the marvelous stand of virgin oaks and elms around the school cut down. Then the green lawn was defaced with trenches and piles of dirt. The troopers requisitioned lumber, doors and whatever else they could from the townspeople to reinforce their earth works.

Still, Stifel had left the town virtually free. And they could take heart that the news from their troops in the south was good. Price had been joined by hundreds of volunteers as he marched south. There'd been a clash at Carthage which set the Federals running. The U.S. general had been killed at Wilson Creek and lost 1,300 men. The Federals were retreating to St. Louis to lick their wounds.

The summer heat was just beginning to lift in early September when the people in Lexington heard the whispers. Price was on his way north to win back the state! The town rustled with excitement, but obviously the Union commanders had also heard the rumors. Susan and her friends watched as another column of Federal troops marched down Main Street and on north to the college campus. Flaunting the Stars and Stripes and the green and gold flag of the 23rd Illinois Infantry, the file swung through the college gates.

The campus now suffered further insult. The new federal commander, an Irish colonel named Mulligan, at once set his men to digging entrenchments to make the site safe from a cavalry charge from the east, the only exposure not protected by steep slopes. Soon the felled oaks had been sharpened into ugly, threatening abatis.

Their champion Price was rumored to have 12,000 men. The townspeople could see Mulligan had less than a third that many. Their excitement grew. When they learned the Irish colonel had requisitioned $900,000 from the town bank to support the Union cause, their bitterness grew also.

By September 11 they could see at least part of Price's huge force for themselves as units pulled up and bivouacked at the county fairgrounds a mile south of town. Lexington citizens slipped easily in and out of town through the thin line of Federal pickets to visit the Rebel force. Other Missourians from the surrounding countryside began arriving in wagons and on foot to see the show. Susan found the town packed with people. They sprawled on the courthouse lawn and bedded down in the livery stable. The taverns were

People of the Old Missury

packed with Southerners loudly certain the Federals were in for a whipping.

The two forces began feeling each other out. Mulligan burned the bridge Price would need to approach town; a Union battery set up in Machpelah Cemetery, where Susan's sister lay buried. Small squads of Price's men dashed into town for a brief exchange of shots before racing back to their lines. Susan followed the action from the porch and windows of her home. She cheered the daring of the Southern men, but when a friend was unhorsed and bayoneted before her eyes she was suddenly sobered. As he was carried away by blue-coated troopers, she wondered: was his brave show worth the cost?

Yet more Southerners arrived. Now they camped right in town, on the lawns and in the churches. The Federals withdrew to their trenches. On September 17, with a battle imminent, the citizens were ordered to evacuate the town for their own safety. Women and children, including some wives of Union troops, streamed down the streets and into the country.

Susan did not go. The next day, a clear, golden fall morning, she heard the strains of the new popular favorite, "Dixie," and ran from the house and across the lawn to peer up Main Street. She caught her breath. There down the street came the Confederate flag; neophyte soldiers -- ununiformed but moving with purpose -- were falling into position all along the road. She could hear the noise of shouted orders, of horses hooves, of drums and bugles, and the rumble of guns being wheeled into place.

One battery set up only three lots away from where Susan stood. Farther away she could catch glimpses of other troops moving to surround the college. As she stood watching, a family friend marched by, he, like the rest of the volunteers, still in civilian clothes. "What are you doing in town?" he asked in surprise. "You would better go to shelter at once. We are to fight now, right away!"

Almost as he ceased speaking the guns began to thunder. Susan shuddered and involuntarily covered her ears. Houses blocking the Confederate line of fire turned to kindling as they were blasted out of the way. Still she refused to flee. She moved to the intersection of Third Street two lots above the battery and, finding a good view of the field, settled down to watch.

To the east was the college, ringed by trenches, with batteries at three corners. West of it trenches and breastworks snaked on west and north around the crest of the hill, then looped back east to the headquarters building. Just beyond the western trench stood the home built by well-to-do citizen Oliver Anderson.

Anderson had developed his hemp business until he was co-owner of a warehouse (which stood just below the house on the river bottom), and owner of a rope factory and a newspaper. The stately brick home, just eight years old, was complete with slave quarters, a carriage house, and a substantial brick summer kitchen. A flower garden, vineyards, the vegetable garden and an orchard that yielded apples, plums and peaches stretched between the house and the college.

The Anderson house, whose upper story windows commanded a view of both the sun-bright orchard, heavy with fruit, and the Union entrenchments, bore the yellow flag of neutrality. It had been marked by the Union for use as a field hospital. But as the fighting accelerated there appeared to be rifle fire coming from the bedroom windows.

The crack of Minnie rifles was added to

the cannonading. The ground seemed to shake and Susan could see windows in nearby houses quiver and shatter from the concussion. Old Sacramento was doing her part. The Confederate forces had completely ringed the Union position, with a skirmish line between them and the river. Whatever water there was in the two college cisterns would be all the Union forces would have for 3,500 men and 700 horses.

Already, wounded were being carried to the Union hospital. The call went out for doctors and nurses for both sides. But although the rooms of the house sheltered wounded, there could be no question the entry balcony and upper story also provided cover for Union snipers. The Confederates shrank from shelling the building -- both for humanitarian and practical reasons -- but it could not be ignored.

As Susan watched, a horde of men charged up from the riverbank, not firing on the sanctuary, but racing through head-high weeds towards the building. Land mines exploded as they ran, but most of them made it through the dirt and smoke to the house. Susan tried to imagine the wide hall and curving stairway she knew echoing the boots of angry men. She could see nothing of what went on inside, but it seemed no time at all until there were snipers firing east into the Union trenches, instead of west into the Southern lines.

Then, with a sun that blazed like summer still high in the sky, Susan saw a line of human forms silhouetted for an instant on the top of the Union embankment below the house. As they flowed over it, yelling wildly, they were immediately followed by another line. The Yankees were trying to retake the hospital! She moved to the middle of the street for a better view.

Almost as fast as they moved over the embankment they began to fall. But others ran behind them, yelling defiance and peppering the house with fire. They fell among the apples of the orchard, between the grape vines, among the flowers. Then they were at the entryway and in the east door; the Rebels fled out the other side for cover. For a couple of hours the sniper fire was again directed west. However, before sunset the Confederates had driven the Blue Coats out and reclaimed the besieged house for the South.

As the light faded Susan retreated to her father's home, emotionally exhausted but too upset to get much sleep. The rooms of her home, unlike the Andersons', were not filled with groaning men, its walls were not pocked with bullet holes, its gardens were not littered with corpses. But her bedroom ceiling was washed in red on and off through the night, as town buildings ignited by the hot shells smoldered and flared into fires that kept her tense with fear.

And, in the Union camp, countless fires flickered as the men molded bullets they would use tomorrow.

The second day of the siege was quieter. A morning shower cooled the air and gave the suffering Union forces a little relief for their parched throats. Neither side had plentiful ammunition and the cannons spoke only now and then, but squirrel rifles crackled constantly. Missouri sharpshooters were perched on every roof and tree that gave them a line of fire into the trenches. They waited, at their ease, for a Blue Coat to show himself and be dispatched.

Other Southerners under General Raines on the northeast side of the college aimed incendiary shot at the symbolic Masonic eye painted on the gable, laughing as the heated balls crashed through the gables and the shingled roof, picturing the frantic scramble they caused inside.

The Northern troops aimed a few balls at the town and set some more houses afire. One ball slammed into a column of the courthouse. But it seemed obvious that unless they were reinforced it was only a matter of time; all of their attempts to reach water had been repelled. The stench of dead horses and men began to drift over the town.

At twilight there was activity down at the Anderson warehouse. Men were seen rolling the large hemp bales out of the building and down the riverbank. Then the dripping bales were loaded on wagons and carted up to the hospital.

On the morning of September 20 Susan woke to see a line of bales stretching from the hospital to face the Union trenches. As a fresh artillery barrage ripped gaping holes in the college boarding house and blasted brick and mortar from the embattled headquarters that had so recently been schoolrooms, the line of hemp bales began to move. Over and over the heavy bales rolled, as the men behind the moving cover advanced into withering fire that could not reach them.

The desperate Mulligan tried hot shot, but the wet bales refused to ignite. Direct hits rocked them, but only delayed them for a moment. By noon the Confederates had breached the defenses. As white flags went up, first on the perimeter trenches and finally over headquarters, a gigantic cheer burst from the Southern troops, and the people of Lexington knew the end had come.

Susan watched the weary, smoke-blackened Union troops -- and some soldiers' wives who'd stayed through the battle -- straggle out. Then, from inside the college, she heard a band playing. It was not "Dixie" this time, but the marching song of Mulligan's Irish troops. Soon, their last defiant gesture finished, they, too, moved out the gate to stack their arms.

Susan and the citizens of Lexington celebrated the victory, never doubting the rightness of their cause. It was satisfying to know the courthouse floor was piled with Union muskets, rifles, swords and saddles. It was thrilling to know Mulligan was a prisoner of General Price at the City Hotel. It felt good to find relief in laughter, as the local men who'd fought for the Union were released on their promise not to bear arms against the South again -- provided their wives also promised to keep them out of future mischief. It was exciting to watch the Southern troops march back south, their numbers doubled by enthusiastic volunteers, their steps enlivened by the Lexington brass band's renditions of "Dixie" and "Listen to the Mockingbird."

But Susan's enthusiasm was tempered with the knowledge that William had decided to join the State Guard. He was to leave her, his dry goods store, the Presbyterian Church where he taught Sunday School, and go south with General Raines to fight wherever the fighting was -- perhaps another small town like Lexington.

She knew her town and people would retain scars less visible and more permanent than the terrible rends in the college lawn.

She could scarcely bear to think of some of the tales that filled the town -- they said one of the wounded Southerners left behind in the Anderson house when the Yankees recaptured it had had both eyes ground out. Another young Southerner's body showed gaping holes through both palms -- futile protection against a bayonet.

The townspeople would not soon forget or forgive the brutalities of war. And they'd have to live with the fact there had been Lexington men on both sides of the battle. Gallant, promising young men were dead -- some defending, some attacking the flag she loved.

Long after victorious troops had marched away, Susan wandered through the trenched campus and came upon a human foot protruding from the ground. This soldier's grave, she knew, must have been nothing more than a few spadefuls of earth, thrown over his body under cover of darkness. She found it pathetic. What must it have been like to be on the receiving end of those Missouri squirrel rifles, she wondered. The soldiers in the blue coats, she realized, were human, too.

The year 1861 was especially hard for Susan McCausland. Besides enduring the Battle of Lexington and sending her husband off to war, she buried both her parents in the newly crowded Machpelah Cemetery.

However, ensuing years were kinder. William came home to stay after the Battle of Pea Ridge, and when peace came they built a comfortable life together -- he a city councilman, a church elder, a trustee of Wentworth Male Academy that took form in 1881 not far from the grounds of the college ruined 20 years before. She was known for her quick intelligence, liberal education and refined Southern ways.

In 1912, when Susan wrote her reminiscence of the Battle of Lexington, many of the six score men who'd died in the battle lay buried in the town cemetery; others had been carried away by their families to rest at home. The girl with the flag, then 73, mused that others, in graves undiscovered, would probably be forever part of the hill where they fell.

To the Golden Hills

While some men fought their brothers along the lower Missouri for the sake of principles, word of new riches at the river's source tempted other men to leave the settlements in search of a better life. Fifty years before, the lure of soft, brown pelts had convinced men to take their chances in the domain of the Blackfoot. This time the area called Three Forks (in the southeastern corner of present Montana) was blessing the daring with the sweet, hard weight of gold.

Some took the river route -- steamers now made their way past Fort Union and on to Fort Benton -- and worked their way south to the camps springing up in Grasshopper Creek, Alder Gulch and the Gallatin valley. Others traveled the Platte River Road to Salt Lake and headed north. By 1864, others were turning off the Platte Road above Fort Laramie to follow a trail marked out by a young Georgian named John Bozeman. It was shorter, with good wood and water and plentiful game. Few of the eager emigrants thought at all about whose land they would have to cross to reach the hills of gold. Fewer yet wondered how those inhabitants would feel about their trespass.

On May 17, 1864 a small train of wagons set out from the little prairie town of Geneva, Kansas. Ahead, Frances Wiggins Kelly was sure, lay a romantic and delightful journey to "the golden hills of Idaho," better health for her new husband, Josiah, and a better life for her and their daughter, Mary.

Slim, dark-haired Fanny was not a privileged southern belle. She had spent her first 11 years on a Canadian lake shore before her father joined the migration to Kansas in 1856 and established a home for them in the new town of Geneva. He'd returned to Canada for his family, full of enthusiastic plans for their new home, but cholera had taken his life just as they'd reached the Missouri. Her mother, true to her husband's wishes, had continued on to Geneva and they'd managed as best they could. Fanny was 19 now and a new bride, but she'd already taken on the care of her sister's young daughter, adopting the child when the need arose.

She and Josiah had heard all the news about the rich new gold fields in the year-old Idaho Territory. Miners had fanned out from Washington, California and Colorado to explore the mountains which gave rise to the Missouri and its westward-flowing sisters. There were already 35,000 people burrowing into the hillsides around Virginia City in Alder Gulch; a new town of Gallatin City was forming at the Three Forks. There was talk that Idaho Territory would soon be split to form yet another government.

Fanny and Josiah were filled with optimism. With their two Negro servants, Frank and Andy, and friend Gardner Wakefield, they had taken the trail west along the Platte River toward the Rockies. Many others had caught the fever and a few days from Geneva they were joined by a Methodist minister, the Reverend Sharp, and a Mr. Taylor. When they overtook a large train of emigrants a few weeks later, they were joined by their friends the Larimers, and Fanny welcomed the pleasure of another woman's company to help pass the long days.

Mrs. Larimer had an eight-year-old boy, and was an ambitious, accomplished woman. She was a daguerreotype photographer and her wagon was carefully packed with the chemicals of her craft. She hoped to make her fortune photographing the miners and their camps.

Fanny, like most of her fellow travelers, was impressed with the "wonderfully clear and transparent sky," and she rejoiced in the vibrant wildflowers spotting the grasses with purples, blues, yellows and whites. With Frank and Andy to set up camp and tend the cattle, she had time to enjoy their journey, time to read and sing songs with Mary and write letters to those back home. Josiah even laughed and indulged his bride's sensitivities by purchasing wood whenever possible so they'd not have to eat food cooked over buffalo chips. During noon rests and after evening meals, the two women entertained themselves and the children by gathering flowers, picking berries and examining the natural curiosities of the prairie. On Sunday, which they observed as a day of rest, Reverend Sharp presided at worship services and Fanny took comfort in the familiar words and tunes in this unfamiliar land.

The landscape was growing increasingly strange to her. At night, listening to a silence deeper than she'd ever known, she tried not to think of her mother's fearful farewell. The older woman had a presentiment they'd never meet again, and Fanny had tried to comfort her with promises that when the railroad across the West was in operation they could easily visit each other.

Mary, the niece who was now her daughter, was a good traveler and a joy to Fanny. She kept the train entertained with her chatter. But as they began to meet Indians she grew fearful.

Most of the Indians along the crowded, dusty road were harmless beggars, pleading for some sugar or a biscuit. Both Fanny and Josiah tried to reassure the child by showing friendship for the natives; Josiah bought her beads and other trinkets. Still Mary could not get used to the faces that looked so strange and fierce to her; she ducked her blonde head and retreated behind Fanny whenever Indians were near.

Early in July, with the yucca blossoms shriveled and the scattered clumps of grasses turning brown in the heat, they reached Fort Laramie. It was time to decide which route to take to the gold fields. The route on to Salt Lake and the Pacific coast was like a wide highway, its hard-packed ruts a testament to the thousands of feet, hooves and iron tires it had borne, its edges littered with discards, its campsites crowded.

The road north along the eastern foot of the Big Horns would scarcely be a road at all. At the last bridge of the Platte (present Casper, Wyoming) a few wagon ruts would turn off at right angles to the river. This trail had first been used successfully by wagons only the summer before. But it was shorter, they were told, and wound through beautiful country, blessed with wood and grass and game. The Kellys with their servants, the Larimers, and the Misters Wakefield, Taylor and Sharp decided to turn north.

They gave no thought to savages. Everyone knew about the terrible massacre the Santee Sioux had committed in Minnesota in 1862 that had left over 500 people dead, but they were only vaguely aware the army had chased the Santee west to the Missouri country and chastised them. On their way up the Platte they had seen troops building new posts at Cottonwood Creek and Scott's Bluff. However, at Laramie and at Horseshoe Station the word was the same: the Indians' quarrel was with the soldiers, they were told. They would not be molested. Convinced they could make better time if their small party remained alone, Gardner Wakefield sang out, "Ho for Idaho!" Little Mary joined the chorus and they moved on up the Platte.

On July 12, the wagons wound through the trees along Little Box Elder Creek (near present Glenrock, Wyoming), splashed across the small stream and pulled up the far side. Fanny noticed gratefully that the sun was finally setting. She paused to admire the evening sky, more than ready for a breath of cooler air, a simple meal and a night's rest. It had not been an unpleasant journey, but it had not been easy, either, and she was weary of the heat and dust and constant travel.

She'd not heard the slightest sound, but as she reached to untie her sunbonnet the bluffs ahead were suddenly covered with Indians -- at least 200 Indians, painted Indians who gave a wild whoop, fired their guns in the air and galloped down on the train. The main body of warriors pulled to a stop a short distance from the wagons, and before they could think, smaller parties were circling their train.

Recovering from the shock of their appearance, Josiah ordered the wagons corralled and grabbed his rifle, determined to resist.

Fanny, with a trembling Mary pressed against her leg, begged him to be cautious and do nothing to provoke their anger. With a reassuring nod, Josiah walked out to meet the chief and demand his intentions.

He was an Oglala, the Indian said, and friendly. He and his people were good friends of the Whites. He walked to the wagons and began shaking hands and in moments the whole party was crowding around the wagons, smiling and nodding and shaking hands with them all until Fanny's arm ached. The Indians seemed cheerful enough, using signs and a few English words to make themselves understood, but their first request was that Josiah trade his fine horse for one of their ponies. Afraid of antagonizing them, he reluctantly agreed. Still not satisfied, they asked for flour. When handed a sack they dumped the contents on the ground and saved only the cloth sack. Then they asked for clothing.

With resistance impossible, the white party granted their requests, offered other gifts and played for time. Josiah tried to give Fanny hope; if they could keep the Indians feeling friendly perhaps another train would appear and scare them off, perhaps they'd get tired of their game and go on their way. But she could clearly see the despair that underlay his cheerful words.

Struggling to keep things in a friendly mood, Fanny smiled and asked if she could have a pair of moccasins in return for the clothing. A young Indian cheerfully handed her a beautifully beaded pair. However, other Sioux were becoming bolder and more insolent in their demands. A warrior laid a hand on Josiah's rifle, but he curtly shook it off. Then at last the chief gave them permission to move on and they were on their way.

But instead of riding off, the Indians went with them. They insisted on driving the small herd of livestock, and Josiah decided to halt the train. When he refused their demands to move on, the chief decided his men needed supper. If they were fed, he promised, they would go to the hills to sleep. Hoping to appease them, the Kelly party agreed. Josiah told Fanny to stay in the wagon and took Andy with him to gather some wood. Fanny, fighting to control her mounting fear so that she could comfort Mary, tried to think if there was anything she could do. Glancing around the wagon, she reached for her purse and stuffed it into a pocket in her skirt.

Mr. Larimer and Frank had started the fire. Mr. Taylor was tending his team, and Mr. Wakefield was getting food from his wagon when guns exploded in Fanny's ears. She watched Wakefield collapse in slow motion. The minister, his hands full of sugar he was distributing to appease the Sioux, fell a few feet away.

Taylor's forehead became a bloody hole and his eyes stared wildly at her as he toppled backward. Frank crumpled at the front wheel, his body bristling with arrows. Suddenly braves were in the wagons, smashing crates and trunks with axes and tearing their belongings apart.

Fanny was yanked down from her seat, her legs catching cruelly behind the footboard. Hoping they weren't broken, she crouched with a hysterical Mrs. Larimer and their frightened children on the ground under guard as their wagons were emptied and put to the torch. She had no idea where Josiah was or what his fate had been.

Fanny was sure the four of them would be killed as soon as the Indians were ready to travel, but she determined to stay quiet and not provoke any act herself. When the chief came near she touched his arm and pleaded for protection for them and their children. He shook her off and told her to be quiet.

She caught her breath when a wagon appeared down the trail. But none followed it, and when the Indians saw it was alone they galloped toward it. The man driving managed to wheel it around and whipped up the horses. Then he handed the reins to his wife and threw their possessions out the back as they fled to safety.

The faint hope of rescue died away.

Then Mrs. Larimer, watching her trunks of photographic gear fall to ruin, gave a wild cry, and the chief was at their side with a knife in his hand. Fanny, affecting courage she did not feel, begged again for their lives. He handed her a clump of feathers he wore on his head, but she could see no change in his fierce expression. As night came on, the women huddled with their children on the ground, certain their fate was already decided.

Then a young brave gave Fanny a handful of clothing and a pair of shoes for her and Mary. They would need these, he indicated. They were to live -- at least for now. Fanny wrapped a bright shawl around Mary and allowed herself a small hope. When the same brave brought her some letters and books from their wagon, she hid as many as possible in her clothing. Josiah might be alive out there somewhere. She would use the papers to mark their trail.

The Oglala loaded up their plunder and set fire to what was left. The Indians ordered the women to mount horses, and in the flickering light Fanny could see the horse they'd picked for her was a crippled one that belonged to the Larimers. She tried to tell her captors, but they did not understand and forced her to mount. The horse immediately fell, pinning her beneath his weight, and she felt sharp pain. By the time she was mounted on another horse, Mrs. Larimer had disappeared in the distance and Fanny came close to panic for the first time. To be alone with these savages was almost more than she could bear to think about.

Yet she was not entirely alone. Mary's arms gripped her waist, and as she rode further into the dark night and the line of march stretched out, Fanny developed a plan. She was toward the rear of the party and no one had noticed the papers she was dropping. Perhaps at least Mary could be saved. She whispered to the terrified child, convincing her this was the only way. Then, watching her chance, she slid the girl to the ground in some brush and rode on.

Her whole body tight, she waited for the cry of discovery.

There was none. The train moved on as before.

At first she was weak with relief. But as each thud of the horse's hooves carried her farther from the child she began to wonder. Had she done the right thing? Could Mary wade the creek they'd crossed, see the papers in the dark, find her way alone? Were Josiah or any of the other men still alive to help her? Or would she wander helplessly until she died of thirst or hunger?

Had she given her daughter a chance for life or assured her death, abandoned and alone? Unable to bear the torment, she risked everything. Slipping as quietly as possible from her horse she dropped to the ground and lay quiet. Her horse walked on.

But not for long. Soon there were excited cries and the line of march halted. Then the Indians formed a line and began beating the ground to find her hiding place.

They might have missed her, crouched in the dark undergrowth, but the horses did not. The animals reared in fear and she knew she was discovered. Immediately she stood and took the offensive.

The child had fallen asleep and slipped from the horse, she told them. She had tried to tell them, but they had not heard her. She had gone back to find her child.

The Sioux were not fooled. They beat her, and warned any further attempt to escape would mean death. They would find Mary themselves, in the morning. On they pressed, to ford a river and split into smaller groups. When they finally camped, Fanny slept on the bare ground without any cover, but under guard.

The next day Fanny's mind turned every breeze and bird cry into Mary's voice and she determined to try escape regardless of the cost. She strove to keep track of the direction of march. But that night she was tied securely and could not wriggle out of her bonds.

When she was untied in the morning she was rocked with the news that Mrs. Larimer and her son were gone. A sympathetic Indian had helped them escape during the night. Now she was truly alone; her desolation complete. Could she retain her sanity, she wondered? How could she survive this? She began to pray and with the prayer came hope. Perhaps Mary had reached safety. Perhaps Josiah was alive and already searching for her. As long as she had one small hope she could live. She had a pencil and began keeping track of the days.

Robot-like, she went about her duties, for she was expected to work now -- to gather the Indian-spooky settlers' horses in the morning, to carry the elderly chief's arms on the march and to lead an unruly pack horse.

Struggling to hold his gun, bow, and arrow case and still control the horse, she accidentally dropped a long, ornate pipe. It broke and she left it behind.

That night the Indians built a huge fire and began to dance. Fanny was wondering if she was about to be burned alive when the chief thrust his face into hers, demanding something she could not understand. Anxious to obey, she glanced around for a clue to what he wanted, and the boy who had given her the shoes motioned as if he were smoking a pipe.

When the chief understood that she had broken it, he sentenced Fanny to death. She would be tied on a wild horse and used for target practice, they told her. She sank to the ground in terror, praying her final prayer, while the Indians readied the horse and waited for the signal. Then she remembered the purse still in her pocket. She pulled it out and began distributing the money.

Miraculously the rage faded from their faces. They lowered their weapons and asked her to explain its worth. She began, raising trembling fingers to indicate each bill's worth, but before she could complete her task she collapsed into an unconscious heap.

Once again they let her live, but the next days she was sorry they had. Fighting to stay on her mount without losing the erratic pack horse, bruised, exhausted, hungry, suffering terribly with thirst as they moved north across dry, sandy hills, she longed for the release of death.

She nearly found it. She was so near succumbing to heat and thirst by the time the Sioux reached one river on their long trek northeast, they had to lay her body in its cool waters to revive her.

On the ninth day of her captivity the tribe came on a buffalo herd. After the kill they handed her a knife and urged her to share in the raw meat. Weak and hungry as she was, she could not bring herself to do it.

But at last their journey was coming to an end. As the Sioux neared their village (between the Heart and Cannonball Rivers in North Dakota) they paused to dress for their triumphal entrance. Fanny watched the braves deck themselves out in clothes from the wagons. One Indian wore her hat. The war chief topped his grotesquely painted black and yellow face with a crown of eagle feathers, then draped one of Fanny's colorful quilts around his shoulders.

As they entered the village, she was astonished at its size. It stretched for several miles along a stream, and the travelers were immediately engulfed in celebration. Songs and glad cries filled the air as she was marched between two columns of warriors to the old chief's lodge. Five smiling women came to meet him; then stared at Fanny in silence. She was escorted into his lodge, where she discovered a sixth wife -- the eldest -- and watched the women "*ooh*" and "*ah*" over the spoils from the wagons.

She had looked forward to reaching the village, remembering the noble savages she'd read about, hoping the Indian women might be more understanding and merciful. Now there was a frightening squabble over a piece of cloth, during which she learned Sioux women could wield knives as well as men. Shrinking terrified from the fray, she thought the chief's old wife at least as fierce as he and dreaded being left alone with the women.

However, once the eldest wife had established her authority, they all treated her kindly. One brought her a bowl of meat and soon women and children from other lodges were crowding in to see her and give her food. After she'd eaten they examined her body again and again, exclaiming over her dress and her hands and feet.

When they discovered bruises and cuts she'd suffered when she was jerked from the wagon they dressed her wounds. And when they saw her fright at an order for her to join the chief for feasting, the eldest wife sent one of the chief's daughters, a little girl named Yellow Bird, with her for reassurance.

At the feast the chief himself spoke to her for the first time with kindness. She could have Yellow Bird for her own, he told her, to replace the daughter she had lost. The little girl was warm and open, and Fanny did find comfort in her presence. That night the chief's old wife brewed a special tea to help her rest, showed her to her bed of buffalo robes, and gently took the moccasins from her feet. Curled on the furs with Yellow Bird beside her, Fanny had the first real sleep she'd had in nearly two weeks.

As the celebration continued the next day, she was invited to join the chiefs, medicine men and warriors in a huge tipi for a feast. The women in her lodge were impressed at the invitation and let her know that she was being extended a rare honor. Seated in the lodge and again the center of attention, she observed that a pole in the middle of the circle was hung with scalps, and food simmered in kettles at its base.

As the chief and others spoke they often gestured toward her, and she began to fear they were again debating her death. After the chief had lit a long pipe and offered it to the four directions, the earth and sky, he passed it around the group until all had smoked. She remembered the pipe she had broken on the trail and began to understand its significance.

Then, in silence, the lids were lifted from the kettles and a stew of dog meat dished into bowls. Given her share, she realized she could not refuse and managed to eat a few bites before passing it on for others to finish. When the food was gone, the guests all departed in silence. Relieved that she had misinterpreted the Oglala's intent, she decided the feast must be a religious ceremony which required the Indians to sacrifice their faithful friends in testimony to the Great Spirit.

The dance that night seemed dedicated to baser gods. For hours she was made to stand in the center of the circle of wild dancers, holding high a pole from which dangled human scalps. The dancers' fury seemed intense, yet when it was over, the chief's three sisters kindly led her back to her lodge.

She was a quick young woman and she was already learning some of their language. She realized that, like the other females, she would have regular duties in the lodge and she did her best to do them well. Pleasing her captors seemed her only hope for safety.

As ordered, she kept the lodge supplied with water and peeled kinnikinnick for the braves to smoke. She befriended the children, singing to entertain them, surprised at how many of the small ones had fair skin and light hair.

One squaw she met could speak a little English. Her husband was a soldier from Fort Laramie and her little boy was dressed in a miniature uniform. However, the soldier's white wife was at the fort now, and the Indian family had been sent away. Her child and the other half-breeds were always the last to fill their bowls, and Fanny was grieved to see their hunger.

After only a brief stay at the village, Fanny was awakened to help pack the contents of the lodge. They were moving. The noise and commotion made it seem as if the world were coming down with the tipis. Yet to her surprise, in spite of squalling children, barking dogs and screaming squaws, the tipi skins were soon packed on lodgepole travois, the horses and the dogs were loaded and they were on their way. Eventually, she found out why. The warriors had gone to fight the white soldiers; the camp was moving to a safer location.

When they reached a group of clay-topped knolls (the Killdeer Mountains) they set up another camp and waited the coming battle. Fanny had many hours to wonder whether defeat or victory would be more dangerous to her. The camp looked south over a rolling plain and she thought it a forlorn place. There were trees and brush in the gullies around the butte's base, but the upper slopes, yellow and barren, shimmered with heat. Worthless as it looked to her, she was beginning to understand why the Indians fought. If they gave any more ground they would have no game to live on. The new trail the Kellys had planned to take to Idaho and the troops pressing west from the Missouri were intrusions that could not be tolerated. On August 8 the warriors set out again.

Suddenly there was great commotion among the tribe and Fanny realized she could hear the guns of battle. Was rescue that close at hand? Would the Sioux let her live to be rescued? In her anxiety the day seemed endless, but as the hours passed the sound of firing grew louder. And now she could see smoke rising above the hills. The Sioux began throwing their belongings together and rushing to get the women and children away from the line of fire.

Fanny was ordered onto a horse near the head of the column. They snatched off her sunbonnet so she would look more like an Indian woman. She was not to look toward the fighting, they told her fiercely. She couldn't resist a quick glance. Blue-coated troopers were advancing while bronze-backed warriors dodged from rock to tree, fighting a desperate delaying action. Then blows rained on her head and shoulders for her disobedience and she could see no more.

The Winter of the White Woman

Fanny Kelly's trip to Idaho had ended in a Sioux camp just as the Teton Sioux were caught up in the growing conflict with the white man. The army, determined to punish the Santee for the uprising which had left 500 dead in Minnesota, had pushed most of them west into the recently organized Dakota Territory just as word of the magnitude of the gold strikes in Montana spread, and more and more argonauts wanted to use the Missouri as a route to and from the gold fields. Others, familiar with Isaac Stevens' railway survey, decided to go overland from Minnesota. Both these groups and the budding plains towns on the east side of the river were demanding the government do something to control the increasingly hostile Sioux. In response, the army moved upriver from its most northerly post at Fort Randall to build a new fort which was named for Dakota District Commander Gen. Alfred Sully. It was the first of a string of posts the army intended to establish on the upper Missouri.

In the parched summer of 1863 the Hunkpapa had gone east across the Missouri to find buffalo, not battles. But there on the hunting grounds was the Santee Inkpaduta and his people, who'd been pushed out of the lake country by the angry Whites the summer before. The Santee had a sad story to tell, of waiting for annuity payments that did not come, of years of broken promises, of insults and humiliation while their children cried with hunger. They had finally rebelled and attacked the agencies and settlers, but the soldiers had prevailed. Troopers were right on Inkpaduta's heels, and he'd invited the Hunkpapa to join the fight.

For the first time Sitting Bull tried his skills against this new enemy, who came with wagons and marched in lines. Although the big guns the soldiers used kept the Indians too far away for a proper fight, he had scored one satisfying coup. Charging down on one of the mule keepers, the warrior evaded the bite of his long black whip, touched the infuriated man and galloped away with a mule, yelling his triumph. The soldiers had followed the Sioux to the Missouri, but had not crossed it. Sitting Bull headed back west with his trophy and a new honor, his confidence unshaken.

But this summer of 1864 the soldiers were on the west side of the river, invading the Hunkpapa hunting grounds. There were thousands of them, the Indians learned, with hundreds of wagons and several of the big guns which rolled on wheels. The soldier chief had made it clear they wanted war. When three Sioux had killed one of the invaders who'd wandered off alone, the soldiers rode them down and killed them in return. But killing them had not been enough. The soldier chief had ordered their heads cut off and stuck them on high poles on a hill, an obscene taunt against the prairie sky. The Sioux knew, now, what to expect. The white man evidently wanted to kill all the Sioux. They withdrew to the edge of the badlands, where they never saw white men, and pondered what to do.

By the time Fanny had reached the Sioux encampment in July of 1864, the army was building another post, Fort Rice, a few miles north of the Cannonball River, and Sully was on the march with 2,200 men to find and subdue the Sioux.

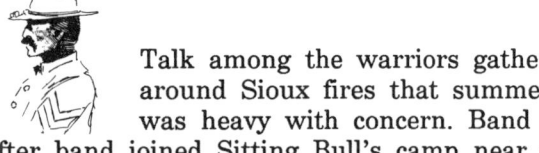 Talk among the warriors gathered around Sioux fires that summer was heavy with concern. Band after band joined Sitting Bull's camp near the Killdeer Mountains just south of the Little Missouri. Sans Arc, Miniconjou, Oglala and Blackfoot Sioux gathered with the Hunkpapa to talk of the outrage. Where were the soldiers going and what were they doing in the Indians' country? Many of the Hunkpapa were frightened at what was happening and had no wish to fight the soldiers. They had only a few guns and little ammunition.

While the councils were debating what to do, Inkpaduta's band of Santee and Yanktonai rode into the large camp of Teton Sioux. He had fought the soldiers many times, so the Hunkpapa and other tribes sat down to listen to his words. He advised moving back into the hills to a more protected site. The Sioux moved their village, which now housed nearly 1,600 lodges, to a place of Inkpaduta's choosing, a flat piece of ground near a spring on an open slope at the mouth of a canyon. There was good water, wood, plenty of game: surely here the people would be safe.

Sitting Bull had never intended to fight the white soldiers. He was content in his own world, where buffalo provided food, and enemies provided wealth and honors. His adopted brother had repaid his charity by growing into so fine a warrior the Hunkpapa listed his coming to the tribe in the winter count, a friend so true that he was seldom more than a few steps from his brother's side. Sitting Bull's graying father had fallen to a Crow knife the summer after the young Assiniboin found refuge in the warrior's lodge, and the young brother now bore the honored name of Jumping Bull. With his father gone, Sitting Bull became leader of his band. All he wanted was for his people to live unmolested, to follow the way of their fathers.

The women were still settling their families' belongings a day or two later when a hunting party returned to report soldiers were coming. Anxious for the people's safety, the chiefs sent out scouts to watch the troops, and before long they returned to report the soldiers were closer yet and would be at the camp the next day. The next morning Sitting Bull's nephew, out to care for his family's horses, galloped in to report, "The soldiers are here now!"

Sitting Bull ran for his war horse and rode with Jumping Bull, his uncle, Four Horns, and other Sioux to a hilltop, where they could see the troops approaching. The prairie was dark with them, foot soldiers marching in a wide line, then bunches of horse soldiers, then a long line of wagons. As the warriors waited to see what the troops would do, a man named Long Dog shouted that he would find out if they'd come to fight. Calling on the special charm which made him bulletproof, he dashed forward and raced in front of the line. Although the line of soldiers spurted with smoke, Long Dog rode back unharmed. His medicine was strong; bullets could not harm him.

As the line approached, Sitting Bull's young nephew, who as yet had no coups, rode forth to challenge the soldiers and draw their fire. In moments he was back, breathless, triumphant, untouched by the bullets. Sitting Bull was proud the boy had wanted to prove his courage.

By now all the warriors were riding down to meet the threat, each fighting in his own way. One bunch of Sioux grouped to charge the army's flank. The horse soldiers managed to drive them back, but as they galloped after the Indians they were suddenly set upon by Sioux with fresh horses and had to wheel and ride for their lives. Several were pulled from their mounts before they reached the line. However, as the white men drew closer and the fighting became general, the soldiers began to use the big guns that boomed twice and shot so far. Whenever the Sioux managed to separate a bunch of soldiers and move in for the kill, the guns boomed and bodies went flying. As they were pushed back, a few shells flew over the braves and into the village. The women had already started packing, but as the lodgepoles shattered and tipis collapsed in smoking ruin they scrambled to save what they could and flee.

Then a thing happened that made all the Sioux proud. From the camp came a yellow horse pulling a travois and in the basket of the travois sat The Man Who Never Walked. He had never fought either, for his crippled limbs could not support his weight. His hands could not grasp weapons, but today he was determined to face the enemy as a man of the tribe, he said. If death came, it would be a man's death and better than life as a useless cripple. Understanding, Sitting Bull whipped the yellow horse toward the enemy line.

For a moment the soldiers held their fire, not certain what to make of the strange contraption. Then guns blazed and the horse fell dead. The cripple rolled into the dirt. Slowly, painfully, he managed to right himself and began singing his death song. It was not yet finished when the bullets found their mark.

Sitting Bull and the others had little time to admire his bravery for the troops were almost upon them. Knowing their families needed every moment, they fought fiercely, using their arrows, ancient guns and small supply of ammunition with desperate skill. Suddenly the soldiers charged the spot Sitting Bull's family defended. In a burst of fire, Jumping Bull's horse was hit and Four Horns cried out that he was shot. Sitting Bull grabbed the bridle of his uncle's horse and galloped out of the line of fire to cover, where he could examine the wound.

The ball had plowed into the back of the older man's rib cage, and he gasped that he could still feel it in his body. Unable to extract the bullet, Sitting Bull bound the wound with some of the remedies he always carried and led his uncle's horse back to the camp.

It was about noon when they rode into the abandoned village. The women and children were gone -- fled into the protection of the gullies and canyons -- but they'd left much of their lives behind. Many tipis still stood and there were signs of hurried flight all around. Bundles of buffalo robes ready for market, parfleches full of meat and dried fruit, soft folds of deerskin, racks of saddles, stacks of travois poles, brass kettles, dogs, even horses had been left in the panic. The warriors stayed near the camp long enough to keep the soldiers from advancing any farther. Then they took the trail the families had left as they fled toward the badlands that lined the Little Missouri. About sunset Sitting Bull found the Hunkpapa camp; the women were unharmed, but he was only too aware what the loss of so many goods would cost his people.

The next day scouts discovered the soldiers had taken time to turn their village and the whole mountainside into a smoking pall, leaving not even a pup alive. Every kettle was punctured, every horse was shot and two babies lay crushed on their carrying boards.

In a few days the Sioux had a chance to avenge their loss. The troops were moving west to cross the Little Missouri and the Hunkpapa joined the Sans Arc to attack the train. Taking advantage of the chaotic expanse of eroded buttes and gullies they moved through, the braves preyed on the soldiers. The troopers never knew when a bullet would whiz from a stunted juniper, when a ravine would spit a score of charging horsemen, when the sky would rain arrows into a narrow canyon.

The Sioux watched the soldiers sweat to heave their impossible wagons over boulders and carve out passes between rocks, their shirtbacks dark with moisture their bodies could not afford to lose. And they waited near the infrequent water holes to ride down on the furtive figures tying to fill canteens.

Although the troops sometimes found places to mount their big guns and blast the cliffs ahead of the column, most of the time the guns were impotent and the warriors could fight in the way they knew best. Sitting Bull studied the tempting herd of horses that moved with the train and watched his chance. Finally he worked in as close as cover would allow and kicked his horse into action. Plastered on his mount's neck he charged toward the herd.

The soldiers saw him coming and bullets pinged on the hard ground, but he was quickly in the herd and away with a chestnut and a fine buckskin. The army could provide him riches as well as the Crows, he decided, as he rode away unscathed.

He did not think much of the white soldiers' skill as warriors. At night their jumpy guards fired at everything and nothing, making the Indians laugh. They stood in one place or ran in a straight line, instead of ducking and dodging to avoid fire. Fighting them was just shooting, not fighting, he thought. The tedious exchanging of bullets at long range could not compare with daring to touch your opponent's body.

And they seemed so unfeeling. Where the Indians openly mourned a fallen brave -- and sometimes ended the fighting for the day -- the soldiers fought on among their wounded as if nothing had happened. It was hard to understand such heartless people.

Across the 40 sun-scalded, tortuous miles of Little Missouri badlands and on toward the Yellowstone the two groups dueled, the pursuer now the pursued. The trail was littered with carcasses of horses and mules bearing the army brand, some felled by arrows but a larger number victims of thirst and hunger. More than once men and animals forgot discipline and raced headlong into a gravely needed source of water. Behind them, smoke swirled from piles of charred lumber the animals could no longer pull.

However, all the soldiers were not easy conquests. One day Sitting Bull watched a Blue Coat take on two braves, one after the other, and best them both. Without a thought he charged into the fray and gave a yell of victory when his arrow thudded into the soldier's back. But this soldier did not die easily. Though his mouth and body spurted blood, he twisted around and fired his pistol at Sitting Bull. The Indian felt the bullet tear into his hip. By the time he got back to his friends his left leg and the horse's side were lathered in blood.

Jumping Bull, who was never far from his side, tied up his brother's gaping flesh wound as best he could and led him to the Hunkpapa camp.

For Fanny Kelly and the Hunkpapa women, the running battle with the soldiers had provided no triumphs. Most of the comforts of life had been left behind, and men busy with war could not provide meat. Fanny's moods swung from ecstatic to depressed as she heard the cannons -- now close, now far -- and wondered if she'd live to see Josiah again.

She'd stumbled through the badlands, overwhelmed by cliffs and canyons of red, ragged country that seemed as hard and savage as her captors, who made a point of tormenting her with grisly trophies of the battle. Continually threatened with death by the ravished, angry Indians, she was ordered to treat wounded as they were brought into the camp. She had little knowledge of what to do, but she tried to help them, sure her life balanced on her ability to please.

When the fighting broke off in mid-August the bands separated and went their individual ways. The Hunkpapa could now take time to mourn, and she watched their wild grief in horror. The bereaved walked through the village with blackened faces, shorn hair, and arms and legs which bled from self-inflicted gashes. Soon they were focusing their grief on her.

Early one morning a council debated her right to live. Knowing they admired bravery, she stoically pretended to accept whatever fate Wakan Tanka decreed. While one faction demanded the vengeance of her death, another pointed out that she was innocent of her people's wrongs and had been helpful to the tribe. It was decided she could live. She was surprised to discover how much she still cared.

Stripped of their food supply and unable to follow the game, the people traveled on through starving times. Fanny went for days with only what food she could gather. She plucked leaves and hips from the rose bushes and chewed on grass to quiet her stomach. She was not the only one who suffered. Dogs went unfed and died, to provide a meal for their masters. Horses collapsed and were cut up immediately for the village pots.

One day while Fanny was scavenging food along the trail a strange warrior rode past her. Her eyes fastened on a bright little shawl that hung from his saddle. Numbly she stared as a long, blond scalp lock swung with the horse's gait. She tumbled unconscious from her horse.

Now, when she wished to die, neither the Indians nor Wakan Tanka would oblige her.

In September the heat broke and the rain finally came, but now its cold was penetrating. She huddled near the fire and thought about the winter. Her hand strayed, as it often did, to one of the papers she'd saved since her capture. It was Josiah's discharge from the Union army, her link to their past together. She reminded herself he might still live.

Her other comforts were a reader and a pencil. To distract herself she often showed the pictures to the Indians, explaining her world to them as best she could. She found them apt pupils with good memories, and she tried to explain how life was better on a farm with a permanent home. But when she attempted to make them understand the white man's numbers, they called her a liar.

Yet more of those numbers were already traipsing across the Hunkpapa's territory. As the band moved on through the puddled countryside, Fanny suddenly learned the Indians had a train of 100 wagons surrounded near a Little Missouri crossing to the south (near present Marmarth, North Dakota). In spite of a soldier escort, the Indians had overwhelmed two straggling wagons and killed several men. They came singing into camp with whiskey bottles, cigars, silverware, stationery and jars of pickles.

The wagons of the threatened train had corralled now and the Whites were throwing up dirt walls to hide behind. Further attempts to take it would be costly. The braves, many of them drunk by now on the liquor, told Fanny to write a letter to the captain telling him they were tired of fighting and it was safe to leave his fortified position and move on.

Once again help seemed so close. Her mind raced as the Indians dictated the words she was to write. By condensing what they told her to say, she managed to say that she was a captive. Plagued with anxiety and the need to deceive the Indians, she found it a struggle to be coherent, but she inserted a warning to the wagons not to move and ask them to help her if they could. Forcing herself to appear unconcerned, she waited while the chief studied the note and counted the words. It passed inspection. A brave carried it out and stuck it on a stick near the soldiers' camp and waited on a nearby hillside for the results.

The captain's reply made it clear he did not trust the Indians, but he offered three horses for her ransom -- *if* she really was a white woman, and he could do so without risking his men.

Fanny was crushed. But that afternoon the Indians asked her to write again. They had their own ideas about the worth of their prisoner. This time they asked for four wagons and 40 cattle, sugar, coffee, flour and gunpowder. The soldiers were on their ground; they wanted them to "go home and come back no more."

She again warned the captain, who was named Fisk, to beware of trickery and not move the train.

The next day the Hunkpapa gathered on a hillside within view of the white's fort. They let Fanny look at the white men through a glass and she prayed someone was looking back at her. Her face was painted -- they painted her every day -- and her arms ringed with tight brass bracelets. Her sunbonnet was long gone, her feet in moccasins, and her dress a simple length of material tied with a red sash. Could they still tell she was a white woman? Or would they think it all a trick?

Before long she knew. Captain Fisk wrote again. The letter began "Dear Madam:" Blinking back involuntary tears, she skimmed it quickly. Just as quickly her hopes collapsed. The captain was explaining she had his sympathy, but he had neither the authority nor the goods to negotiate with the Indians. However, he'd add a load of food to the horses he'd offered in trade for her. Fanny read the letter to the Indians and explained the terms, but in the necessity to please, she had made herself too valuable a property. The chief did not want to give her up; three horses and a little sugar and coffee would not feed the hungry tribe.

When it became obvious the wagon train was not going to expose itself, the Hunkpapa and a despairing Fanny moved on.

Sitting Bull had many things on his mind that fall as his people tried to recoup their staggering loss. The soldiers the Sioux harried across the Little Missouri had limped away up the Yellowstone, where they'd been rescued by the steamboats sent to support them. While many of them had marched back east, others were settling in at the new fort on the Missouri, within a few days' march of most of the Sioux campgrounds.

The encircled wagon train had also gone back east, the women white-faced, the men looking over their shoulders in fear, but Sitting Bull did not need his oracles the birds to tell him they -- or others like them -- would be back. Especially now that everyone would know they had a white woman in their camp.

As he recovered from his wound, he'd watched the young woman in Brings Plenty's lodge, and now, well enough to ride horseback again, he pondered what should be done. She was a good woman, so good that her owner, Brings Plenty, had named her Real Woman, a title of honor. The people liked her. She had many skills and tried hard to be of service. She was bearing the increasing cold without complaint. He felt pity for her as he had often pitied Indian captives. His people still talked about the time he had killed a captive Crow woman with an arrow rather than see her burned alive. And how he'd asked that three Crow women and a baby, captured in the battle where his father was killed, not be killed to revenge Jumping Bull's death, but instead be returned with gifts to their people.

Moreover, he was certain she would bring trouble. Other braves had already tried to buy Real Woman, eager to return her for ransom, and Brings Plenty would not consider their offers. One day there was sure to be a confrontation. More important, the traders would be coming in the spring. Perhaps the Hunkpapa would be unable to obtain goods if they held a captive white woman. He urged that Real Woman be given more food and care so that she could be returned to her people. Perhaps the band could obtain some food and supplies in return.

Then one morning, in camp at Laughing Wood on the Grand River (near Bull Head, South Dakota), he saw a delegation of Blackfoot Sioux ride in to parley. After they had been greeted, warmed and properly fed, their spokesman, Crawler, who was a good friend, explained their mission. They had been to the soldiers' fort at the mouth of the Bad River. The army chief was angry about the white woman captive in the Hunkpapa camp. He'd asked them to bring her in -- warned them all the Sioux would suffer until she was returned. They were ready to pay for the woman with horses.

Sitting Bull was pleased, and the other leaders agreed it was the best thing. However, Brings Plenty would not listen. He did not want horses, he wanted Real Woman. He took her into his lodge and sat by the fire, and an excited group of Hunkpapa began to surround the tipi, ready to defend the rights of Brings Plenty.

Then Sitting Bull began to speak and the crowd quieted.

"Friends, this woman is out of our path," he said. "Her path is different. You can see in her face that she is homesick and unhappy here. So I am going to send her back." He turned to Crawler and told him to go get the woman.

The hulking Crawler, known for his many coups, stepped into the lodge.

Three times Crawler asked for the woman. Three times Brings Plenty refused his offer. As he refused the third time Brings Plenty drew his knife. But Crawler was faster. Shoving a pistol in Brings Plenty's face he threw Real Woman behind him and backed from the lodge. Other Blackfoot boosted the white woman onto a pony, but friends of Brings Plenty crowded around to block their way and the camp grew loud with argument.

The leaders withdrew to hold council and Sitting Bull's logic prevailed. The woman was a danger to the tribe. They should get for her what they could. A delegation of Hunkpapa was appointed to go with her to the Blackfoot camp and on to Fort Sully, and Sitting Bull charged them with her care and safety.

As often as she'd longed to leave the Hunkpapa, Fanny was frightened to be sent off with the Blackfoot Sioux. The known terror was better than the unknown. Suspicious of the Indians' intentions, she decided she was to be used to gain entry to the fort so the soldiers could be slaughtered. But, helpless to do otherwise, she rode along, hoping she'd have some chance to pass a warning.

After a long and bitterly cold journey, she was surprised to be welcomed into the Blackfoot camp with a feast and rejoicing.

Suddenly she was a guest of honor, and her head spun at the change. But the day had a bitter edge: it was, by her count, the first anniversary of her marriage.

Close to freedom now, she was held prisoner by the weather. December blizzards swept the landscape, and even the new robes the Blackfoot had presented her were no barrier to the biting cold. With travel impossible and the wind rattling the lodge skins, she waited and wondered how she could warn the fort.

Her chance came when a young Hunkpapa came to visit and, to her astonishment, to declare his love. As she listened to the unwelcome proposal, she realized this was her opportunity. Using a bullet she sharpened to substitute for a pencil, she wrote a letter to the fort's commander. Then, convincing him the message would not harm his people, she persuaded her suitor to carry it to the fort. He disappeared into the ice-bound hills.

Several anxious days later she herself was on the trail, part of a column of hundreds of Indians who chanted a farewell song as they moved off south toward the fort. She had never known such cold. The pony's hooves slipped on the surface of the frozen drifts, breaking through only in the gullies. The wind grabbed at her buffalo robe and her hands froze when she struggled to hold it to her. Often she walked as the Indians did, realizing only exercise would keep her from freezing.

She had nearly despaired of surviving the journey when she saw a flagpole and a huddle of buildings by the river. As her escort dressed for their entrance, she scooped up a handful of snow and tried to scrub the paint from her face. Dimly she realized she could not feel her fingers on her cheeks. Placed in front with eight chiefs, the rest of the tribe to the rear, she rode toward the fort. Her chest was clamped in bands of anxiety; it hurt to breathe. The Indians broke into song. As the chant carried through the crackling cold air, the Stars and Stripes was run up the flagstaff. She could see the roofs of the buildings inside the stockade now; they were thronged with soldiers. The gate opened and officers stepped forward to greet them. Then the gate closed. She and the chiefs were inside, but the rest of the Sioux were locked out. For the first time in five months, she was safe.

Fanny spent several weeks at Fort Sully while the doctor cared for her frozen hands and face and she recovered her health. One day in early spring the mail wagon arrived and Josiah jumped down to take her in his arms. He had survived the attack and had been trying to ransom her ever since. Sadly, he had to confirm her fears regarding the fate of their daughter Mary.

The Kellys went back to Kansas and built a hotel in Ellsworth, but Josiah died of cholera less than two years later, shortly before Fanny gave birth to their son. She spent some time in Wyoming, writing an account of her adventure, but her ambitious companion on the wagon train, Mrs. Larimer, somehow managed to publish it under her name rather than Fanny's. It was 1871 before Fanny's account saw print.

Fanny went to Washington and asked to be rewarded for her aid to the Fisk train and Fort Sully, and to be paid damages for her suffering. In 1870 the Sioux acknowledged they had kept Fanny captive, and asked that she be paid damages from their annuity monies.

Sitting Bull's compassion was neither understood nor appreciated by the young white captive, but his own people added it to their list of his great deeds. That year was entered on their calendar as The Winter When the White Woman was Rescued.

Deprived of Glory

While the Blue Coats on the upper Missouri had a formidable opponent in Sitting Bull in the fall of 1864, their counterparts in Kansas faced an adversary of overwhelming proportions.

The War Between the States, which had begun with such heady victories for southern forces, was now going badly for the Confederate cause. Gen. Phil Sheridan had raided Richmond, a Union fleet had sailed into Mobile Bay and Gen. William Tecumseh Sherman had crossed the Chattahoochee River and taken Atlanta. However the Rebels had the strength for one final push -- one they hoped might yet change the complexion of the war.

Union forces in the West had been depleted to swell their armies in the East. They were also distracted and plagued by the wide-spreading Indian uprising on the plains. A thrust up through Missouri to Kansas City and Fort Leavenworth might puncture the Union's ballooning success and drain off the troops that were threatening Confederate forces in the East. Missouri champion Gen. Sterling Price was given 10,000 men to do the job.

By October he had sliced his way north past Pilot Knob, reached the Missouri, and was marching toward Lexington, which he had left in such triumph just four years before.

 When 23-year-old Capt. Henry E. Palmer marched his 250 men into Lexington at dusk on October 19, 1864, he knew it was again in Rebel hands. Women on the outskirts of town, celebrating the arrival of Price's army, waved at his men and shouted. Their words were of welcome, but they were not words Palmer's men wanted to hear.

"That's right, you old Lincolnites, come in and surrender", they called in glee, "we welcome you."

For Palmer was a Union soldier, a member of the 11th Kansas Volunteer Cavalry, and he'd been fighting the Rebels since 1861.

For the past five days he'd been engaged in a desperate attempt to slow Price's march on Westport and Kansas City, to buy time for the imperiled Kansas citizens to arm themselves and organize to face Price's veterans.

James G. Blunt, who'd been fighting slave-owning Missourians since John Brown's days in Kansas, was the Union general in charge of the delaying action. He had ordered Palmer to take his own men of Company A, along with Company F, a company of the Second Colorado Cavalry and 65 men from a Missouri regiment and hold the Dover Road east of Lexington "until ordered to retreat."

In the confusion of battle the order never came, and now Palmer's 250 men were surrounded. With the Missouri on the north, Price's army a mile to south, and the cavalry he'd been dueling with behind him, there was no way to go but west into Lexington, where they would be forced to surrender. It was a sorry prospect, knowing surrender meant a long, hungry tramp clear to Texas for imprisonment. Death was preferable, Palmer thought, and he was sure at least half his men agreed. He passed an order as they rode.

"Load your revolvers and carbines, if they are not loaded, and shoot only when you hear me fire the first shot at the head of the column." Just what they could do was problematic, with half of Price's army between them and Blunt's force, but Palmer ordered his men to keep cool and be ready. They would not volunteer to hand over their guns.

Palmer rode at the head of the long column with his 20 scouts. He and the scouts had been chasing Missouri bushwhackers for 16 months, and they were dressed in a combination of Confederate butternut and Federal blue so they could more easily move between the states. As they reached the head of Main Street, Palmer saw with surprise the whole street was taken up with stacked rifles.

He turned through an alley to Market Street. This street was clear -- except for hundreds of Rebel soldiers. But the soldiers, having stacked their arms, were milling about, looking for supper. No one moved to challenge Palmer's column.

With a surge of hope Palmer ordered the bugler by his side to sound the trot. As the horses speeded up their pace, their hooves kicked up dust which rose to envelope the column and its telltale guidons and blue jackets. Before long they were hearing shouts of encouragement from the lounging Southerners, who mistook them for a Rebel force riding to battle.

Incredulous at their luck, Palmer thought they were going to ride through town unchallenged. Then a Confederate major rode up and demanded they halt. A private stuck his pistol in the major's side and fired; the rest of the column heard the signal and their guns exploded all along the line. "Sound the charge!" Palmer yelled, and with Rebel troops diving over stone fences and behind buildings to get out of the way, the column galloped through the center of Lexington and out of town.

The men were exultant as they headed west, but Palmer knew the next obstacle was the Sni bridge, three or four miles away. The covered bridge was their only way across the quicksand bottom of the river, and they could hear muskets and artillery fire in that direction. Evidently Blunt's rear guard still fought Price's advancing line. As dark came on they could see the flash of rifles and artillery less than half a mile away. Price's men were on the near bank of the Sni; Blunt's on the far. Somehow they had to get through both lines -- their own as dangerous as the enemy's. Palmer gathered his men, ordered them to reload and told them his plan.

The column started at a trot, then broke into a gallop. Urging their mounts to top speed and firing to the right and left, they broke through the rear of the Rebel skirmish line. It took a moment for the surprised

Southerners to realize these were Yankees riding through and by that time, screaming the Kansas yell at the top of their lungs, Palmer's men had galloped onto the bridge.

Their voices reverberated from the graywood tunnel with the echo of a thousand hooves and there was scarcely time to wonder if they rode to death or safety. But the Kansas troops heard the yell in time to hold their fire, and Palmer's command burst triumphantly from the bridge into their lines.

Moments later the bridge was ablaze and Palmer was surrounded by a group of astonished, congratulatory officers. He was supposed to be a prisoner and here he was reporting without the loss of a man. Ordered on west to the Little Blue River, his men rode all night before bedding down for a few hours sleep.

However the young officer was used to the demands of war. He'd been in Denver in July of 1861 when he'd learned about the war, and he'd hitched and walked and trotted to Fort Leavenworth in 18 days to enlist on his 20th birthday, worrying only that the war would be over before he could take part.

Four days later he was in a battle, and in late September -- at Osceola -- he learned the nature of war on the Kansas-Missouri border. While his drunken comrades revenged the fall of Lexington by looting and burning all but three houses, his commander put seven secessionists "on trial," found them guilty and sentenced them to death. The new soldier watched as the blindfolded men were forced to kneel by newly dug graves for their execution. It was in retaliation, he was told, for the hanging of six Union men by guerilla Charles Quantrill.

The hatred rampant in the Kansas border country in the days of John Brown still festered. Quantrill, Bloody Bill Anderson, Jo Shelby and others struck mercilessly into Kansas from Missouri. The Grim Chieftain, Jim Lane, along with Charles Jennison, James Montgomery and other Kansans answered in kind. Palmer, who had imagined the glory of noble battlefields, found himself in Lane's command.

He had seen atrocities on both sides. On picket duty on the Kansas line one morning in October 1861, he'd watched a woman walk up the road in a drizzling rain. She held a baby to her chest, and four children under the age of seven trailed behind her. All were shaking with cold, clad only in their nightclothes. Her husband had been a wealthy slave owner but had remained loyal to the Union; he'd freed his slaves and joined the Union army. After he left, Missouri guerillas had systematically raided his farm and stolen his stock. Finally they'd pushed the new mother out in the rain in her nightgown, burned her home and shot the oxen she tried to use to flee to Kansas. By the time Palmer and his men discovered the family, the baby was dead and the mother dying.

Palmer had joined a special force to fight Quantrill. He headquartered in Westport, and before long he knew every wood road and trail from Independence down to Fort Scott. He'd learned to drill by signs and signals, lie in wait at river fords, hide by day, strike by night and travel with the stealth of an Indian. Yet neither his nor other units had been able to prevent Quantrill's deadly raid on Lawrence in 1863. Palmer had arrived the morning after to find the air still sharp with smoke and 183 unarmed men and boys dead in the ruins.

He'd seen the bitterness and heartache that followed Federal Gen. Thomas Ewing's retaliatory Order Number Eleven, which evicted everyone, loyal or disloyal, from the farms of the four Missouri border counties. In two weeks the rich countryside had been transformed into the Burnt District.

Each act of violence precipitated one in answer. Some Kansas cavalrymen had led a raid on a defenseless old Rebel sympathizer who lived in Jackson County. The man and his two daughters were about to bury their wife and mother when the Jayhawkers interrupted them. They took the 60-year-old father out to his own orchard and alternately hung and revived him until convinced his valuables were in Canada as he said. Leaving him more dead than alive, they ransacked the house anyway, slashing open bedticks and axing open trunks and drawers. Not satisfied, they forced open the lid of the casket which rested in the parlor.

There was nothing but a gold ring on the dead woman's finger. They sliced off her finger and took the ring. Then they fired the house, leaving the two daughters to drag their mother's coffin from the inferno.

Palmer had two of his men scalped by Quantrill's men; watched five of the guerilla's men hanged in Kansas City. It was a relief, really, to be facing regular troops along the Little Blue, in uniforms that did not belie their loyalties, where he might expect his body would be given an honorable burial.

He knew death was a likely prospect. He did not want to think about it, for he had a young wife in Westport. But the Union generals had had to hurry back from fighting Indians on the frontier, and their army was little more than a crowd of untrained civilians. Only 10 days before, the Kansas governor had ordered all businesses closed and called the men to arms. Union commander Maj. Gen. Samuel R. Curtis had declared martial law and called all able-bodied men from 18 to 60, Black and White alike, to help defend the state. They were still reporting, with whatever guns they possessed, their tin cups and their frying pans, to the nearest county seat. Ununiformed, with only sprigs of blazing sumac to identify them as a military force, shopkeepers, lawyers, preachers and doctors were digging trenches and rifle pits at Kansas City and along the Big Blue east of the town.

Palmer and his men spent October 20 at the Little Blue, eight miles east of Independence, cutting trees along the small river and sharpening them into abatis. This would be the first line of defense as Price's troops moved west toward Kansas.

ASA BATTLES

Morning light on October 21 was slow in coming. A cold gray fog enveloped the woods along the stream and Palmer slept late. About nine o'clock he was sitting on the chilly ground trying to sew up a rip in his pants when enemy shells began to land around him. He jumped for his horse, threw the pants across the saddle and raced, with the wind whistling through his drawers, to see that his men were in position.

Again his men could only delay superior numbers. For an hour or two they held the high, wooded ground west of the river. But by 11 o'clock it was obvious they could stand no longer. Palmer's regiment ran a wagonload of hay onto the bridge and set it on fire. Even as they did it, they knew it was a futile gesture, for the Confederates had already forded the stream to the north and south. In jeopardy of being cut off again, the Kansas boys yielded slowly and began a disciplined withdrawal toward the rear.

The whole line was falling back. They'd gone a couple of miles when the 11th came on the Colorado battery. The artillerymen were struggling to get their six Parrott guns across a plowed field. As the horses strained against the weight, the Rebels moved closer and closer. Something had to be done or the guns would be lost.

Palmer's Company A got the order. They were to counterattack and buy some time. Forming his 88 men for a charge, Palmer led them down the narrow road past the Little Blue church. Ahead he could see a brick house and a stone wall. Rebel rifles blazed at them from both. Then the road dipped into a small hollow and they were out of range for a few paces. When we top that hill, Palmer thought, we'll be shot.

As his horse scrambled up the slope he threw himself flat on her back. Shots peppered the line. His horse staggered and fell, but he rolled clear. The man beside him fell dead on the captain's back and the charge evaporated as his men retreated to the hollow. Through a hail of bullets he dodged back to join them and assure them he wasn't dead, after all.

They'd have to dismount. Leaving their horses in the road they jumped a fence, ran through an orchard and charged the house. Before long they had cleared both the house and the stone fence of Rebels. But without help they were trapped there. Palmer was trying to think of some way to save his men when he heard a roar and saw the white-horsed Colorado Cavalry coming to rescue them and the battery. Although its commanding officer was shot dead at the head of the charge, the be-sashed and gauntleted Colorado boys covered the Kansas boys' withdrawal. Nearly out of ammunition, yet ordered to stand once more, they raised a defiant cheer and threw a chorus of "Rally Round the Flag, Boys" at the Rebel lines.

Company A had just retreated through Independence when Palmer saw two friends riding up. They'd come for his body, they told him after delighted greetings. One of Palmer's command had ridden all the way to Palmer's home in Westport to report him killed. His wife was wild with grief. Promising his colonel he'd return to his command before dawn, the young captain spurred his horse ahead down the road to Westport to prove he was still among the living.

Back at duty as promised on October 22, he joined his men in fortifying the Big Blue River. Again they cut trees and sharpened branches, piling Byram's Ford and all the crossings of the deep, narrow river with tangles of debris. The Rebels would have to ford the stream, get up the bank, and take a second rock ledge. The Union troops would be waiting.

Again the Colorado Battery took its position in the center. Behind breastworks that stretched more than 10 miles north to the Missouri River and south to Hickman's Crossing, men crouched for a final stand. Some were seasoned troops; more were untested civilians. Some, like one unit of the 2nd Kansas Militia, were Black. All heard the rumors: Price was coming with 37,000 men.

Whatever the true number, they found they could not hold him. Shells screamed back and forth across the river as the artillery dueled. Rifles and muskets cracked until the air was black with acrid smoke. Tree branches splintered and fell. In late afternoon some of the militia finally broke, and Price was across. The Union troops, forced to retreat again and leave their fortifications to the enemy, fired and fell back, fired and fell back, until Palmer found himself once more in Westport.

The town seemed to wait with resignation for whatever fate had in store. It had seen many raids, was home to soldiers for both sides; there was no rush to evacuate. Certain the Rebel cavalry was not far behind, Palmer galloped to the gate of his father-in-law's house. Twenty women and children milled in the yard and on the porch, some crying with fright. He leaped down and ordered them all to the cellar. Catching up his wife, he carried her down the ladder into the icehouse and set her on a pile of sawdust. Giving her a quick kiss, he guaranteed she'd stay there by pulling the ladder up behind him. If the Confederates shelled the small town, she should be safe there. If his loyalties inspired darker deeds -- who could tell?

In the chill twilight of the short afternoon the Union forces regrouped for a stand south of Westport along Brush Creek. Palmer and his company rode as part of a cavalry charge near the red brick buildings of the Shawnee mission. This, Palmer thought, was the way war should be fought.

But in camp that night he assessed their chances of surviving the battle to come in the morning and lost hope. They'd done nothing but retreat for five days. They were exhausted and hungry. He huddled near the fire as the night rustled with the sounds of food and ammunition being passed, of men moving into position, some on his side of the line, some on the enemy's.

Farther east the dull thud of artillery went on for hours. They could retreat no farther without sacrificing Kansas City. Tomorrow's battle would be decisive, he was sure. Without relief there was no hope.

Before dawn on October 23 they were on the move, the thin ice on Brush Creek crackling underfoot as they moved across it and to the edge of the barren trees along its banks. With dawn, bright and clear, lighting the frost-rimmed brush, came the Rebel attack.

The Kansas men could not hold their ground. They fell back across the creek. Then General Curtis arrived on the line and ordered another advance. With him were the militia that had been held in reserve at Kansas City. Shells from cannon after cannon began to open holes in the Confederate line. Yet in spite of it all, the Rebels clung to the high ground south of Brush Creek.

Near noon another charge was ordered, and this time Palmer and his men sensed things were different. Some of the Rebels had turned to the west to face fire from Curtis and a battery which had worked up a gulch. With a shout the Blue Coats overran the stone fences at the edge of the plateau.

But it was not to be easy. All through the heat of midday the two sides dueled over the dry grass. Charge was answered with countercharge, cannon with cannon, rifle with musket, saber with pistol until smoke darkened the sun. As horses screamed and men collapsed in bloody contortions around him, Palmer decided his only hope of seeing his wife again was to get a serious wound. Perhaps then the Rebels would not immediately march him to Texas. Still holding the reins, he held his left arm high up in the line of fire. But before the Confederates could oblige him, his men began to waver. He abandoned his scheme and rode up and down the line to rally them. "Keep on firing! Fire Low! We'll whip them yet!" he shouted, trying to believe his own words.

Suddenly he was face to face with the man who'd left the field at the Little Blue and reported Palmer's death. Why, the captain demanded, had he run away? Before the man could answer a bullet cut open his chest and he fell dead. Then a carbine dropped at the captain's feet. One of his boys had been hit in the right arm and dropped it. Palmer retrieved it for him and ordered him to the rear. On his next pass the soldier was still there, trying to fire with his good left arm. Before Palmer could repeat his order a bullet tore into that arm. Again the captain retrieved the gun, tied it to his saddle and ordered him to the rear. But the teen-aged soldier refused to leave the line without the other men.

Through the day the men had become increasingly aware of battle sounds to the east. Suddenly a blue-coated column broke over the ridge from the Big Blue. Guidons waving, it galloped to attack, and the Rebel line began to crumple. Relief had come after all.

Palmer soon found out who had turned the battle in their favor. Sent to General Curtis' headquarters he was ordered to take his 20 scouts and report to Gen. Alfred Pleasanton. He worked his way east across fields and stone fences, through orchards and farmyards, trying to ignore their grotesque harvest of splintered guns, blood-wet hats and bodies piled like obscene haycocks.

Pleasanton, he learned, had trailed Price clear across the state of Missouri, attacked his rear and fought across the Big Blue to penetrate the Confederate flank. With Pleasanton's army, Palmer followed the Rebel force as it retreated south. He rode with Missouri militia and volunteers from Illinois, Iowa and Indiana. Now it was the enemy who was forced to fire and fall back, fire and fall back, until darkness at last stilled the guns.

Near Little Santa Fe on the Kansas line that night, Palmer's men stood watch while the Union cavalry marched south. It was raining, a cold, relentless rain that drenched them to the skin and set their teeth chattering. For hours the horses plodded by in columns of four, saddles squeaking and bridles clinking dully, while their riders nodded in the saddle. There had been, finally, nearly 20,000 men in the Union force.

Two miserable, blustery days later, on October 25, they overtook the Rebels at Mine Creek. Palmer was to remember the final charge as "a grand, inspiring sight." Before it was over Confederate General Marmaduke was a prisoner, along with 10 cannons and 1,000 of his men. Some of the Kansas troopers shared the contents of their haversacks with the hungry captives.

Palmer was with General Curtis as he chased Price across the Arkansas River, destroying forever Confederate hopes of a new front and a new day. Then he was ordered back to Fort Riley. By February 1865, he was in Fort Kearny fighting Indians. Mustered out of the service in September, he went to Montana to look for gold. For 20 years he lived on the Missouri in Plattsmouth, Nebraska and then moved to Omaha, where he was postmaster in 1906.

That year he recorded his memories of his "strenuous times" in Kansas nearly 50 years before with the 11th Kansas Cavalry. A loyal member and officer of the Grand Army of the Republic, he noted that his men had helped save Kansas and Nebraska from the Rebels and preserved the right wing of "that grand phalanx of army corps that stretched from the Atlantic to the crest of the Rockies."

He knew the nearly 29,000 soldiers who'd fought at Westport made it the Civil War's largest land battle west of the Mississippi. He knew some called the Battle of Westport the Gettysburg of the West. He knew he'd faced Jo Shelby and Swamp Fox M. Jeff Thompson.

He had done his duty and served where ordered.

Still, when he looked back on the dirty, vengeful war he'd been part of in Kansas and Missouri, a mere footnote of the major campaigns, he felt deprived of glory. "If I had but dreamed of the possibility of such a fate," he wrote, "I would have walked to Washington before enlisting."

Up the Rainwater Creek

Henry Palmer's glorious war ended with a celebration of bells on April 9, 1865. But even though peace was declared in the East, a part-time soldier in Colorado assured the West would remain aflame. In November 1864 Col. John M. Chivington led a company of Colorado Volunteers in slaughter of an unsuspecting Cheyenne camp at Sand Creek. The pitiable survivors fled north to their more fortunate cousins, the Sioux, and told their story.

To Sitting Bull, his goodwill gesture of returning Fanny Kelly spurned, the choice seemed more obvious than ever. Dealing with the soldiers was full of peril. The Indians could fight to keep the white man out of their country or they could end their days at his mercy -- without buffalo, land, freedom or pride.

As he drew the smoke of the war pipe into his lungs, he knew this war would be different. This enemy would not be satisfied with stealing horses and counting coups, or even destroying a village or two. Still he was confident that if their hearts were strong, the Sioux could succeed. Those who invaded the upper Missouri country of the Hunkpapa by any route would quickly discover they were not welcome.

 In spite of all Capt. Grant Marsh could say, the nervous clerk looked as if he might shake himself to pieces. He'd been hearing stories ever since they'd chugged past Fort Randall. Every boat they'd met heading back toward St. Louis that June of 1866 had had a tale to tell. The Sioux were ranging the river banks, firing on big boats and small. The pilot house might be sheathed with boiler iron for protection, but the rest of the boat wasn't. It was suicidal to try to get the *Louella* clear up to Fort Benton.

Restraining his impatience, Marsh tried to reassure the young man that steamboats were relatively safe on the upper river, especially now that owners were covering the topmost tier of their vessels with iron until there were only slits to peer ahead. They had men and guns enough to fight off any Indians. The killings he'd heard about were usually miners who tried to run the river in unprotected mackinaws and canoes, or woodhawks who lived along the shore to supply fuel to the boats. It was natural for the clerk to be a little nervous, important they take care, but he intended to fulfill his first assignment as captain and deliver his boatful of would-be miners and their equipment to Fort Benton before the end of June.

Some of the other passengers were concerned, but they'd already made their decision to risk life in the Montana goldfields and they were not about to turn back now. As the *Luella* steamed past the walls of Fort Union they welcomed every westward mile, even though the hills stood more barren, the sage more stunted, and landmarks bore forbidding names like Wolf Point. The clerk, without visions of gold to outshine his fears, was close to nervous prostration by the time they reached the Milk River. When they met another steamer heading back south he ignored the catcalls of his fellow passengers and scrambled aboard the down-river vessel. Marsh shook his head in disgust and turned his attention back to his real opponent -- the river.

He was both pilot and captain of his boat, and navigating the unpredictable river was an all-consuming task. He'd never been this far before, never turned the giant arc to follow the riverbed 1,000 miles west to the mountains.

But he knew the Missouri was so changeable that past experience had little value; sandbars and shoals moved weekly, if not daily. A pilot had to read and react to what he could see with his eyes; he had to know in his gut where the channel crossed, and feel from the vibrating deck just how far he could push the boilers.

A captain had to control the 30-some men in his crew, see to the business of booking freight, make sure the crates and boxes were loaded in the dark hold so that the craft was bow heavy and would drag before they were irretrievably stuck, oversee meal preparation, be host to the passengers, and decide when and where the boat would move.

Not many men took on both jobs, but Marsh was confident in his ability. Although he was only 32, he had worked on rivers nearly 20 years. From his first day on a steamer as a 12-year-old cabin boy, he'd loved the river life, moving from the Allegheny to the Ohio to the Mississippi and, at 19, on to the Missouri. Before the Civil War had interrupted his life, he'd been up as far as Omaha. He'd taken a load of Sully's troops as far as Fort Rice in 1864. Now he was taking his own ship back north.

North to Fort Benton and the head of navigation on the Missouri. Steamboats had been tying up at Fort Union for 34 years, but they'd only threaded their way through to Benton for five years now. Two or three made it in a good season; more gave up the battle two, three or four hundred miles from their goal, some renaming the 175-mile stretch below Fort Benton the "Rocky River." This year, with the Bozeman Road endangered by the Sioux and the gold trade too rich to ignore, many more were attempting the run. It required a substantial investment but the rewards could be just as great. The settlers and miners in Montana were eager for every kind of goods from door knobs to dog collars, from cow bells to Dr. J. Hostetter's Celebrated Stomach Bitters. Customers waited for pipes, matches, ink, buttons, thimbles, shoes and crockery, as well as for lead bars and powder kegs.

There was no greater challenge for a steamboat pilot. Mississippi pilots might sneer at the plainer, smaller, nearly flat-bottomed mountain steamers, with their paddle wheels in the stern to keep them safer from the Missouri's logs, but few volunteered to try their hand at navigating "that rainwater creek."

The boat Marsh had been asked to captain was far from the fastest on the river, but she was sturdy and reliable, with the shallow draft the Missouri demanded. Since April 18, when they'd cast off at St. Louis and pushed into the ice-studded current, she'd fended off logs, bounced off snags, and crawled over sandbars in search of the channel. Gulping wood from every pile of driftwood, from every woodhawk's stash along the bank, she turned it into steam to fight the current as smoke from her twin stacks belched black into the sky.

Beyond the hardwood country fuel was a constant problem. Almost a cord disappeared into the blazing furnaces every hour. Green cottonwood would barely keep up the steam, so they searched for fire-deadened stands and water-felled giants. Each stop was filled with tension, for both the men ashore and the sitting boat made easy targets. Often it seemed they spent more time gathering wood than moving up river.

Yet sometimes, even when Marsh yelled orders down the tube from the pilot house to fill the doors of the furnaces clear across, the *Luella* could not force her way through the sand. Then the winches began their din as long heavy spars on each side of the bow were winched up and set in the sand ahead of the boat.

Looking like huge, hinged legs of the grasshoppers they were named for, they lifted the boat up and forward a step at a time. It was slow but effective -- unless a spar shattered or a hemp cable snapped under the strain. That could cost lives as well as time.

If the sand or rock beneath the bow refused to be breached, nothing would suffice but unloading gear enough to reduce the draft so she could float over a bar to deeper water. Then the grim-faced roustabouts lowered the mackinaws, loaded them with cargo, took the load to shore and left it on the bank. After a few such trips the lightened steamer could float across the bar; then the crew would unload more cargo, so the boat could double back, reload the first batch, return, reload the second batch and they'd be on their way. A man needed patience, as well as strength, to conquer the Missouri.

Marsh had the combination of temperance and daring it took to challenge the river. Tall, broad-shouldered, reserved, he did not play flamboyant cock of the walk like many of the pilots, but his presence at the wheel or at the dinner table was commanding. Engineers, firemen, cooks, and the brawling roustabouts knew who was boss. Even the fuming miners who crowded the decks, more impatient at every delay, tempered their complaints in Marsh's hearing.

The Missouri never acknowledged a master, but luckily this June it held the three or four feet of water needed to float their flat bottom through the pine-crested cliffs at the Musselshell's mouth and past the open mouth of Judith's canyon, named half a century before by explorer William Clark. Then they chugged for miles, open-mouthed with wonder, between soaring bluff faces that shone white and fanciful as fairy castles, blocking out everything but a strip of blue sky above. Finally they were over the last of the rock rapids to Fort Benton. They'd been 60 days on the way.

Coming from the vastness of the fantastic canyon to tie up at the waterfront at the fort was like sailing from the doldrums into a hurricane. It was June 17, and 18 steamers had touched bank before them -- triple the number that had come up the year before.

Everywhere within sight and sound bullwhackers, muleskinners, teamsters, mules, oxen, wagons and crates of freight were melded into a hectic scramble of commerce. The crumbling old adobe fort and the traders' posts had been joined by a freight yard with corrals and barns, a stage office, a hotel, stores and saloons. It was the levee of St. Louis, Franklin, Independence, St. Joseph all over again; the jumping-off place for the West.

But this town was at the back door of the gold camps. Last Chance Gulch was just west of the river a hundred miles upstream. Above Three Forks, Virginia City and Alder Gulch were pouring out millions of dollars of the coveted dust. The *Luella's* passengers nearly ran off the boat in their eagerness to get ashore and fight with hundreds of others for a meal, a bed and a way to the gold fields.

More steamers arrived and departed until the bemused old timers tallied the unheard of total of 31. The town swarmed with Southerners, looking for a new start, ex-Union soldiers, miners from the west coast and every kind of adventurer. The neophytes mixed with others, who only a year or two before had been as green as they, now swaggering into town with plump leather sacks swinging from their saddles, ready to catch a boat home.

Marsh was surprised, in the crush of men with all manner of morals, to see miners leave their pokes unguarded on a merchant's floor for days at a time. Yet they remained untouched until their owners reappeared. One of his crewmen found out why. He stole a bottle of patent medicine from the cargo and somehow the word got around. When Marsh saw him again he'd been whipped nearly to death. The Vigilance Committee, whose members had spent the past two years ridding the gold camps and trails of robbers, had impressed another lesson on the dishonest. Marsh, shocked at the harshness of the punishment, was told his crewman came within three votes of hanging.

Most of the steamer captains were in a rush to be off on the journey south, afraid they'd miss the June rise and be stuck on the river for the winter. The rush of water from snow melting high in the Rockies could last six weeks, or it could be gone in a few days -- no one ever knew. Yet when Marsh was asked to make a trip down to Fort Union and back, he weighed the odds and agreed. When he returned again to Fort Benton, the accumulation of 37 years of life at Fort Union lay on his deck. The famous walls that sheltered fur man and Indian, artist and scientist, sportsman and soldier had outlived their usefulness. Men traveled the rivers now to harvest gold instead of beaver, and the American Fur Company was no more.

Again Marsh was asked to delay his departure. This time it was to rescue the passengers of the *Marion*, wrecked 70 miles below on the rapids. Confident he and the *Luella* could survive where other boats met disaster, he went down and ferried the disheartened passengers back to Benton.

But time was running short even for the *Luella*. It was almost September. No other boat had ever stayed so late. The riverbank thronged with miners building mackinaws to carry them down to the states, and onlookers scoffed that those foolish enough to ride a 200-foot steamboat would spend the winter on a sandbar for sure, freezing and starving, sitting ducks for the Indians. Nevertheless, Marsh found 230 miners ready to take the chance.

Now he faced the problem of booking a boatload of passengers and freight without a clerk. He was a literate man and kept careful notes on the course of the river, but bookkeeping was not his forte. However he was a good judge of men, and when an intelligent-looking passenger named MacNeil volunteered for the job Marsh hired him.

As the bearded, boisterous miners filed aboard with their belongings, -- the most important of which bulged noticeably around their waists -- MacNeil took charge. Quickly figuring the amount each man owed, he demanded payment in gold dust. But in spite of angry protests he was not about to accept their dust at face value. While the miners glowered and grumbled, MacNeil dumped each sack into a pan and ordered the owner to swirl it in water. Then he bagged the results, minus the black sand some had tried to pass off as gold. When he had finished and totaled up the columns, Marsh learned the *Luella* would carry 2-1/2 tons, $1,250,000 in gold dust, down the river.

Underway with a blast of the whistle on September 2, they passed the wreckage of the *Marion* and picked their way through the canyon. Even Marsh was surprised at the ease of the journey as they rode the shallow current. Then, at the mouth of the Milk, they felt the familiar, dreaded jolt of the boat running aground.

While the crew went about the business of winching up the spars to work over the bar, the anxious miners crowded the rails. Had the scoffers in Benton been right? Would they be stuck and frozen in here for the winter? They jostled each other for a better view.

Then Marsh heard a shout and laughter. A miner had fallen overboard. It seemed of little consequence. The water was only two feet deep. But the shouts became more frenzied. The man couldn't seem to find his feet; he was being carried along in the swift current, thrashing and gasping. By the time they began to realize the weight of his belt made him helpless, he was out of reach. Before rescuers could splash to his aid he disappeared in deeper water. Though they mounted a search, he was never seen again.

Expecting to find Fort Union deserted, Marsh was surprised to see an army unit camped below the old fur fort at the mouth of the Yellowstone. The troops were hard at work building a new military post; palisades were rising around the beginnings of frame quarters for the men. He nosed the *Luella* into the bank for a quick visit and discovered the unit of infantry, under the command of Capt. W. G. Rankin, had been ordered to erect a post named Fort Buford, one of several the army hoped might protect river travelers from attacks by Sitting Bull and the Sioux.

Marsh welcomed Captain Rankin and his charming Cuban wife to his quarters for a pleasant visit, but as he listened to their tales he felt no envy for their position. They'd been left, with only their orders and a few axes, two months before and had been attacked by Indians almost daily since. The 70 men had rifles in their hands more often than tools, and progress was slow.

Before they pulled away Marsh saw proof of Captain Rankin's claims. Mrs. Rankin had lingered on board after her husband returned to work. When she mounted her horse and headed alone along the bank for the fort, a gang of Indians galloped toward her from a draw. She spurred her horse toward safety, and her husband and some men raced out to cover her retreat. Thanks to a fast mount she reached the fort safely, but the passengers on the *Luella* had seen convincing proof that the Sioux had no fear of the soldiers sent to tame them.

Nor did they fear the boatload of miners. Seventy miles past Fort Buford the *Luella* ground to a halt on another sandbar, this one at the mouth of the White Earth River. The crew had just started to hoist the spars into position when bullets suddenly splintered the deck and pinged against the armor plate. As they dove for cover they realized Indians were firing from the bluff above them.

The Indians, far above, could watch every move they made. Every time a crewman showed his head he drew fire. The boat could not move without setting the spars. They were stymied. Yet with September more than half gone Marsh could not afford to wait for the Indians to tire of their sport; the water level was dropping some every day. Winter on the boat was unthinkable, even if the *Luella* survived the crush of ice. Marsh knew Fort Buford would be lucky to sustain its own men through the bitter weather. And he'd seen enough of the bug-infested, rat-plagued, rotting log quarters at Forts Rice and Sully to know their resources were hardly greater. They had to move whatever the cost.

Considering his situation, he was sure the miners far outnumbered the Indians, and their guns were probably of longer range. If they raked the bluff with fire, he thought, the Indians would have to keep their heads down and the deck hands could work. Briskly he ordered the miners to the upper deck with their weapons. Marsh carried no gun, had no real authority over the miners. But many of them were ex-soldiers, used to obeying orders, and all of them wanted to get home. Soon guns barked from the upper rail while the crewmen raced to set the spars.

It was an agonizingly slow process. The decks throbbed as the steam winches strained to wind the cables from the spars around the capstan and hoist the bow above the sand. Praying that everything would hold together, they greeted with a muffled cheer the sudden lurch that meant they'd taken the first step.

Immediately the crew moved to reset the spars. Every so often an Indian crept near enough to send a bullet whining past someone's ear, and the crewmen ducked for cover while the miners peppered the cliff top with fire. Eventually the crew's frantic efforts dragged them far enough forward that Marsh thought the engines could force the boat through the bar. With the paddle wheel churning wildly and sand and water flying, they broke through and were on their way.

Before long they were turning south. Stopping only to snatch driftwood from the sandbars and cut timber in yellow-leafed island groves, they steamed triumphantly into St. Louis on October 5, steam streaming in a white column above the whistle, as Marsh blasted out a long and two shorts, a long and two shorts, to announce their arrival. There they unloaded the richest cargo that had ever come down the Missouri. The *Luella* had cleared $24,000 for her owners and Capt. Grant Marsh had established himself as one of the most skillful navigators on the Missouri, a man who would be called on again and again to set the prow of a steamer against the Missouri's current.

A Humble Niche

While Grant Marsh was making a name for himself on the upper river in 1866, a man with a very different heritage was establishing a reputation of his own in Missouri. His battles would not be with painted warriors. In fact, he might well have been sympathetic to the Sioux cause, for the white man had done his people even greater harm, and he intended to redress their losses. However he fought back without guns or arrows. His weapons were a book, a slate, and a piece of chalk.

 The man who stood facing a roomful of quietly nervous children on an April day in 1866 was not remarkable in appearance. He was slender and of medium height. The children could not help noticing that when he moved about the room he walked with an obvious limp.

However, that was a sight Missouri children saw often now, with so many soldiers returned from the war. He did have heavy eyebrows above black eyes that gazed at them intensely. But it was the color of his skin that surprised them. He was Black, like they were. They'd never known a black teacher before. In fact few if any of the Negro children in Kansas City, Missouri had ever known *any* teacher. For almost 20 years the Missouri constitution had forbidden teaching any Negro to read or write. For them to be in a schoolroom on this spring day in 1866 was an experience more frightening than pleasant.

For the teacher, James Milton Turner, the sight of the class was an immensely satisfying experience. He was young enough, at 26, that his own struggle to learn still burned in his mind. He could well remember the furtiveness and fear it cost him to learn to read. How they'd had to sneak into Reverend Meacham's Baptist Church on Almond Street in St. Louis and meet out of sight in the basement, with smoky, smelly tallow candles for light. How one day, when he was sunk in concentration over his speller, the police had burst into the room, making him jump with fright. How he'd watched with a pounding heart while they'd arrested the teacher -- then had run in panic with the rest. Some time after that he'd studied with the nuns in the Catholic Cathedral on Walnut Street. There in the stone church near the riverfront, with the children of slaves, he'd tasted more of the forbidden treasure of knowledge.

He had not been a slave himself since he was about four, when his free father had purchased his and his mother's freedom. James hadn't really understood what was happening when he stood with his mother on the broad, stone steps of the St. Louis courthouse that late winter day in 1843, but his father had often told him the story.

His father was a bright man who claimed he could trace his line to a Moorish prince. Whether or not it was true, he had accomplished success beyond the imagining of most Negroes of his day. Of course he'd been lucky in his owners, a young master who'd taught him the rudiments of veterinary medicine and brought him to St. Louis, and there another owner who allowed him to pay her for free time in which to practice his skills. Gradually becoming known as Black John, the horse doctor, he'd finally earned enough money to buy his freedom.

The teacher's mother had led a more circumscribed life. She was of the Vai tribe in Africa and she'd come to Missouri from Kentucky, where she'd been presented to a minister's wife as a wedding present. Later, in St. Louis, she was purchased by the Loring family and taken to their plantation about 12 miles west of St. Louis on the road to St. Charles. By law, although her husband was free, any children she bore automatically became the property of her owner; James Milton had been named for the young master born the same day he was.

However John Turner, aware his wife and new son, like any slaves, were ever at risk of being sold and shipped to distant states, was determined they would be freed. It had seemed an impossible goal, with the price of $3,000 set on his wife, Hannah.

Still, while little James Milton learned to crawl, to toddle, to run, John Turner worked and saved. Then, when James was about four, Hannah had an accident. A broken wrist, and the suggestion she would lose her hand, convinced Loring to put her up for sale. Few in the courthouse crowd were interested in bidding on such damaged property, and no one topped John Turner's offer of $400.

James cost his father an extra $50. By December 4 the family could glory over the neat script on the coveted manumission paper which declared the servant Hannah and the boy James Milton, "also of brown or copper color," emancipated and "forever set free."

However being free did not entitle James to an education. He was still a captive inside his black skin.

The teacher moved around the classroom now, reassuring the anxious students, showing them how to handle a book, explaining that they could and would learn to make sense of the marks on the page. He was not trained to teach, but he could share what he knew. More important, he was determined to reach through their doubts and convince them they could understand -- to give them the confidence to try. The classroom might be makeshift, the few books battered, but if they wanted to learn, they could.

Once he'd learned to read, James had not been able to keep his hands off books. The nuns and the Baptists had taught from the Bible, more concerned about his future life than his present one.

But there were other books, he discovered, books full of all kinds of knowledge. Risky as it was, he'd kept reading anything he could find. He'd gotten a job working for a doctor as an office boy and contrived to read whenever there was a chance he'd be unobserved for a few moments. The more he read, the more he wanted. For a while he'd been able to attend a tuition day school across the river in Brooklyn, Illinois.

He'd done so well at his studies that in the mid-1850s the family had managed to send him to Oberlin, Ohio, where he was accepted by the preparatory division of the college. There, a few miles south of Lake Erie, where both Blacks and women were welcome in the classroom, the 14-year-old boy roomed in a professor's home and breathed the heady atmosphere of a town and state awakening to the cause of abolition. Northern opponents of the Fugitive Slave Law were adamant and vocal. Volunteers risked imprisonment as they whisked slaves north through the state on the Underground Railroad. Newspapers were full of news about the Kansas turmoil between the proslavers and the Free-Soilers.

However James had been called back to St. Louis after only a year or two of learning so that he could help support his family. There, in a city which was frantically growing, a city which housed both slave holders and abolitionists, where plantation owners and German and Irish immigrants confronted each other in the streets, a city that boasted a new railroad, symphony, opera, theater, library, literary lectures, and a public high school -- for Whites -- he looked for work.

In March 1857, not long after his return from Oberlin, he learned with the rest of the nation that the Supreme Court had decreed St. Louis slave Dred Scott was a property and not a person.

James knew who Scott was. Most of the city knew about the lawsuit to free him and his family on the grounds he'd been taken to live in free-soil states. James saw Scott in church and on the streets as he ran errands in his good-natured, unhurried way, quietly enjoying his mild celebrity. The possibilities and ramifications of his case had been debated, examined, celebrated or condemned by all segments of society. But the simple man had grown old these past 11 years while the lawyers' case to free him moved from county to state to Federal court.

Finally the decision came: the highest court in the land declared Scott had no rights -- that no one of Negro blood could claim to be either a person or a citizen -- that from the time the Constitution was framed Negroes were "so inferior that they had no rights which the white man was bound to respect." It seemed a stunning defeat for all the grand concepts that had fed James' soul at Oberlin.

James was not a slave. His treasured manumission declared him "forever set free." But freedom for a black man in St. Louis was a relative thing. There were three dozen slaves for every free Black like him, but he and the 3,000 other free Negroes in Missouri were still considered dangerous. With the legislature threatening to expel them from the state, they had to tread lightly. While a few owned barbershops or meat markets or worked in the river trade, most of them held jobs as domestics, or toiled as laborers on the levee.

For a time Turner worked for the army officers at Camp Jackson west of the city, fetching and carrying and blacking the officers' boots. Then he'd been lucky to find a job in the office of a railroad promoter and politician named Madison Miller. When the war broke out, he'd gone with Miller into the Union ranks as the colonel's body servant. A few weeks later he'd seen crusty Union General Lyon fall before Sterling Price's Missouri boys at Wilson's Creek. Then on an early April day in 1862 he and the colonel had camped near the Shiloh church on the Tennessee River.

They were as unprepared as the rest of the Union forces when the Confederate attack came, and before the day was over Turner was among the 7,500 Federal wounded. The colonel had vanished.

Left on his own, Turner grabbed the colonel's knapsack and crawled away from the Confederate fire. Taking cover in brush and streams, he thanked heaven as he dove into one and lay submerged to his chin that his face was black instead of white. Nursing his wounded hip, he made his painful way back to St. Louis, where he sadly reported to Mrs. Miller that he believed her husband was dead. He gave her what he had of the colonel's possessions. He could still hear her expressions of astonished gratitude when she opened the soiled bundle he handed her and discovered $4,000.

His act of honesty earned him a reward later when Miller surfaced from a Confederate prison and -- more important -- the respect of some influential white families.

While Turner readily demonstrated his loyalty to white people who'd been good to him, he felt no compunctions about working against a society based on slavery. For the rest of the war years he worked actively in the Underground Railroad, spending many dark nights fighting the Mississippi's currents to deposit fugitive slaves on the free Illinois shore.

The war was over now; his people were free, at least in name. He'd celebrated with the rest in January 1865 when the state constitution finally freed the slaves -- two years after Lincoln's proclamation declared those in the Confederacy free. The St. Louis streets echoed with a 60-gun salute and fireworks lit the night.

However, when the flags and banners had been folded away, few of the slaves had any idea what to do or where to go now that they were suddenly on their own. Many of them congregated in the cities but, unschooled and unskilled, they could not find work. With no concept of self-discipline, many who found jobs soon lost them or squandered wages they had no idea how to handle. Often they ended up back on the farm or plantation they'd left, working for minuscule wages or a share of the crop. The Federal Freedmen's Bureau helped as many as it could; northern philanthropic groups sent a handful of teachers. Still the need was overwhelming.

Turner could see his people must help themselves. He was one of the few Blacks in the whole state who had the knowledge they needed and he was determined to help them step into their new world. Looking at the bewildered young faces before him in the classroom that April morning, he had a new appreciation of the leap there was to be made, the effort it was going to take, before the black man could realize his potential.

Another essential right he knew Blacks must have was the vote. One might be emancipated and still held in subjugation by a society in which he had no voice. The southern governments were quickly moving to pass codes which deprived Blacks of all rights before the law. In his state's largest city Negroes could ride only on the platforms of streetcars; in the country, Blacks could still be cheated, whipped or even killed while the law looked the other way.

Turner had spent much of the past year helping to organize the Missouri Equal Rights League and traveling the state to speak for the cause and gather signatures on petitions requesting the vote for Negroes. Sometimes his audiences were Black, sometimes White. Sometimes he looked into black faces on one side of the room, white faces on the other. Strike the word "white" from the new state document, he challenged. Make it a constitution for *all* the people. While many of the league members were Whites who were devoted to the freedmen's cause, Turner also encountered audiences who did not appreciate his efforts. In one southeastern Missouri town the home where he slept was attacked by a mob, and he'd been forced to flee barefoot into the winter night to save his life.

He was not to be scared off. He was an articulate man, and the more he spoke the more confidence he gained on the platform. He began to use his knowledge of classical literature, and work quotations he admired into his speeches. His appearances brought him prominence and by the mid-1860s politicians in the state began to accept him as the spokesman for Missouri's Negroes.

By March 1866 more than 3,000 citizens had had the courage to sign their petitions. Gratified by the numbers, League members had carried them to Jefferson City the month before, daring to hope the legislature would admit the justice of their cause.

It was a vain hope. Still, the state which refused them the vote did decide to grant Negroes free public education, and when the Kansas City, Missouri school board asked Turner to teach in their school, he'd readily accepted. One had to start somewhere, and this nondescript schoolroom -- the first public school for black children in Missouri -- was a beginning.

Turner saw to it that many more than a roomful of children in Kansas City took the road to knowledge. Before there could be schools for the Negroes, there had to be teachers. Where were they to come from? They couldn't all come from the North, as had most of those for the freedmen and missionary schools operating here and there in the state. He joined forces with a teacher from New Hampshire who'd served as an officer for an infantry company of black Missourians, and a local minister. They collected nearly $7,000 in contributions from colored infantry companies from Missouri and Louisiana.

Although many white people resented even rudimentary education for Negroes, Turner and other Blacks canvassed the state seeking additional support. Before long the college-to-be had purchased farmland near the state capital, where Negroes could work to support themselves while they studied. They named it Lincoln Institute, and Turner watched it grow from two students in a ramshackle building to 70 within a few months.

After moving that fall to Boonville to begin a black school there, and teach the four-month term the statutes allowed, Turner was appointed an assistant superintendent of schools for the state and charged with establishing classrooms for Negroes. He knew he'd have to fight for teachers and materials and against both subtle and overt opposition. In some counties black schools had been burned; black children had been stoned as they walked to school. In others there was simply little interest in educating white children, no willingness at all to pay school taxes for Blacks.

While larger towns such as Kansas City were already building schools to replace the rented, makeshift quarters they began with, others sent their children to endure heat and cold in dilapidated log cabins. Few schools knew the luxury of desks. Many were grateful for a few benches along the walls, a blackboard and a globe. Others had even less.

In a year's time things were already changing. Many towns and counties were accepting their responsibilities under the new law. Enrollments were growing and attendance improving. Where the local government was slow to act, the freedmen were establishing and supporting their own schools. They held picnics and fairs to raise money to support them. Three public schools in St. Louis were crowded with 437 students, 45 of them adults. His people wanted to learn! Turner threw himself into the work with passion.

He also served on the board of Lincoln Institute in Jefferson City and, in 1870, his oration to the legislature was instrumental in persuading the body to underwrite the school -- providing the institution could match the legislature's contribution. Again he helped plead for funds for the college, and before another year passed watched it dedicate its first building.

Increasingly active in state politics, he amazed both white and black audiences throughout Missouri with his abilities as an orator. And in March 1871, at age 31, he was appointed United States minister and counsel to Liberia, the second black American accepted into the diplomatic corps. He served seven years, during which he learned his mother's tribe, the Vai, were accomplished people who had developed their own alphabet and grammar; he noted the Vai working around the legation asked for pens, ink and paper rather than tobacco or rum. Yet he did not encourage American freedmen to immigrate to Liberia as some Blacks advised; he thought their future, like his own, lay in the United States.

When he returned in 1878, after exemplary service, Negroes met him in Boston, New York, Philadelphia and Washington with demonstrations and banquets to celebrate his success. One of their own -- a former slave -- had moved in the circles of power, become accomplished in international law, been welcomed to the homes of European royalty. If anyone questioned the wisdom of emancipation and the 15th Amendment they could point to Turner's career.

Home in St. Louis, where he'd had to steal knowledge to feed his mind and polish boots to feed his body, Blacks took the horses from his carriage and used their own power to pull him through the streets.

However, in spite of the citizenship granted in the 14th Amendment and the suffrage guaranteed by the 15th in 1870, he found many of the freed slaves still under the yoke. In 1879 he became involved with the great exodus of Blacks to Kansas; later he worked to find land in Oklahoma for refugee Blacks with nowhere to go. He spent years in the courts and government chambers to secure land payments for former slaves of the Cherokee nation in Indian Territory and traveled the territory to find land and jobs for a colony of Choctaw freedmen.

In 1882 he was invited to speak before the Missouri Historical Society as it accepted a portrait of Dred Scott into its collection. Aware of the honor the invitation implied, Turner limped to the lectern and praised the society for recognizing the fact that Blacks were part of the state's history. With quiet irony he noted that no state's history could now be complete without mention of this unschooled, unpretentious man.

Ever a champion of his race, he did not hesitate to remind the old-line Missouri audience of the contribution his people had made to the state -- felling forests, draining lagoons, building cities, toiling in the fields -- serving beside them in the war.

"Surely," he reasoned, "the Negro must somewhere, at some time and somehow, have carved his humble niche in the temple of time." He hoped placing Scott among its records was a sign those unmindful of black contributions might become aware, and hoped the differences between the races were "disappearing beneath the healing touches of humanity and time."

In later years he admitted that in his own experience during a long and active life he dealt with "...very few white men...who did not, either wittingly or unwittingly, compel me to feel that I was a Negro." He accepted the fact that slavery was as old as history, but he pondered why society was so slow to realize that human slavery is not "the crucible to refine and ennoble human nature and befit it for grand undertakings."

He had escaped the bonds of ignorance and broken the mold designed for him, but he was always aware of those who'd been less fortunate. His efforts on behalf of the freedmen were sometimes described as self-serving, but he was able to use his political knowledge and influence to help them achieve their goals, as well as to earn financial success for himself. When he died in 1915, friends had to schedule two services to accommodate the numbers who wished to recognize his accomplishments. One among numerous editors who paid him tribute described him as "a leader who moved among the masses -- none being too lowly; who marched with intellectuals, none being his superiors."

Of Neither World

As the 1860s drew to a close and at least some in the South moved to mend their broken society, the northern Missouri remained in turmoil. No one raised the question of whether the 14th Amendment should apply to red men as well as black.

By 1868, Sitting Bull's honors and character had earned him the title of chief of the Teton Sioux. When the missionary Father Pierre-Jean DeSmet came to his country to establish a peace, he was willing to talk. He had no reason to war with the Whites, he told the Black Robe, as long as the soldiers left and the forts were abandoned. Representatives of the Hunkpapa went in to Fort Rice to sign the Treaty of Fort Laramie, which recognized all land north of the North Platte and east of the Big Horn Mountains as Sioux property. No Whites were to occupy any of the land without Sioux permission.

Convinced he had secured the homeland of his people, and confident of their strength, Sitting Bull continued to live and war as he pleased. Although steam engines now clanked along the Platte and the valley of the flat river curled up behind plow blades like leaves shriveling in the sun, he closed his mind to the thought that the same things could happen in his country.

But other tribes were not as sanguine. Miners -- and now shopkeepers, freighters, gamblers, preachers, soldiers, ranchers, newspapermen, wives and children continued to pour onto the levee at Fort Benton. The Blackfoot who'd signed Governor Stevens paper 13 years before, and even some of those who'd given their hearts to Father DeSmet's god, began to wonder what place there would be for them in this new world. In the summer of 1869, some of the young Piegan men had a glimpse of their place in the white man's world and decided they would not accept what they saw.

 On Malcolm Clarke's ranch in the Little Prickly Pear Valley they were worried about the cattle. They'd not been seen for a day or two, and though the sky promised nothing more than another hot August day, Clarke was uneasy. The Indians were on the prowl. Several outfits hauling freight from Fort Benton to Helena had been attacked and a couple of white men had been killed.

In retaliation, without waiting to find out what braves or what tribe had been responsible, some fools in Benton had shot down the unarmed brother of the Blackfoot mountain chief and a teen-aged boy who'd been sent to the fort on an errand. The Blackfoot, outraged at the murders, had struck back by stealing horses up and down the Missouri. The Clarke's horse herd had been run off two weeks before, and now the cattle were missing. While he was sure they had just wandered farther than usual, Clarke decided to send his young Indian herder to find them.

Helen Clarke knew her father was concerned because he'd not been able to ride to the Blackfoot camp since the murders. He could not offer much but sympathy, but he hoped the sincere regret of a long-time friend would help ease their hurt and anger and defuse a dangerous situation. He might be 52, his hair white, but he was still the vital, compelling man he'd always been; she was confident he could handle any situation. He'd survived in the West for nearly 30 years and the last thing he was afraid of was Indians.

In fact, none of Clarke's children was afraid of Indians because they all had Indian blood in their veins. Like many of the fur traders, Clarke had married into a tribe during his years as an employee of the American Fur Company at the upper river posts. Helen's mother was a Piegan woman, Cothcocoma, and all of her siblings were of mixed blood.

Not that Helen, or Nellie, as the family called her, felt much like an Indian. Although she'd been born at the mouth of the Judith in 1848, where her father was trading with the Indians, she'd been sent to live with his sister in Minnesota when she was old enough for school. There in a Catholic school -- called Helen, rather than Piotopowaka -- known as the granddaughter of Maj. Nathan Clarke who had commanded Fort Snelling, rather than of Big Snake who ruled a Piegan band -- she absorbed the Catholic faith, social graces and her ABCs.

Except for yearly visits, when his compelling, bearded presence flashed in and out of their lives, the children had rarely seen their father. It was only since she'd come back west to live on the ranch a few years before that Helen had come really to know and love him. Though she was 21 now, a tall beauty with upswept hair and deep-set black eyes, she'd taken readily to life on the Montana ranch. Her father had chosen an area of park-like grassland on the west side of the Missouri, not far from where the river burst between the huge gray cliffs Lewis and Clark called the Gates of the Mountains.

Renewing acquaintance with her Piegan mother, whom she now saw with adult eyes, she realized Cothcocoma was a good wife to her father, a person who gave readily of both herself and her possessions. Her childhood feelings of love deepened with admiration for the good woman. And the more she learned about the Blackfoot, the more she empathized with their problems.

She all but worshiped her father, delighting in his stories of the early days when he'd come west to work for the fur company. She was proud that the Blackfoot had first named him for the striking white lodge pole which was the center of attention in the sacred tipi. Later, when he killed four grizzlies before breakfast, part of 30 he dispatched in one month, they renamed him Four Bears, a name they'd never before given either to White or Blackfoot.

She loved to hear him tell about the time the Arikara had attacked Fort Benton. How, while a fellow trapper plucked the infant Helen from a Ree's arms, Clarke had ridden to the rescue of a young Blackfoot boy and brought him to safety through a rain of arrows. Listening to other stories of his adventurous life she decided he led a charmed existence.

Busy with their morning chores, they realized after a while that it was noon and the cattle had not appeared. Then it was four o'clock, and still no herd; no herder. They scanned the empty hills and speculated how far the herd could stray.

Though they were anxious about the welfare of their animals, they had no concern for themselves. There'd been some trouble with the Piegans over stolen horses two years before, and her father had had to make peace between a young hot-blooded cousin of Cothcocoma named Netuscheo and his own rash son, Horace. But Clarke had spent the winter in their camp and he felt confident the hard feelings had been soothed. He'd put his persuasive skills to work and was convinced he'd made progress in his campaign to be appointed their trader.

He'd listened while the mountain chief voiced his hatred for the Whites and the way they killed the buffalo and mistreated his people. Because Whites could or would not differentiate between the tribes, his people were often made to suffer for the wrongs of others, the chief said. He announced he would no longer take responsibility for keeping rein on his young men. He didn't want to deal with Whites except at the trading posts. He didn't want to see them in his camp.

But Four Bears was different, he said. He'd married into the nation, treated his two wives well, taken care of his children. He was a friend. It was possible they would grant his desire to act again as their trader. Clarke had returned to the ranch convinced the bond between them was secure, hopeful he could earn some extra money as a trader.

They'd finished supper and the sun was low on the horizon when they finally heard the tinkle of cattle bells and the lowing of the herd. Clarke and Horace checked them over, found them in good health, and decided they'd just wandered farther than they had before. Everyone relaxed, and Helen accepted her father's challenge to a game of backgammon. Her quick mind made her a good match for her West Point-educated father, and the two were soon engrossed in their contest.

About nine o'clock the dogs barked. They both glanced up. Too late for a neighbor. Must be an Indian. They might knock on the door at any hour. Helen had often heard her father answer such knocks in the middle of the night, listen to their stories and decide whether they needed help or just wanted a meal. It was probably some of Cothcocoma's relatives. Father and daughter started another game.

But more voices and more barks ruined their concentration. Helen went to the back of the house to find who'd come to visit.

She found Netuscheo, the mountain chief's son and two other young braves greeting her mother and her mother's aunt, Black Bear. Her younger sister, Isabel, excited to have visitors, chattered a welcome while the youngest daughter rubbed sleepy eyes and stared up at the large men causing so much commotion.

Helen greeted Netuscheo by name, made a joke about the Clarke's horses being stolen again, and watched him shake hands with her father and give Horace -- whom he'd not seen since their squabble -- a quick embrace. Her father, ever the generous host, welcomed them, ordered a meal prepared and sent his personal invitation out to a brave named Shanghai who was said to be too bashful to enter the house. Then he filled his pipe, passing it to the tall Shanghai and the others, one of whom Helen had nicknamed Richard the Third. The Indians asked after Nathan, Clarke's other son, who was out hunting the horses and not expected to return until morning, and the Clarkes told the mountain chief's son how sorry they were that his uncle and the teen-ager had been killed at Benton.

When the courtesies had been taken care of the braves announced the purpose of their visit. They'd come, the Piegans said, prepared to discuss Clarke's wish to be their trader and to return some horses the Bloods had stolen from the Clarkes three years before. They wanted Horace to go out and identify the horses. It was welcome news to the nearly horseless family.

Horace picked up his hat and automatically glanced around for his gun belt. But when he did not find it after a brief search, he decided he did not really need it and followed the chief's son out the door.

Helen noticed the braves all seemed restless and excited. The mountain chief's son paced about the room, fingering first one thing and then another. Netuscheo kept a blanket across his lap and she wondered briefly if he was cold. Two or three times he asked her father to step outside so they could discuss something in private and her father had obliged. Helen knew the Indian had recently killed his father-in-law and supposed he was asking her father for sanctuary. She knew that idea would not be popular with the neighbors, but Netuscheo was a relative and it would be difficult to deny him.

Once again the two men rose to go outside. But this time the door had scarcely closed when a shot broke the quiet.

Isabel rushed to the door to see what had happened, but Netuscheo appeared and pushed her back inside, telling her it was just some target practice. He lifted Clarke's gun and powder horn from their hook near the door and went out again. Helen noticed his action without alarm, for her father followed the Indian custom of freely sharing his belongings with all family members.

But then there was another shot.

Helen, on her feet now, swayed dizzily, suddenly sure who had been the target. She ran toward the back of the house to find the other women. The door stood open and through it she could see dozens of Indians riding wildly about the house. She gasped. Her relatives had been transformed to demons of hell. As she crossed herself and asked God for mercy another shot sounded. Just then she heard Horace's voice call in the distance.

"Father! I am shot."

Yelling for Isabel to go check on their father, Helen ran toward Horace's voice, unable to believe what was happening. She found him crawling toward the house, his face a mass of blood.

Even then she could not believe the Piegans were responsible. Surely it had been some other Indians. Tell me it was the Pend d'Oreille, she pleaded irrationally. Not until Horace had told her two or three times could she accept the truth that their own people had betrayed them.

"Father?" he asked.

"Gone." she said. She had not seen him, but she knew.

By now the elderly Black Bear had hurried out to help her get Horace back to the house. They made him a bed on the floor of her father's room and Helen tried to staunch the bleeding and see the extent of the wound. There was too much blood. She asked a little Piegan boy who'd been staying with them to go for water, but he was too frightened to leave the house. Helen rose to go herself but Isabel grabbed the bucket from her hand and ran for the stream. In a little while the young girl was back, white-faced but whole. The chief's son had feinted as if to grab her, but done her no harm.

Helen, sure her brother was bleeding to death as she watched, tried desperately to think of some way to stem the flood. Her frantic mind settled on tobacco and she grabbed her father's pouch. The bullet had gone through Horace's nose and cheek and come out in front of his left ear. While Helen wet the tobacco and applied it to Horace's face, the little girl went out again to search the dark ranch yard for their father.

In only moments she was back to confirm their worst fears. He'd been shot down within a few feet of his door. Helen went out to where he lay, a bullet through his heart and the gash of a tomahawk in his forehead. The weight of his lifeless hand in hers said it all. She whispered a prayer that he had found peace.

Then, between them, she and Cothcocoma and Black Bear managed to lift him, carry his body into the house and place him on the floor of his room. Cothcocoma and Black Bear began to keen their high, wild cry of despair and the little girls started to cry.

Helen, fighting to keep her own emotions under control, whirled on them sharply. "It is no time for crying," she snapped. "It must be stopped! Pray!"

"Yes, Nellie, pray," Horace answered weakly.

For they were all in peril. There was no

reason to hope the angry warriors would stop now. Black Bear offered to go see if she could influence the braves or find a chief who could stop them. The chances of success were slim, the risks great. The old woman slipped from the house and disappeared.

Suddenly aware the doors were still open they rushed in a panic to shut them. But there were no locks -- they'd never needed any. Cothcocoma tugged one of the beds from its place and pushed it across the room to block the door. As she passed the window it shattered and a bullet whizzed by her head.

They decided it might be safer to barricade themselves in Helen's room, which opened off her father's in a wing of the house. While the trader's room was familiar ground to the Piegan, Helen's was not. That this would make any difference to the vengeful braves was the smallest wisp of possibility, but they needed to believe it might. Isabel grabbed up blankets and Cothcocoma a knife, and they herded the little children before them. Horace, grasping a hatchet, crept unsteadily after them.

Helen brought up the rear with another knife, the crucial tobacco and the pail of water. Rushing across her father's room, slopping the water in her hurry, she glanced at his body on the hard floor. How could she leave him unprotected? She picked up a blanket and threw it over him. It was not much -- it was nothing, if his enemies were bent on mutilation -- but the gesture made her feel a little better.

Gathered with the three young children in Helen's small room, the two women and the wounded man wondered who was still out there in the darkness. Cothcocoma nailed the door shut, but they all knew their defenses were more imagined than real. They heard the sound of horses galloping away and for about an hour all was quiet. Perhaps the Piegan, shocked at their deed, would not return.

However, in an hour or so they heard hoofbeats, this time approaching. Then the sound of steps in the house. They held their breath, smothering the exclamations of the little children. The next instant they jumped as one, when the dishes were swept from the table, to crash and roll on the kitchen floor. The noise escalated as trunks were dumped, furniture smashed, mirrors broken. Helen could follow their movements through the house as they laid claim to the family possessions they wanted and destroyed the rest. Then the familiar voices gathered in her father's room to argue about what should be done with them.

Some wanted prisoners. Netuscheo wanted them killed. "Horace is alive," he said. "He is in that room." The doorknob turned and the door began to creak as he threw his weight against it.

But then they heard another voice. Black Bear had returned and was trying to reason with the braves. "Oh, no," the old aunt said. "He is dead. The Four Bears is dead. Have pity."

Bravely she told them they'd murdered their best friend. That the deed was so dark the trees would whisper it. That dawn would bring a hundred horsemen to avenge The Four Bears.

Gradually the others agreed enough blood had been shed; that they warred now on women and children. All but Netuscheo. He finally left with the rest, but under protest, yelling back threats, promising the family huddled inside he would be back to finish his task.

As they rode away the warriors drove the cattle herd before them. Frustrated and helpless, Helen and Horace listened to their animals bellow with confusion and fear, while the sound of gunfire told them the braves were expending their emotions and their unused bullets on the stock.

The family sat in darkness and silence. Nothing more was heard from the old aunt.

About one o'clock Horace vomited blood. Helen, fearing his end was near, dared to light a candle and tend him. But when they heard a noise they quickly put out the candle. Again they sat silent and tense in the black room, aware of every breath, every heartbeat. Any moment Netuscheo could return and make good his threats. Helen thought how easy it would be for the Indians to fire the house.

About 4 a.m. she struck another light to check Horace and help him apply the tobacco and water. She had never been so tired. Isabel leaned against her. Her youngest sister curled in her lap. And the little Indian boy clung to her leg, as he had all night.

But the night was finally ending. In another hour the sky was light and she looked out into the yard. All was quiet, but a trail of flour, sugar and dead cattle stretched away toward the hills.

Hesitantly she and Isabel started for help. Aware of every trembling leaf, expecting any moment to be seized, the sisters worked their way through the brush nearly a mile to an outbuilding where they found one of their ranch hands who still had his horse. She sent him to Helena for a doctor and they walked on to a neighbor's home. Helen ran to the door and began to pour out her story to the women inside. She'd done what she could for Horace, but he needed better care. Would one of them come and look at his wound?

Astonished, horrified, she heard them refuse. They were too afraid to leave their house. Understanding their fear, she tried not to hate them. She and Isabel returned home alone and she began to wonder why her brother Nathan had not returned from hunting the horses. Walking numbly through the chaos of her home, she automatically began trying to put things right, to return their lives to some semblance of order. But there was so little left she could not disguise the damage. She sat dejectedly while the family dog licked her hand as if to offer comfort.

It was mid-afternoon when the doctor finally came, but after he'd examined Horace's wound his news was good. Her brother had no broken bones in his face. He'd not suffered serious damage.

She had one other trial to endure. Nathan rode in late in the day. She walked down to the corral to prepare him for what he'd find in the house. By evening the house was filled with her father's friends, and two days later they buried him on the rim of Little Prickly Pear Canyon.

Helen went back east after her father's death, but she did not reject her mother's people or waste herself in bitterness against the Piegan. She knew the tribe as a whole had not wished his death. She'd watched them mourn. Understanding the pressures on the tribe and knowing that any race could harbor vengeful members, she realized Malcolm Clarke was a victim of circumstances no one could control.

She decided to attend drama school and for a few years she made use of her rich, deep voice in a successful acting career that included performances in Europe. However, it did not bring her happiness. In 1875 she returned to Montana to teach in the Benton and Helena schools. A popular, accomplished woman, she was elected the Lewis and Clark County superintendent of schools in 1882, becoming the first woman superintendent and the first female to hold elective office in the state.

Yet she never forgot her mother's people or tried to deny her heritage. For most of the 1890s she worked in Indian Territory, helping the Ponca, Oto and Pawnee understand and accept a law which required them to choose a plot of ground to farm. Interpreting, mediating, cajoling, persuading the reluctant men, she helped them realize they had no choice but to comply.

Sadly, she decided her own choices were equally limited. An attractive, vibrant woman who did not lack suitors, she chose to remain "Miss Nellie." Her experiences convinced her that as a half-breed she would never find a white man who would neither pity nor patronize her, but would consider her an equal. She could accept no less.

Required by her choice to support herself, she taught elocution classes in San Francisco in the early 1900s. But again the whirl of society, concerts and theater soon palled. She could endure the city only so long. For her, home was always Montana and in 1902 she applied for permission to live on the Blackfoot Reservation. There at the foot of the Rockies (present Glacier National Park) she ranched with her brother, Horace.

Ever a champion of education, she maintained a large library, and her door was always open to anyone who needed a friend -- Indians, Whites and especially those, like her, who belonged to both worlds and neither.

When she died in 1923 a friend mourned Piotopowaka with the Blackfoot chant:
Ake u, ake u, ake u; Ma cante maseca.
Ake u, ake u, ake u; Ma cante maseca.
Come again, come again, come again,
For my heart is sad.
Come again, come again, come again,
For my heart is sad.

Goodbird's Mother

The Blackfoot who punished the Clarke family were just one of the tribes feeling pressured by the Whites. By 1870 settlers were pushing across the Big Sioux River into Dakota Territory, and soldiers had piled from steamboats to man eight posts between the Niobrara and the Yellowstone. Even the Sioux and Cheyenne peace chiefs, who'd agreed in 1868 to live on reservations west of the Missouri, were grumbling about the proliferation of white men.

Some bands, such as the Hunkpapa, disdained the reservations and continued to believe they could maintain their lands as their fathers and grandfathers had, by striking fiercely when and where they could. Others looked around them and wondered how to find a place for themselves in a world of which their ancestors had never dreamed.

The young Hidatsa woman named Waheenee sat quietly with the matrons grouped in one side of her father's roomy earth lodge in Like-a-Fishhook Village on the north bank of the Missouri (in present McLean County, North Dakota). Their work done, she and her mothers, Red Blossom and Strikes-Many Woman, her grandmother, Turtle, and her two sisters-in-law could relax and enjoy the feast with the rest. She'd had a busy day, boiling what was left of their favorite green corn and helping the other women pound ripe corn in the gray wooden mortar and mix it with buffalo fat until they had more than enough meal balls to feed all their relatives. But it was pleasant work, with everyone in the good mood a successful buffalo hunt inspired.

The four pony loads of meat she and her husband, Son of a Star, had brought home to her father's lodge would make an important difference to their large family, for their cache holes were nearly empty, and although planting time was near it would be months before another harvest. Fourteen people -- even though the men were good hunters and the women good farmers -- required a lot of food, and it was a matter of pride that Small Ankle's family supply other relatives whenever they could.

Although Small Ankle was aging, Waheenee's father was still a leader of the 70-lodge village, keeper of the medicine bundle for the Big Birds' ceremony and responsible for the welfare of families beyond the walls of his own lodge. Waheenee, as the wife of the hunter who'd brought in the meat, had already prepared bundles of dried meat for each guest to take away. She was proud she and her new husband could make such a substantial contribution.

Waheenee had good memories of her first young groom, who had come to share her bed in her father's lodge before she'd completed her sixteenth winter. She'd grown and learned much in their dozen winters of marriage, before she lost him to the coughing sickness.

But after her seasons of mourning, Son of a Star had wanted her for his wife, and he was proving to be a good husband. Son of a Star was a Mandan, one of the few who'd survived the terrible scourge of smallpox that had killed most of their kinsmen shortly before either of them were born. The Mandan who lived had fled north with the Hidatsa to establish a new village on the river bank and begin to rebuild their lives. Son of a Star might not be Hidatsa, but he could carve brave deeds on his canoe paddle and was entitled to wear two eagle feathers for being among the first to strike an enemy. Even Small Ankle was impressed that three times this hunter's arrows had sped clear through a buffalo's body to fall on the prairie beyond, and he had welcomed him into the family lodge.

Always anxious to excel, Waheenee had redoubled her efforts to be a good wife to her new husband. She was one of few women in the village entitled to wear all three honor marks -- the blue-beaded belt for tanning skins, a gleaming yellow-tin ring for embroidering a robe with porcupine quills, and a bracelet reserved for those who'd decorated a tent cover with quills of the gull.

She took pride in constructing sturdy bullboats and extended herself to carry ever heavier loads. An ambitious, accomplished matron, she contributed her share to the family goods. She'd learned the craft of weaving bark baskets from an older relative and found many customers for her attractive black-and-tan designs. She'd paid to learn the art of tipi making and was paid in return to measure and cut the skins for a snug skin lodge.

However she was proudest of her right to superintend the construction of an earth lodge, a skill she had acquired from Red Blossom. It took the strength of the men to set the *ipsi*, the four huge center posts for a new lodge, but they were only placing timbers she had selected and cut to measure, and only she could dictate just how they'd be placed and trimmed. She was the one who sighted in the correct slant of the rafters that spread from the central square, marked the circle for the puncheons that formed the outer walls and decided when the roof had sufficient willows to hold the final layer of sod or dirt. The finished product, large enough to hold an extended family (and horses when the need arose), would last at least seven winters after smoke first curled up through the square-cut smoke hole.

Unlike some braves, Son of a Star appreciated her efforts and sometimes scolded her for doing too much. She hoped before too many moons to be able to give him a son, or a daughter who would sing to the corn, as she had as a little girl.

Yet now, as people relaxed after eating their fill and the laughter and talk began to subside, she heard her father, seated near her on the right side of the fire in the men's circle, talking with a friend about the changing times.

"Every spring, when I was young we fired the prairie grass around the Five Villages," Small Ankle was saying, speaking of the great congregation of lodges near the Knife River that Waheenee could scarcely remember. "Green grass then sprang up; buffaloes came to graze on it, and we killed many."

"Those were the good days," his friend agreed.

"But it is now seven years since a herd was seen near our village," her father continued. "The white men's guns have driven them away. And each year we kill fewer deer."

Waheenee knew how true his words were. Her people had always been farmers, raising corn and squash on the rich Missouri bottom, but their staple was still buffalo and other game. When meat was scarce the caches of dried crops emptied far too quickly. As they'd prepared to go on the hunt just completed, Son of a Star had remarked that even if they did not find much game to bring home, they'd at least be able to feed themselves instead of eating from the supplies of corn and beans needed by the children and old people.

"I heard some Sioux families starved last winter," Small Ankle's friend was saying.

"They starved because they are hunters and raise no corn," Waheenee's father answered. "We Hidatsa must plant more corn or we shall starve. And we must learn to raise white men's wheat and potatoes."

Wheat and potatoes? Waheenee thought of her father as a progressive man, but still it was hard to imagine her people growing wheat and potatoes like the traders and soldiers in the forts. Traders had been part of the Hidatsa's lives for longer than she could remember; the log houses they called Fort Berthold stood behind a stockade at the edge of the village and the Indians visited freely to trade and socialize. They were used to seeing steamboats unload barrels and crates at the river's edge and watching the trader trundle everything from flour to farming tools up the slope to his post. Twice a year the shipments were special, for these contained the blankets and clothes the government had promised the three river tribes at the great treaty conference.

Soldiers had come half a dozen winters before, their uniforms a welcome assurance that the Sioux would keep their distance from the village, until they moved on east to build another fort (Fort Stevenson) three years later. In fact, Son of a Star had been so taken with the soldiers' coats that she'd spent weeks making him one like theirs -- knee length, with sleeves and pockets. But his was made of three of her soft buckskins and her colorful beadwork trimmed the breast and back, the pocket flaps and wrists. Like many Hidatsa men, he often wore a shirt of cloth and a white man's leather belt, but his breech clout, skin leggings and moccasins were like those his father and grandfathers had worn.

The next few days, as Waheenee sharpened her hoe and sorted her seed corn, she gave thought to her father's words. She had loved the corn fields from the time she was old enough to toddle out and watch Grandmother Turtle wield her bone hoe. Some of her favorite memories were of days spent there after she was old enough to learn the words of the corn-growing songs. Sitting with her sister on the platform in the field, singing to encourage the young plants and let them know they were loved, had been not a duty but a pleasure. Through the years she'd helped her energetic old grandmother steadily enlarge the family fields on the Missouri bottomland until their plots were among the biggest of the village.

A few days later, when the gooseberry vines were in leaf and it was time to plant again, Waheenee convinced her mothers they should work even harder. While they planted the field that had rested the year before, she and old Turtle worked with their hoes at the edge, breaking new ground. They planted for nearly a month, and spent more than a week drying and shelling their corn.

Harvest, with its huge pile of ears and the

young men coming for the husking feast, was always a joyous time, but this year it was especially meaningful for Waheenee. As she sorted out the best ears to save for seed, braided some ears in strings and hung them to dry, stripped the kernels from others, gathered sacks of sunflower seed and laid great strings of dried squash rings in the grass-lined cache pits, she felt the child she had hoped for move in her belly. It was indeed a fruitful year.

However not everyone in the village had been as wise or industrious as Small Ankle's family. Assessing the results of the meager summer hunt, the leaders decided there simply was not enough food to winter as they usually did on the Missouri bottom.

It was an unsettling decision. They were used to leaving their permanent earth lodges and camping on the more sheltered lowlands in winter, but the site was never far from Like-a-Fishhook Village. Now village leaders were saying they must follow the buffalo to the Yellowstone country and spend the winter there.

This plan was so unsettling that no one wanted the responsibility of being winter chief. Many things could go wrong on such a journey. They'd be exposed not only to the risks of weather and hunting unfamiliar territory, but to the hazards of living in a land traversed by Blackfoot and Sioux. A winter chief was expected to keep his people safe and bring them good hunting. The blame was his if the village experienced bad times, and none of the men believed his medicine was strong enough to ensure its safety.

The Black Mouth society collected donations and offered gifts and the pipe to all the head men, but each refused, afraid he would "lose the people." After several meetings and much consultation the council solved the problem by dividing the responsibility between two men. Each would lead on alternate days. Both accepted the pipe and prayed to their medicine bundles for food and safety through the winter. The crier walked through the village, alerting the people to prepare for a journey five days hence.

Waheenee climbed down into the cache pits and, bending awkwardly over her distended belly, gathered up strings of corn and squash and began to pack. To pack all the family would need for several months was a strenuous undertaking. She and the other women scooped corn into double bags that would hang over the mules' saddles, filled parfleches with dried squash and corn ears, ladled green corn into the calfskin bag. Although Waheenee had already made 12 pair of moccasins for herself and her husband, she packed skins with fur for making new winter ones and the sinew and awl she'd need to sew them together. She gathered her elk horn scraper, sharpening stone and knife, the pestle and their wooden bowls, tin dishes, horn spoons and prized shiny yellow-tin kettle that came up to her knee. The bright kettle and the sugar and coffee she packed had come into their lives with the traders, as had the ax she added to the pile.

Some of the gear went on the backs of the two Big Ears -- they could carry more than ponies, she knew, and she had recently bought her own for that reason -- or on the travois that dragged behind their three large dogs. The ponies would drag the tipi poles and carry the heavy square of the folded tipi skin -- she'd made that too, of 13 new skins. The bullboat and paddle would top a mule's travois. Working with the skill of long experience, she was finished when the crier warned them to be ready to depart the next morning. Preceded by the two winter chiefs and their medicine bundles, the village filed out of the stockade and headed west.

For 11 days they followed the Missouri west, the line of marchers stretching out along the bluff tops, dipping into the ravines, cutting across the prairie where the river bent to the south. There were two wagons, another innovation that came with the traders, and a few rode ponies, but most were afoot, their horses needed to transport their camp gear.

Waheenee, alternately sharing a pony with Son of a Star, led one of the mules. Her two young nephews shared a horse and her mothers took turns riding another. Small Ankle, nearing 60 winters, was still a good walker and disdained to ride. The warriors ranged ahead and to the side to hunt and guard against attack as they advanced to Narrow Hill, Good Point, Shell Creek and Flint Steel Creek. A few miles below the Yellowstone's mouth, they pulled in to camp on a sandbar and prepared to cross the big river.

They had fought a chill wind all day, and Waheenee was glad to reach the shelter of camp. With practiced skill the women had Small Ankle's tipi up in a few moments. Minutes later he'd struck fire in one of the puff balls he carried and they had meat set to boil in the kettle. As the aroma filled the tent, Waheenee's mothers spread dry grass around the walls to cushion the robes for their beds. They ate hungrily in the early twilight and later welcomed some curious soldiers who'd come down from Fort Buford to visit and trade. Some of the troopers gave bright coins to the Hidatsa children, and Waheenee thought they seemed like good people.

However her thoughts were soon drawn inward, and she knew this night would be a special one. She told her mother Strikes-Many Woman of the contractions in her belly, and all but this mother and Waheenee's father left the tipi to spend the night in other lodges. Kneeling on her bed of grass, she felt the pains take hold. Birth on the march was trickier, she knew, than if she'd been safe at home in Like-a-Fishhook Village. She'd be unable to enjoy the 10 days of quiet and special consideration always granted a new mother after she gave birth. However, she knew Strikes-Many Woman, who had the power of the River Ceremonies, had seen many babes into the world. Small Ankle began the quiet chant of his mystery songs.

As the hours passed, Waheenee turned from the softly glowing coals of the fire and lifted the blanket over the door. The wind had died; the air was still and cold. She pulled her robe tight around her shoulders and looked up at a crescent moon which gave just enough light to glimmer on the tops of waves in mid-channel.

She listened to the river, picking out the lap of its waves on the beach where they camped, the swish of an eddy around a point. Yet under and over all other sounds she could hear the power of the main current pressing on toward Like-a-Fishhook Village, past the village and on to the old Five Villages on the Knife River where she was born, past those bluffs and on -- she knew not where.

Tomorrow they would cross this river.

By midnight the pains were gripping her body. Strikes-Many Woman whispered words of encouragement and Small Ankle gave her a medicine to ease the pain. One of her dogs, sleeping curled against the outside of the tipi, roused, pointed his nose at the sky and howled. Her other dogs joined in and soon the whole camp was enveloped in the chorus. From the dark prairie a lone coyote answered. Finally they were quiet again, and when the sky was barely gray above the smoke hole, she gave birth to a son.

She and Son of a Star, called in to greet his new son, watched fondly as Red Blossom gave the infant a bath. Laying him on a soft fur by the fire, the older woman used a horn spoon to fill her mouth with water. Holding it until it warmed, she then blew it over the baby's body. Waheenee winced at his indignant cry, but Son of a Star laughed and said such a lusty cry must presage a great warrior.

Red Blossom wrapped the baby in furs and with a hot rock warmed some clean sand to place in the bottom of his cradle bundle. She slipped him into the skin pouch, packed cattail down around his form for extra warmth, and tied a wildcat skin around him and over his head like a hood.

Even as she finished bundling the child and handed him to Waheenee, the walls of the tipi sagged above them. Old Turtle was already pulling the pins. The river was running ice this morning; there was no time to waste. They must be on the move. As soon as they were clear, her grandmother bundled the tent poles and tied them to the tail of the boat.

It was frightening to step into the unsteady bullboat with Son of a Star and watch him stroke into the current. She'd ridden the river many times, often paddled herself across with loads of meat, but never feeling so weak and carrying such a fragile cargo. They could not hug the ice-free shore; they had to brave the main channel. She clutched her baby with one arm, trying to shield him from the wind and spray, and held fast to the rounded rim with the other.

It was a rough ride, but Son of a Star, kneeling opposite her, paddled fiercely and soon she felt the welcome grating of the boat bottom on sand. Her husband helped her up the steep bank and built a small fire so she could have some hot broth. Then he returned to help the rest of the family.

Wrapped snugly in a robe, Waheenee sat watching the others cross. There were only a few boats, and they were kept busy ferrying the old people and children, so most of the tribe had to devise other ways to cross. Like the others, Waheenee's mothers piled their belongings in the lodge skin, gathered the top to make a large pouch, tied the bundle to a pony's tail and drove him into the water. Many of the men, and some of the women, swam across in the icy water, clinging to their bundles or their horses. For three days the current of the Missouri was spotted with the Hidatsa and their goods, until finally the far bank was empty and the hundred tipis were reunited on the south shore.

With the threat of snow in the air, the winter chiefs were anxious to move on. Unwilling for Waheenee to walk, Son of a Star hitched a travois to her docile mule. Seated in a travois basket with her son in her arms, wrapped securely in skins, Waheenee knew her mothers would have walked in the same situation. She thought how lucky she was.

For nearly a week they moved on. Conscientiously Waheenee removed the cattail down as it became soiled and pulled fresh down from the slender, brown heads she carried in a sack to replace it. Hugging the tiny bundle inside her furry buffalo robe, she strove to keep it warm with the heat from her body and the milk of her breasts. She was relieved when the winter chiefs found buffalo bones on Round Bank and were satisfied the omens were good enough to make camp on the small creek.

The day after they were settled Waheenee prepared a dish of venison and green corn -- her father's favorites -- and set it before him. For a moment she was back in her childhood, hearing his voice sing her to sleep by the fire, snuggling her ankles in his warm furry cap. Looking into his face, which was showing the lines of age, she said, "I want you to name your grandson."

Small Ankle smiled and began to eat. Waheenee waited, knowing he was giving the matter careful consideration. When he had finished the bowl of food he rose and cradled the baby in his arms. "I name him Tsakahta Sukkee, Goodbird," he said.

Waheenee nodded in satisfaction. Small Ankle's gods were the Thunder Birds. The name was a prayer that those gods protect and assist her little son.

The months in winter camp were long and cold, but the hunters managed to find enough deer and buffalo to keep them fed. When Goodbird was about three months old she began to loosen his wrappings so he could kick and stretch. Often she sang him to sleep, her hand patting his small bottom while she crooned, "*A-ho, i-lo, a-ho.*" Like other Hidatsa mothers, she hung a skin sling near her bed, where she could pull it gently to and fro, and he spent contented hours swinging.

As always, Waheenee grew impatient with the confinement and she was glad when the women of the Goose Society declared an early spring. The water birds, who had carried the corn and other garden spirits south for the winter, were bringing them back. The society members brought out their duck-beak head-bands with the iridescent green feathers and began their ceremonies. Joining with the elderly women in celebration to welcome the growing season, she prayed to the goose spirits for good weather to plant the corn.

However before they went home to plant, they needed to conduct their spring hunt.

Small Ankle decided to push on up the Missouri in search of the big herds which had eluded them. Grateful they had all survived the winter, delighted to be breathing the brisk, clean air, Waheenee's family moved up river. It was all so familiar. The gaiety and joking on the march, the men ranging ahead, the children frisking beside the column, the scrape of the travois poles on the earth, and this year, the small, warm weight on her back. Where had Goodbird lived before he came to her, she wondered. In one of the hills that were the Babes' Lodges? As a sweet-singing meadowlark? A fierce hawk? A cactus flower? A pungent sage? Perhaps someday he would look in the magic pond and know.

In a few days the scouts came back to report a small herd, and the hunters hurried away. Waheenee sat with the other women in the quiet camp, shushing any dog that thought to bark, entertaining the children to keep them still. Soon they heard the distant pop of guns and a little later Son of a Star was presenting her with the tongues, kidneys and a paunch of blood from his kills. Later, with the treat of blood pudding warming their stomachs, they harnessed the dogs and went out to get the rest of the meat. Ten animals had been butchered. The gods had provided them with a good hunt. Back at camp the women roasted the meaty bones, stripped off the flesh and cracked the hot bones to scrape out the rich, yellow marrow. Then they built racks, cut the flesh into narrow strips and hung it to dry.

With her meat curing in the sun, Waheenee began work on the boats. The ice of the river had broken. Geese and ducks were streaming by overhead. It was time to plant the crops. She collected willows along the river's edge and used rawhide strips to lash them together into two hoops, one tall enough to reach her eyebrows, one slightly smaller. While these were staked to dry, she bent longer pieces to form a knee-high curve at each end and lashed them so they would hold the shape when dry. That accomplished, she used strips of rawhide from the unneeded leg skin to tie the ribs and hoops into a tub-shaped form. A green hide to cover the flat-bottomed frame had to be scraped free of flesh before being stretched and lashed in place. With one done she began another, for she needed four; they were going to ride the river home.

Son of a Star loaded one of the boats to the rim with packs of dried meat, partially filled another and lashed both in a line with a third. Again Waheenee climbed into a bullboat, but this time the breeze was warm, the grass greening and their minds at ease. Waheenee joined her husband in the first boat and knelt to help paddle the small flotilla. She glanced back to check on Goodbird in the second boat, content in the arms of her teen-age half-brother, and they pushed off. Several other families had joined them for the trip to Like-a-Fishhook Village and calls and songs skimmed the river among the 11 boats. Small Ankle and her uncle herded the horses along shore and were joined by the boaters to camp under the stars.

Then one afternoon as they neared the mouth of the Little Missouri the sky grayed and a burst of cold wind raked the water. They rounded a bend to feel sleet sting their faces and see ominous white-capped waves. Ordinarily they tried to ride through such squalls by holding to each others' boats, the combined fleet being more stable than individual crafts. This time they had no chance to join forces. Waheenee and Son of a Star found themselves alone in a curtain of white, their three boats pitching crazily and threatening to capsize. As water sloshed over the sides he shouted something she could not hear above the wind, but she knew what he wanted. Their only chance was to pull for shore.

She was leaning into her paddle, stroking as she never had before, when Son of a Star suddenly dropped his paddle and leaned far out over the water. Tilted into the air, she screamed and grabbed for the rim, sure they were going over, wondering if he'd lost his mind. Then she saw that he was pulling something in toward the boat. "I-na!" she exclaimed as she realized it was their baby boy. He handed her the dripping, screaming child, who seemed more frightened than hurt, and they made their way to shore. There, cuddling the child they had so nearly lost, she learned what had happened. Her half-brother had just loosened the child's wrappings to give him room to move and stretch when the storm caught them. A violent lurch had knocked him across his boat and he lost hold of the baby. Evidently the loosened wrappings held enough air to keep Goodbird afloat. Surely Small Ankle's gods had heeded his prayers.

With the sleet and rain turning to snow, they quickly set up camp. For four days it snowed. As the drifts piled up around the tipis Waheenee had ample time to wonder if her father and uncle had reached home with the horses. It was so like the time she waited as a child, wondering if his war party had survived another spring blizzard.

When they finally stepped out into a world dazzlingly white, it was to find the shoreline littered with the bodies of birds, come north too soon; small, frozen testaments to the weather's treachery. It was a subdued group that climbed again into the bullboats and rode the Missouri to Like-a-Fishhook Village. Pulling their boats in below the village, they climbed the bank to hear a cheerful answer to their anxious questions. Small Ankle and his brother were safe. Many horses had died in the storm, but no people had been lost.

It had been a strenuous, uncertain winter, chasing the buffalo, trying to maintain their old ways. The horse herd was smaller, the village poorer, but they'd been lucky. It was time to plant the corn and look ahead. As Waheenee and her mothers pressed the kernels into the hills of warm earth, she wondered what the next years would bring her family. It was hard to imagine a future without the great buffalo herds, difficult to believe there were enough white men to change the whole world. But perhaps, as Small Ankle advised, the time was coming when they'd have to learn to eat wheat and potatoes to keep themselves alive.

Die Auswanderer

People who already depended on wheat and potatoes for their sustenance were beginning to share the Dakota prairie with the Hidatsa and the Eastern Sioux. In the early 1870s railroads cut the prairie to Bismarck and Yankton, and farmers in the east pored over the land grant companies' checkerboard maps to choose the 160-acre parcel on which they would risk their family's future.

They all would have adjustments to make, new ways to learn. However some who came to sow their seed in the prairie faced deeper changes; changes as elemental for them as those Waheenee pondered for her people.

Thirty-year-old Paul Tschetter braced himself at the rail of the steamship *Silesia* and stared at the waves rolling through the English Channel. It was a magnificent ship, he thought, but the wind was throwing mountains of water against her and he was frightened. Without need for thought, his mind invoked the Lord's protection for the trip he and his uncle were just beginning over a wide and angry ocean.

Behind him he could hear the merriment of other passengers, too absorbed in their music, drinking and dancing to take note of the storm -- or perhaps afraid even to acknowledge their fears. Their behavior amazed and disgusted him, but he was not surprised. He had seen enough of worldly people since he'd left home to know what to expect. He did not understand them, but he knew they would understand him no better. His people, the Hutterites, had been different -- and had been persecuted for their differences -- for 350 years.

From the days of Luther, when Jacob Hutter had embraced the Anabaptist cause, they'd been on the move. Their positions that church and state should be separate; that no one should be baptised until he was old enough to make a free choice, often brought violent reactions. Gradually they'd been forced east, from Austria to Moravia to Hungary to Romania, and finally to the Ukraine. Each time they'd been welcomed for their skills in agriculture, their productivity, their thrift, their moral lifestyle. Yet eventually each country had decided they were too different, too threatening, their beliefs too demanding.

They asked only to be left alone -- to speak their native German, teach their children their own way, own their lands communally (if they chose) and live unsullied by more worldly people. However they believed men should obey God, not man; they would take no oaths, hold no offices, take part in no courts. Most important, they would not bear arms for any country -- to take a man's life was a sin.

Southern Russia, where Tschetter lived in the dorf of Neu Hutterthal, just north of the Sea of Azov, had been a happy home for Anabaptists for nearly 100 years. But Prussian-born Catherine the Great, who'd invited her countrymen to come farm in Russia, was no longer in charge. In 1872 Alexander II had ended their exemption from military service and declared all Germans must leave off their separate ways. Their language, their schools, their exclusivity would no longer be tolerated.

Hard as it was to think of leaving their prosperous farms, verdant gardens, established orchards, and neat villages to begin again, they could not abandon their pacifist beliefs. To give up their language and the right to educate their children was to give up their faith. They must seek a new home.

It was daunting to cross the sea to America to search out land for his people. Neither Paul nor Neu Hutterthal's other delegate, his uncle, Lorenz Tschetter, spoke English. They had all heard terrifying things about the violence in the United States -- there were savages, outlaws, and frontiersmen with pockets full of guns. Could men of peace survive in such a place?

Finding comfort in unity, as they always did, half the village accompanied the two delegates on the first leg of a journey that would take them by ship and train from the north shore of the Sea of Azov, across Europe to the seaports of Germany, over the Atlantic and into the heart of North America. Paul's father and mother had wept and clung to him until the last moment. The cries of Uncle Lorenz's daughter had followed them until the faces they loved blurred into dots in the distance. Paul's wife, Maria, left behind with five children, his brothers and sisters -- the whole village -- wondered if they'd ever see either of them again.

On their way they'd been joined by two other delegates, these representing nearby Mennonite villages. The religious beliefs of the two sects were nearly identical; the only difference being the communal organization some Hutterites preferred. The Russians, thinking the two groups the same, had settled them near each other and the brethren had grown close through the years. Now all of them were looking for a new home. A total of 12 delegates were making their way to America that spring.

As the channel wind plastered Tschetter's narrow black trousers against his stocky legs and parted his wiry beard, he breathed deeply. Slowly the air, still chill in late April 1873, cleared his head and settled his queasy stomach. His unspoken prayer put his spirit at rest, for it was always his habit to put his cares in God's hands. The Lord alone would determine their fate. He turned toward his cabin, ready for sleep.

Thirteen days later, Paul stood at the rail again. But this time he was part of an impromptu congregation and there was a song of thanksgiving on his lips. God had brought them across the Atlantic safely, and his face radiated a joy that belied his somber dress.

After debarking at Hoboken, the men boarded a train for Elkhart, Indiana, for the delegates sent to spy out the land were not without connections and friends in America. They'd never met those who offered them help, but they were all of the same brotherhood. European Mennonites had been moving to America since 1683 and those already established in the New World were ready and willing to assist a new migration.

However the Old Mennonites in Indiana were almost as foreign to the two Hutterites as the godless rabble they'd been thrown with on the ship. They preferred English to German, fastened their clothes with buttons instead of hooks and eyes, parted their hair on the right instead of the center. The women dressed in bright colors and some smoked. Paul was amazed to find red rugs on Mennonite floors and walls papered and hung with mirrors. Worst of all, one of the ministers had three guns in his house and unabashedly went hunting.

A visit to an Evangelical Church shocked him still further. The minister began his sermon calmly enough, but soon he was yelling and pacing the floor. He gestured wildly and pounded on the pulpit until it was all Paul could do not to run from the church. Paul was a minister himself, elected by his people to the unpaid position at the unusually early age of 24, and he had often preached, but Hutterite sermons were read from prepared texts. He tried to present his in a calm and simple manner, in his home or another brother's, because his people chose not to have church buildings. He thought the vociferous minister was "like a mad man," the truth of his words drowned out by the dramatics of his performance.

Happily, visits to Amish Mennonites were less stressful. A service among these dark-garbed brethren in an unadorned house, with no music except the human voice, felt almost like home. Paul quickly came to like John Funk, a Mennonite publisher who offered to serve as their guide and interpreter during their trip west to hunt for land.

At 4:30 a.m. on May 22 they boarded the train for Chicago. By the time they reached St. Paul two days later, Tschetter had marveled at the high echoing tunnel he'd walked under the Chicago River, while boats and steamships passed over his head, and the seven- and eight-story buildings which had sprung up in that city in the wake of its great fire. "One's mind can hardly comprehend what man is able to construct," he wrote in his diary. A high-speed printing press and a paper mill he'd visited in Indiana had left him similarly impressed. Yet to him the marvels meant that the end of the world must be nigh, for the scripture said that after worldly wisdom had achieved perfection in all its things, God would destroy them. In His eyes it was all folly, Tschetter reminded himself. The noise and tumult drove him to his room, where he rested his aching head and imagined his peaceful home.

In St. Paul they met a Northern Pacific Railroad representative who told them America had all kinds of land; the railroads themselves had millions of acres to sell. They would transport the prospective customers at modest or no cost, lodge them in special immigrant houses, and provide them with agents who'd guide them to the land. On May 25 they were on their way.

For the next seven weeks the Tschetters, sometimes in their original group of four, sometimes united with the other eight Mennonite delegates, traveled the Great Plains to assess the land. From ice-filled Lake Superior they moved to the Red River valley that divided the Minnesota woodlands from the Dakota plains. Then it was north to the prairies of Manitoba, south again to Fargo and back east to Worthington, where the hot wind reminded Paul of home.

From the towns they rode out in wagons, their black caps set firm against the west wind, their coats and round-collared vests gray with dust. What color was the soil? How rich was it? Did it crumble properly between the fingers, or compress into a rock-hard ball? Was it too sandy to hold the water?

How did the land lie? Was it too rocky and hilly to plant? Too wet and low to plow? And what about the weather? As the season advanced the wheat began to head and they could judge its size. Was it bigger or smaller than theirs at home this time of year? Did spring come too late? Would fall be too early?

How far was it to lumber? Was there a fast stream that would turn a mill? Was there rich grass for cattle? A road or railroad to get to market? There were so many things to consider and their people's lives would depend on their decision.

By mid-June Paul was fairly certain he'd made his choice: the Red River valley. One night he walked out alone from Grand Forks, admiring the fine, level land, the black soil, the good growth of grass. By the time he got back, well after dark, he had written a new song, "The New Jerusalem." He rode the mail coach from Grand Forks to Fargo, admiring the clear streams, the blooming roses. From then on he compared what he saw with the Red River country.

On south to Council Bluffs and across the Missouri on a substantial bridge to Omaha, they moved unknowing through prosperous towns whose first residents had also fled religious persecution. But the Mormon hovels of 25 years before were ancient history, forgotten in the bustle of supplying homesteaders and railroaders. Nebraska had joined the roll of states six years before. The Union Pacific line, which had stitched Nebraska to the Union and the east coast to the west, carried them on to Columbus, where they met with newly settled immigrants from Odessa before moving on west to the village of Hastings and south almost to the Kansas line. By now Paul was noting distances in American miles instead of Russian versts.

Worn out with traveling, lonesome for his family, he sometimes sequestered himself in his room, where he found comfort in writing a letter to Maria or composing a hymn. Their days always began and ended in prayer, and they never partook of food without thanking the God who provided it. Sometimes he found solace and courage in reading his *Martyr's Song Book*. Reminding himself other brethren had suffered far more for their faith, he reconsecrated himself to his Father's care.

When they were lucky enough to meet other Russian settlers they could talk to, they had a hundred questions. When do you plant, they asked. When do you cut? But Russian or not, everyone claimed to be happy he'd settled where he was. Soon Tschetter realized that "everyone praises his own community because he wants it settled." They would have to decide for themselves.

The Mennonites were not intimidated by the great sweep of plains; they were so like the great steppes of Russia. The isolation, the lack of settlement did not disturb them. They had settled empty crown lands in the Ukraine and prospered there. The isolation was appealing; to be separate from more worldly people was their desire. The land was cheap -- $3 an acre from the railroads -- free from the government for those who wished individual homesteads. There was room for them all to live near each other, as they wished. But would they be free to follow their religious beliefs?

Late in July the Tschetters and delegate Tobias Unruh traveled east to meet with President Grant and find out. Paul had carefully written and rewritten a petition and had it translated to present to the President. On July 27 they left New York City to meet him at his summer home on Long Island. Paul had tried before to meet with a head of state. He was with the Mennonite delegation that had petitioned Alexander to change the law so they could remain in Russia. That mission had failed. He prayed for success on this one.

Their way smoothed by railroad officials, the three German farmers were ushered in to see Grant at 8 p.m. and Paul handed Grant his petition. They asked to be free from military service for 50 years, to form and govern their own colonies, maintain their own German schools, and to be exempt from taking oaths, serving on juries and holding offices. In all matters not against their conscience, they promised to be obedient citizens.

The rotund President seemed warm and friendly, but he said he could not give them an immediate answer. They arranged for his reply to be sent to Russia when it was ready and began their long journey home, where their families greeted them as if they'd risen from the dead.

In the spring of 1875 Paul Tschetter ushered his family off the train at the depot, helping Maria with the baby and the four other children. His older brother, Joseph, had two teenagers old enough to help, and brother Jacob and his wife had only one baby to manage, but his sister Susanne and her husband had five little ones to keep track of. After the fright they'd had in New York City, when a gypsy had nearly made off with one of Susanne's year-old twins, they were all inclined to count noses more than once.

For several minutes they were busy with the bustle of getting their belongings off the train, but when Paul had a moment to look around he stared about in confusion. He was in a small town, he could see -- about two dozen buildings, some of frame and some of sod, were grouped on the north bank of a river that looked to be the Missouri, as he remembered it from crossing at Omaha in 1873. But he'd never seen this town before.

Where was the river that struck a compass course north, that provided the border between Minnesota and Dakota Territory? Where was the flat valley land with the rich black soil he'd admired and chosen for their home? In consternation he grabbed the arm of the Chicago, Milwaukee and Saint Paul Railway land agent. "Where are we?" he asked. "I've never been here before!"

"Why, you're in Yankton. Capital of Dakota Territory," the agent answered, sounding surprised at the question.

"But where is the Red River valley?" Paul persisted. "That's where we were to go!"

It was north, he was told, 250 miles north.

Whether it was a mistake, a misunderstanding caused by the language barrier, an assumption they wanted to settle near Mennonites who'd come over the year before and settled north of Yankton, or a deliberate deception, they'd never know. But here they were and there was land available. They decided to go out and look at it. The next morning the four Hutterite men bid their kerchiefed, anxious wives goodbye, climbed into a wagon with the surveyor and drove north from Yankton.

For the first 20 miles there was a road of sorts, at least wagon ruts led them to the ford of the James River and cut the prairie north of the river as far as a trading post, where they spent the night. Then they left all signs of settlement behind and moved on north and west through a sweep of land that rolled gently as far as they could see. The grass was just beginning to green down among the stalks of last year's growth, which lay brown and soft from the winter's snow, but it looked thick and healthy. For miles and miles there were no trees, but now they approached a creek that had cut itself deeply into the prairie on its way to the James River. They stopped the wagon.

It was Wolf Creek, the agent said, and yes, the flatland that bordered its valley was available. Enough land that Paul, Joseph, Jacob and Susanna's families could each have 160 acres. Enough for their father, Jacob, to have his own claim when he arrived in the fall. Enough for Paul's 35-year-old brother, David, and teen-aged sister and brother, still in Russia with their father, to have claims when they were ready. Enough that Uncle Lorenz, his sons, and others from Neu Hutterthal could live nearby. Talking excitedly they paced the land and fingered the soil. It was a sandy loam that should drain well. They climbed down to the creek bed to find a stream about 10 feet wide, bordered with willows, cottonwoods, chokecherries and wild plum bushes, and pocketed here and there with deep pools for fish.

The Tschetters were Hutterite in faith, but they had always owned their land individually, instead of being part of a colony. They thought of their village in Russia, where 20 families had lived side by side, 10 on each side of the road, and had traveled out to farm their land. But this was a new country, and as they talked it over they came up with a new pattern. Their claims would be a quarter of a mile wide and a mile long, side by side along the creek. Joseph, Susanne, Paul, Jacob, it would read from north to south, and later John and David. There was room for youngest sister, Barbara, across the creek. They would be close. But not too close.

It was decided. The surveyor paced off the land and marked each claim with small numbered rods stuck in a pile of dirt at the corners. It was time to go get the women.

However as they started to leave they looked at the vast expanse of empty land and wondered how they could find their claims again. Someone suggested a pole they could sight from a distance, and they scrambled back down in the creek bed to cut one. But would it stand out against the grass? They needed a flag. One of the brothers sacrificed a piece of shirttail or a kerchief which was soon waving on the pole. They headed back toward Yankton with prayers of thanksgiving in their hearts.

At first light a few days later they again moved out of Yankton. Paul had left a good bit of his $600 nest egg with the town merchants, but his family had two wagons, two yoke of oxen, a plow and enough lumber to build a primitive shelter. While Maria held year-old Jacob in her aproned lap, 13-year-old Susanna watched over the two little girls, nestled amid sacks of flour, sugar and salt. With 10-year-old Paul proudly driving the other wagon, they left Yankton behind.

The next two days, as they jounced over the plains, there was plenty of time for reflection. Time for 32-year-old Maria, a broad-faced, big-boned woman, to remember how she'd sliced and roasted batch after batch of zwieback, cut and dried boxes of apples to feed her family on the long journey. How she'd packed the family keepsakes in the big old pine chest and watched it loaded into another wagon as they'd left their village. Time to remember the tears they'd shed as they'd left Neu Hutterthal, in spite of the brave words of the *"Auswanderungs Lied:"*

> Welcome, thou fatherland, afar
> Where favored gates stand wide ajar;
> We now our land of birth disown,
> We've chose a home in lands unknown.

They'd sung the verses, line by line in echo of the leader's call, as was their custom, and tried to believe that they were leaving neither the world nor God's care.

She'd married Paul when she was 17, a simple village girl with little education. She was proud of his learning, the early age at which he'd been chosen a leader. He was Prediger Paul, Preacher Paul, to all the brethren. She'd borne him seven children, so far. They'd lost one as a baby and she'd buried another, a six-year-old boy, while Paul was on his mission to spy out the land. Still, for five out of seven to be alive and healthy was God's blessing.

The solid heft of the plain pine chest containing the family's past weighted the wagon behind her. It had moved from wagon to train to wagon to the hold of the ship to ride the Atlantic with other crates stenciled: *"Auswanderungs gepock nach Nord Amerika."* Her people were again *Auswanderer*, immigrants, in a new country. She looked across the land and wondered what the future would bring.

There was time for Prediger Paul to wonder if they'd made the right choices -- to give up their farm at a fraction of its worth because everyone was selling at once; to trust that America was the place to begin again. For President Grant had not given them the answer they'd hoped for. He said they asked for promises he had no power to give: that most of the freedoms they asked for were prerogatives of the states. Some of the brethren had decided on Canada for this reason, but the Tschetters and many others had decided on the United States, in faith and hope they'd be allowed to follow their consciences.

Even young Paul, as excited as he was at the adventure of it all, had somber thoughts as he lay under the wagon that night and listened to the coyotes howl. They must build a fireline, they'd been told, before they did anything else. How would it work, he wondered. Would it hold, and keep them safe when flames raced across the prairie? What would they do if anyone got sick, so far from help? What would it be like when it snowed? Was it true the Indians were no danger?

Well into the second day they spotted their marker, a tiny bright spot against the sky. This, now, was home (northeastern Hutchinson County, South Dakota). The lean-tos went up in a hurry as the brothers helped each other get under shelter. Then they set to work plowing the prairie sod, not to produce growth but to prevent it -- to provide a sterile barrier between themselves and the hungry fires.

Most of the time it took both yoke of oxen to force the breaking plow through the wiry mat of roots anchored to soil which had nurtured them for years without number. Men and beasts strained and sweat, but at the end of a day they felt lucky to see more than half an acre lying brown under the sun. And every square inch -- for firebreak, for garden and for crops -- had to be plowed.

There were so many things to do and they all needed to be done immediately. They couldn't count on much of a crop, but they wanted at least to sow some flax. As soon as the ground was open they moved over it, stooping until they winced at the pain, to pick out the rocks and begin the first pile of many that would grow through the years. Then they walked the field, scattering the grain before them in a smooth, practiced motion.

It was a long, strenuous trip to fetch water from the creek. They needed a well to use until there was time to dig and line a large cistern. Most of all they needed better shelter before the rest of the family arrived in the fall, and winter winds began to scour the prairie.

Much of the rest of that summer Prediger Paul and his namesake watched the tails of the oxen switch as they trekked back and forth to Yankton to get lumber for their house. It was a three-day journey -- if they made them long, hard days. And it was a trial trying to buy what they needed at a fair price when they couldn't make themselves understood. It was always a relief to load up and leave the strange language and strange ways behind.

Maria, left with her daughters and sisters-in-law, hung up a sheet to guide the men back home. The women were too busy putting in their potato patches and vegetable gardens to have much time to worry about the savages and outlaws they'd heard so much about in Russia. With five-year-old Marie and three-year-old Barbara to watch, as well as year-old Baby Jacob, she was grateful Susanna was old enough to be real help.

The lumber the men brought from Yankton, in load after load for 13 trips, was fine and sound. Paul decided to put his house in the center of his claim. Working together, the brothers measured, sawed and dipped into the bags of square-headed nails. One after another the four homes took shape.

Joseph, the eldest, wanted his built like those in the old country, with a house and barn under one long roof. But Paul and the other brothers chose to have their houses separate from the animals' shelters. They were not masonry homes, as in the old dorf, but the Tschetters had the resources to build to last -- substantial houses with high roofs rising over spacious attics which, lit by windows in each end, could provide sleeping space for the children or a loft for hay, if need be.

Prediger Paul's house was 40 feet long, with three bedrooms on the first floor and a large living area where they put a hard-coal baseburner stove. When they were finished, their home boasted both a cellar and a summer kitchen, where Maria cooked and the family ate. It was only natural for her to clasp her hands and breathe a prayer of thanks when at last the big pine chest was carried into their new home and set on its six-legged frame, and she could turn the heavy key and unpack some of its treasures.

They knew how blessed they were, for they were not alone. In addition to Uncle Lorenz and his family, who were farming a few miles to the south, many of their brethren from the Russian steppes were settling the country north of Yankton. Numerous Hutterites who'd settled in nearby colonies, and the other Mennonites who were struggling to get established in the area, were still in sod houses with dirt floors. One

Hutterite colony had spent a starving winter southeast of them at Silver Lake and was now trying to get established west of them on the James River; another group was south at Bon Homme on the Missouri.

The colonists re-created their communal lifestyle, the Bruderhof, jointly buying large tracts of land and sharing all they had. They were known by the names of their leaders or trades -- the Dariusleut, the Schmiedeleut, and later, the Lehrerleut.

But the Tschetters, and others like them who lived independently on their own homesteads, required a new name in this new world, and before long one had been coined. They would be called the Prairieleut.

By summer's end the grass they had yet to plow closed above young Paul's head as he went to explore or to look for stock that had only to lie down to disappear. As it dried they gathered it in great armfuls to feed the animals through the winter, and twisted it in knots to eke out their scant supply of fuel.

Their own fare would be simple: fruit gathered along the creek and dried produce from the garden while it lasted, fish from the creek, eggs from Maria's small flock of chickens, and milk from the cow would have to supplement their sacks of flour and corn. For meat they'd have to depend on a beef or a hog, if they could buy one to butcher, for although they often saw antelope and prairie chickens, no one would consider using a gun to hunt.

It was frightening to know town was three days away -- in good weather -- a world away when the sky turned leaden and drifts piled high. They knew that some of those who'd come the year before had been down to browned-flour soup before the relentless winter released its grip.

Still they were cheered in mid-September when they heard a glad shout and looked up to see the remainder of the family trundling over the prairie. From house and field the brothers, wives and children came running to envelope their parents, siblings, nieces, nephews and cousins in hugs, then raise their voices in thanksgiving. The rest of the village had arrived safely, and Neu Hutterthal was transplanted to America. They were together again. They knew how to work. They knew how to abide. The rest was up to God.

In the next few years, like all homesteaders, the Tschetter family experienced droughts, prairie fires, grasshopper plagues, blizzards, and tornados. Paul and Maria lost another child, five-year-old Barbara, in 1877 when her dress caught in the power rod of a horse-powered thresher. They buried her broken body among the seedlings of the new orchard. However they added four children to their family in Dakota and saw eight of their 11 grow to maturity.

Maria lived until 1915, filling their house with the aroma of noodle soup, and baking apples for her grandchildren on the shelf of the baseburner. Prediger Paul ministered to his people for another 44 years. Ever staunch in his faith, he resisted the changes that came to his church and, although he composed many hymns, he never allowed a musical instrument in his home. He maintained his love for the German language -- and for the jigger of schnapps he took before lunch each day.

Yet while he cherished the old ways, he and the other Mennonites were alert for every improvement in farming methods, quickly moving to mechanize their production of wheat. As the years passed they proved again, as they had in Russia, to be among the best farmers in the country.

For 42 years Prediger Paul, his children and grandchildren lived in peace in the United States, retaining their schools and language and remaining largely apart from the world. He often gave thanks for this "land of promise." Then, in 1917, Hutterite boys were drafted to serve in World War I. Two died of mistreatment when they refused to deny their faith and follow orders. Numerous others were imprisoned and punished. Many of the colonists were persecuted for their German ways and several groups fled to Canada.

Prediger Paul, then 75, lamed by a stroke and sorrowing over the death of Maria after 55 years of marriage, was perplexed and distressed, but he gave no thought to leaving the United States. Here they were, and here they'd stay. One could hope. One must pray. In this, as in all things, God alone would decide the outcome. He died in 1919, and 22 years later when the world was again embroiled in war, his grandsons were allowed to serve their country as conscientious objectors.

A Sad and Terrible Blunder

In 1875 the Tschetters and their neighbors had many worries, but they gave little thought to Indians. The local press trumpeted the fact that all of Dakota east of the Missouri was free of savages. The Sioux, they said, had agreed to a reservation eight years before, and the bands which did not yet live on the designated site, such as Sitting Bull's Hunkpapa, were merely a minority.

When Col. George Custer and his men had toured the Black Hills in 1874, the headlines shouted about the gold the soldiers found and the graceful, green valleys; that the Indians owned the land seemed of minor note and could soon be remedied. In September 1875, as the Tschetter brothers were welcoming the rest of their village to Dakota, a commission was meeting with the Sioux and Cheyenne to buy the hills.

The meeting did not go well. Sitting Bull refused to attend and sent a defiant message that he would not sell so much as a pinch of land, and that he would attack any white man he met in his country. Red Cloud, Spotted Tail and the other chiefs who attended the stormy meeting rejected the commissioner's offer. They would not sell the Paha Sapa.

The rebuffed commission returned to Washington and recommended that the sale become final -- with or without the sellers' consent. Keeping miners out of the Black Hills was a hopeless cause. They also suggested the non-treaty Indians were too well-fed and confident for anybody's good and should be forced to live where they'd been told.

On December 3 the Indians were ordered to report to their reservation by the end of January 1876. On February 1, when only a few had fought their way through the icy drifts, the army was told to find the "hostiles" and enforce compliance. The generals began to plan a campaign to end Indian resistance once and for all by striking their home ground south of the Yellowstone River, territory drained by the Powder, the Rosebud and the Bighorn rivers. On March 17 Gen. George Crook's army opened the campaign by punishing a camp of Oglala and Cheyenne on the Powder, burning their food and lodges and driving the residents into the snow and wind.

The refugees from the Powder River camp fled north to the growing village of those who refused to touch pen to paper and accept reservation life. Sans Arc, Brule, Oglala, Two Kettle, Miniconjou and Blackfoot Sioux, Cheyenne and Arapaho warriors had joined Sitting Bull and the other Hunkpapa bands on the small river named for the wild roses that lined its banks. There had never been a larger camp. Or a more determined and united one.

In early June Sitting Bull, chosen by the Sioux to lead them in the coming war, joined other warriors in the ritual of the Sun Dance, sacrificing 100 pieces of flesh from his arms, and dancing from one morning through the next noon until he had torn himself free from two skewers pushed through the skin of his chest. His people had never seen him with such black and consuming anger. The pain of his sacrifice was rewarded with a vision: he saw soldiers falling into camp with their heads down and their hats falling off; Wakan Tanka would take care of his people; they would kill the invading soldiers.

On June 17 Crazy Horse and the recovering Sitting Bull took 1,000 warriors and met Crook's troopers as they probed north on the Rosebud. When the day was over they had revenged the Cheyenne's suffering and turned that army back south. Satisfied with their victory and needing new grass for the horses, they moved their huge camp, which now boasted 2,500 warriors, toward the Greasy Grass, the river the Whites called the Little Bighorn, aware there would be another battle to fulfill Sitting Bull's vision, but confident their strength and their gods would make them the victors.

They did not realize the Whites had also brought together their largest force of the Indian war; that an army commanded by Gen. Alfred Terry had marched west from the Missouri to meet a force under Col. John Gibbon moving east along the Yellowstone, their men as secure in their numbers, as confident of their superiority, as the Sioux.

On May 27, 1876, river captain Grant Marsh washed his hands and hurriedly splashed water from the basin over his face and neck. He'd spent the morning seeing the cargo of the *Far West* was properly unloaded and he hadn't intended to take time for lunch. But the ladies in the cabin had requested he preside at the luncheon he'd provided them, and he felt it necessary to oblige his guests.

He entered the small dining room to a chorus of feminine voices and took his seat beside Mrs. George Armstrong Custer. She and the wives of the other officers at Fort Abraham Lincoln were enjoying his hospitality and the break in the routine of post life while their husbands were away campaigning.

He knew many of them. He'd transported them from Yankton to their new post, which had been built on the west side of the river opposite the little town of Bismarck, rail's end of the Northern Pacific line, three years before, and he'd worked with Custer in the field since then.

The 600 men of the 7th Cavalry had marched west on May 17, just 10 days before, to the strains of "Gary Owen." They were on their way to the Yellowstone River, part of the three-pronged force sent to settle the Sioux hostiles. Marsh and the *Far West* were to make their way up the Yellowstone to meet them at the mouth of the Powder River in a week or so and spend the summer supplying and ferrying the troops involved in the extensive campaign. That, Marsh discovered, was the reason for the particular warmth of Libby Custer's greeting. She and Lt. Algernon Smith's wife wanted to go with him. Mrs. Custer insisted she had her husband's permission and that he expected to see her at the Powder.

The captain was stunned and momentarily at a loss for a polite way to refuse. One reason he'd chosen the *Far West* for the summer's work was that she had a small cabin. Her low profile made her less vulnerable to prairie winds. But equally important, it accommodated only 30 passengers. Knowing the staterooms would often be occupied by officers using his boat for a command post, and that he'd very likely be transporting wounded men, he preferred not to have room to take along civilians looking for excitement.

He'd have enough to think about without worrying about the safety and comfort of passengers.

He couldn't say that to Mrs. Custer. But he could explain the boat's lack of facilities, and -- with an unaccustomed lack of candor -- deplore the fact he hadn't brought a steamer which could properly assure their comfort. Regretfully, he denied them passage. It wasn't easy -- no one refused Libby Custer easily -- but he remained firm and escaped back to his duties.

The next morning, loaded with oats and bran for the horses, food for the men, medical supplies, tents, tarps and ammunition, the *Far West* whistled farewell to the sizeable post and pushed off for the Yellowstone. Stopping to pick up a company of infantry at Fort Buford, Marsh was at the mouth of the Powder River June 7.

Couriers from Col. John Gibbon, who was moving east from Fort Ellis (near present Bozeman, Montana), floated down the Yellowstone that afternoon, and the next morning Gen. Alfred Terry galloped in. Serving as headquarters for General Terry, Marsh spent the next days ferrying officers and supplies up and down the river to establish a depot at the mouth of the Powder.

By the time he returned with a last load on June 15, the grassy banks of the river had changed from empty prairie to a noisy army camp. Custer was there with the 7th, and hundreds of men and horses moved about the valley. His tent pitched a few feet from the *Far West's* gangplank, the colorful officer stood out among the crowds, his uniform sporting frontier touches -- a bright red scarf at his neck, a broad-brimmed hat over his curly hair. He expressed disappointment that Libby wasn't on board, but he didn't seem to hold it against Marsh.

Energetic, quick-spoken, restless, he was usually the center of a crowd. Marsh could hardly help noticing the contrast between the commanders. Terry, quiet, calm, dignified, spent long hours at his desk on the *Far West*, laying his plans with the careful precision of his legal background.

The deck of the boat continually sounded with steps of booted men as plans were finalized. Officers and couriers came and went. Scouts, both Indian and White, contributed their knowledge of the country. "Lonesome Charlie" Reynolds, Custer's favorite scout, came often to have the surgeon treat his infected hand. Reynolds was one of Marsh's favorites, also. He and his crew had learned how dependable the scout was the summer before when with his usual "Reynolds' Luck" he kept them supplied with more meat than they could eat. The Indians jealously called him "The Man Who Never Goes Out for Nothing."

Mark Kellogg, a law student serving as a newspaper correspondent for the *Bismarck Tribune*, could often be seen bent over his notes. He was a last minute replacement for the newspaper's editor, kept home by a sick wife. Custer's brother, Tom, and a nephew, 17-year-old Autie Reed, were also frequent visitors. His lively 19-year-old brother, Boston Custer, charmed Marsh, and he invited the less-than-robust "Boss" to spend the chill nights in a *Far West* cabin for the duration.

On June 21 the command reformed about 60 miles upriver at the mouth of the Rosebud to compile information. Maj. Marcus Reno, reconnoitering to the south, had found evidence of Indians moving toward the Bighorn. Gibbon's Crow scouts, probing from his camp on the north bank of the Yellowstone at the Rosebud, had discovered old lodge fires of a village that appeared to contain about 800 warriors.

That evening, while hailstones from a sudden squall beat on the deck and piled outside the cabin, Terry, Gibbon and Custer huddled over the maps and papers on Terry's desk. The lanterns burned far into the night. When the meeting broke up, Marsh watched Terry and Gibbon walk Custer to his tent. Then the older officers returned to their cabins for the night. But Custer's tent did not go dark. He ordered the officers' call sounded and, breath white in the chill air, gave the men instructions on how they should prepare for departure the next morning.

However, Marsh had not seen the last of the army that night. Keyed up by the thought of the action to come, several boarded the *Far West* in search of distraction. In minutes a poker game was underway, with Marsh a cheerful participant. Captain Tom Custer, Lt. James Calhoun of the 7th, Capt. W. H. H. Crowell of the infantry and others crowded around for a high stakes game. The several months' pay they'd received after they'd left Abraham Lincoln was heavy in their pockets, and they bet with abandon. Marsh managed to hold his own, but several thousand dollars changed hands and the infantry retired winner of the field.

If Marsh had any sleep it was brief, for he was up before dawn June 22 to unload the supplies the troops would need. His 30 deckhands made trip after trip into the hold and when the soldiers of the 7th woke to reveille, their 15 days of supplies were stacked neatly on the bank.

Marsh knew now what the plan was. Custer and the 7th Cavalry would march up the Rosebud until he found the hostile trail Reno had seen. He was to follow it toward the Bighorn, circling so as to approach the tributary they called the Little Horn (present Little Bighorn) from the south. Gibbon and Terry would march up the north side of the Yellowstone to the mouth of the Bighorn.

Marsh would ferry them across. Then they'd move up the Bighorn to assist Custer's attack on the Indian village. The two forces should arrive about June 26, and the Sioux would be caught between them. The *Far West* would continue to supply troops and carry them and dispatches where needed.

Through with breakfast and their gear packed, many of the men took a few minutes to write a letter home. It might be their last chance for some time. Marsh glanced into Boss Custer's cabin to see the young man at work on a letter. Hating to think of the untrained youth on a forced march and probably in a battle, he urged him to remain with the *Far West*. It took some persuasion, but Marsh reminded him of his duty to his mother to keep safe. Boss finally agreed. He went ashore to tell his brothers goodbye and Marsh breathed a sigh of relief.

Grant was not so persuasive with Charlie Reynolds. The scout's infected hand was in a sling and all but useless, and Marsh tried to talk him out of going. Reynolds would hear none of it.

"Captain, I've been waiting and getting ready for this expedition for two years and I'd sooner be dead than miss it," he declared.

Although George Custer agreed with Marsh that the boat was the best place for Boss, the boy had a change of heart. About noon he mounted with Reynolds, the teen-aged Autie Reed and Mark Kellogg and marched out with the column: 585 troopers, 31 officers, 25 Arikara scouts and four white scouts. Marsh watched Custer bid Gibbon and Terry goodbye and disappear. Then he gathered the letters the men had written, including Boss' message to his mother, and made up a mail sack to be taken down river.

However the three soldiers manning the skiff were scarcely 50 feet from the *Far West* when they got into trouble. With a collective gasp, those on the steamer saw the skiff rock wildly and turn over. The men and the mail vanished in the Yellowstone. Marsh shouted for a boat and went to their aid, but it was too late. The men had vanished and the mail was on the river bottom. Marsh called for boat hooks and began dragging the river.

Undeterred by the apparent hopelessness of his task, he threw the hooks again and again until at last something was snagged. The dripping object he hauled to the surface was the mail bag. Taking it back to the boat he helped spread the letters in the sun to dry. A few hours later they were resacked and put aboard another skiff for Fort Buford. This one progressed smoothly down the river and out of sight.

Early on June 23 the *Far West* clanked away from the now-deserted camp at the Rosebud and moved on up the Yellowstone. On the 24th, rations for eight days were carted out and Gibbon's force was ferried over for its march up the Bighorn. Just before dawn on June 25 Marsh was ordered to follow Gibbon up the Bighorn so that supplies would be closer to the troops.

Marsh was the only steam captain who had attempted to navigate the Yellowstone. He had even poked a dozen miles into the Bighorn. No one had even considered risking a boat farther up that river.

The *Far West* was small, but it was still 190 feet long and had a 33-foot beam. The stream was as high as it ever would be -- swollen by the snowmelt and recent rains -- but there would be no room to manuever, no way to retreat if the Sioux found them. How far he could get was questionable. They could easily be stuck and stranded. But he was there to do a job, and if that's what the army needed he was determined to try. He set the crew to cutting wood, and by noon he was ready for the attempt.

It looked impossible. The already small river bed was studded with islands and sandbars. The current was swift. The steamer was only a little way above the mouth when she met rapids. Marsh shouted down the tube for all the steam he could get, but the *Far West* could only hold her place. Soldiers had to be sent ashore with a warping cable which they fastened to a large tree. While black smoke poured from the twin stacks, one of the capstans slowly wound the cable around its girth, pulling the boat slowly upstream.

If they were lucky, they could steam 500 yards before they met the next rapid. Soon the river was so narrow and the current so fierce they were using both capstans and a cable on each shore. It had never been done before, because no ship had ever been designed with two capstans until Marsh ordered it done. Few captains could imagine tackling a river so narrow that cables could reach both shores.

Only the *Far West's* shallow draft -- somewhat less than 30 inches now that she'd been relieved of some supplies -- made progress possible. That, the nerve of her captain, and the sweat of the straining soldiers and crew. The firemen stoked endless logs into the furnaces. The boilers popped. They all worked this sabbath without question. Marsh, in the pilot house, strained to read the unknown stream, shouted orders, gripped the wheel until his shoulders ached.

They were moving into more broken country, past cliffs and through barren badlands. Though he could seldom take his eyes from the stream, Marsh was conscious of black clouds of smoke to the south as the day wore on. The troops must have found the Sioux village, he thought. By nightfall they'd made about 25 miles and the infantry camp. The exhausted men fell into bed.

But dawn brought another message. The *Far West* should try to reach the mouth of the Little Horn. They began another struggle and by noon, after unstinting efforts, they were at the mouth of a stream Marsh took to be the Little Horn. However the army officer on board did not agree. He ordered Marsh to probe farther. Unable to convince him otherwise, Marsh risked his boat and the supplies for nearly 15 tortuous miles before the officer could be convinced they must have passed the Little Horn. The next day, June 27, they dropped back downstream and tied up at an island across the smaller stream's mouth. The smoke clouds which had smudged the southern horizon for two days were gone. They expected they'd soon receive news of a successful battle.

At rest at last, and without further duties until orders were received, the men could enjoy clear waters filled with fish. They cut willow poles from the bank and scattered under the shade of cottonwoods on the island. Marsh and the officers strolled out to try their luck.

Suddenly, shortly before noon, a clump of willows on the river bank across the water was thrust apart. A mounted Indian faced them. Before the startled men could take cover he raised his carbine overhead, a sign of peace. It was Curly, one of the Crow scouts who'd gone with Custer.

They hurried to the boat to meet him, but once on board he collapsed in grief, rocking, crying and moaning incoherently.

Marsh and the others watched with growing concern. The boy was only a teen-ager, but obviously something was wrong. When he calmed a little they tried to find out what.

The Indian could speak no English. They could speak no Crow. They were unable to fathom his signs. Finally the army captain gave him a pencil and showed him how to mark on a paper. Curly dropped to the deck, stretched out on his stomach and began to draw.

Marsh and the others stared in silence as he drew a small circle. He enclosed this in a bigger circle. Between the two he put dots, dozens of dots. "Sioux!" he exclaimed, "Sioux!" Inside the smaller circle he put more dots. Only these dots he identified with a word Marsh understood to mean soldiers. Then the Indian leapt to his feet, swung his arms wide and began hitting his chest with his fingers. "Poof! Poof! Poof!" he said. "Soldiers."

Marsh and the officers stared at each other. There could be only one way to interpret his meaning.

Curly continued his pantomime. He lost his scalp to a Sioux knife. It hung on a Sioux belt for a war dance. Sickened at the possibilities, almost afraid to ask, they pressed him for details. It took two hours but at the end of that time they knew what his message was. Custer was dead, and the 7th Cavalry with him.

They couldn't -- wouldn't -- believe it. The officer ordered him to go back to Custer and tell him where the *Far West* was.

Curly refused to go. He refused to eat. He returned to his grieving. The rest of the long, hot day they could only wonder and wait.

The next morning they woke to rifle fire, some close, some distant. Marsh ran out on deck to find the night guards providing cover for a lone rider who was racing for the safety of the boat.

Several Indians, yipping in pursuit, pulled up when they saw the boat and broke off the chase. It was Gibbon's scout, Muggins Taylor, carrying dispatches to Fort Ellis. He doused their faint hopes by confirming Curly's incredible story.

They'd come on the battlefield that morning, he said, and wandered among the gory, bloated corpses spread over the grassy hilltop. Custer was there. Near him lay his brother Tom. Young Boss and his nephew Autie were there, too, farther down the slope. A few steps away lay the *Bismarck Tribune* correspondent, his body stripped, scalped and mutilated like the others, but his notes undamaged.

However Taylor's news was not all bad. Reno and some of his men had fought on a separate hill. For 36 hours his seven troops held off the Sioux. Most of them were still alive when Gibbon's approach finally drove the Indians away. Marsh found a cabin for the exhausted scout, and the men, sick at heart -- asking themselves why? how? -- waited to see who would be going home.

Finally, on the morning of the 29th, the men on the *Far West* learned they could do something besides wait and grieve. Word came that 50 of Reno's men were wounded. Marsh was to prepare for their care. Finding relief in action, the soldiers and crew were sent to cut grass from the wetlands along the river. It was spread on the open deck behind the bow until it was 18-inches thick. Then the sweet green grass was covered with tarps, making a huge mattress.

Doctor Williams, the army surgeon on board, placed his medicine chests around the edges and replenished his supplies. Then they waited again, imagining the struggle to make litters for so many men, picturing the rough country through which they'd be carried, regretting the storm which blew up and drenched the valley.

It got darker and later and nobody came. Then Marsh glimpsed the column in the distance and sent crew members to assist it. Blocked by a marsh about three miles above the boat, which they could not negotiate in the dark, the column had halted. When the steamer captain got word of the situation he sent every man out with wood and ordered fires lit along the way.

In the early hours of June 30, 52 wounded, slung between mules on canvas litters made with Sioux lodge poles, appeared out of the gloom. One after another they passed by the flickering fires. Quickly, quietly, they were bedded on the grass mattress for the first real rest they'd had in five days.

Dr. Porter, the surgeon with Reno, had had no rest at all. The only surviving doctor had narrowly escaped death on the battlefield. He had an answer for one of Marsh's anxious questions. Charlie Reynolds had died beside him. Porter had been caring for the wounded ever since, but without pause he went to work beside Dr. Williams on the deck of the *Far West*.

Wrapped in sorrow and pain, the *Far West* cared for yet another wounded warrior that night. Comanche, Capt. M. W. Keogh's horse, had survived his master. The sorrel bore both bullet and arrow wounds, but he'd managed to limp to the steamer. Marsh had no place to put him, but he was determined the only survivor of Custer's battle would be saved. He finally found a spot in the stern between the rudders and had grass laid for a stall.

A civilian veterinarian, working on contract for the army, arrived with the main column shortly after Comanche. Completely unstrung by his experiences, still expecting an arrow in his back, he declared himself unable to do anything for the horse. When Marsh heard about it he stormed over and had a few words with him. Evidently Marsh's anger was as threatening as the Indians'. The vet recovered his composure long enough to dress Comanche's wounds.

General Terry had also arrived with the remaining troops. His force would march to the Yellowstone while the *Far West* carried the wounded. As the dawn blush spread across the summer sky and Marsh ordered up steam to cast off, the general called Marsh to his cabin. The river man found the General, aged past his years, alone. His voice tense with emotion, he charged Marsh to remember what he carried.

"Captain, you have on board the most precious cargo a boat ever carried. Every soldier here who is suffering with wounds is a victim of a terrible blunder, a sad and terrible blunder." Terry, acknowledging the dangers of the river Marsh was about to navigate, urged him to use all the skills he possessed to make a safe journey.

After he'd climbed back to the pilot house, Marsh was suddenly overcome with the scope of his responsibility. He'd always been a pusher, ready to accept the river's challenge, willing to test the dubious channel, sure of his knowledge and his skill. But now he felt weak and afraid. While his engineer waited below for the bell to start the engines, he leaned against the wall, staring at the tortuous river but seeing the countless wounded on the deck below.

He had to turn around in the narrow

channel, get past the island -- and the thousand obstacles downstream. The hand he put to the wheel shook. He knew now what the veterinarian had felt. "Boys, I can't do it," he said to his mate and Dave Campbell, the other pilot. "I'll smash her up."

They reassured him. He'd gotten up the river. He could get down it. "Cool off a minute and you'll be all right," Campbell advised.

Marsh gave himself a long moment. Then he pulled the bell. The *Far West* inched from shore. Slowly, carefully, he worked her around and headed downstream. Almost holding his breath, he eased across one bend and then another. Gradually his confidence returned. By late afternoon he had escaped the claustrophobic waters of the Bighorn and was in the Yellowstone once more. Once there, they were forced to wait for Gibbon's men and ferry them across the river. For a long, frustrating weekend they waited. It was nearly evening on July 3 before they could start again. They were cheered that 14 of the wounded had recovered enough to be left in the field, but they had 38 still on board who desperately needed the hospital at Fort Abraham Lincoln 700 miles away.

Marsh made it a marathon. The hours of daylight were long, but he charged through the darkness as well, calling for every ounce of pressure he dared. The firemen below crammed the furnaces, the engineers read the gauges and prayed, the wheel churned brown water, the timbers of the deck vibrated beneath their feet, sparks streaked the night behind the stacks. With Marsh and Campbell mounting four-hour shifts, the *Far West* careened along, skimming over bars as if they weren't there, swinging through turns that scraped the nose along the bank, then threw the hull against it. More than once they were all thrown to the deck when the keel scraped bottom. But she did not stick.

There was a somber stop to bury one of the soldiers the surgeons had been unable to save. And then, giving thanks for the spacious channel Mississippi pilots called "a rainwater creek," they were in the Missouri. There was a hurried stop at Fort Buford to leave a wounded Arikara scout and another at Fort Stevenson, their news leaving these posts in an uproar. Draped now in black, her flag at half-mast, the *Far West* charged into Bismarck at 11 p.m. They had made 710 miles in 54 hours.

The blast of her whistle woke those sleeping in the scraggly line of cabins that was Main Street. Lights began to show. Then she touched bank and men were running up the street, shouting out the news. Stumbling out, groggy with sleep, half-dressed, the townsfolk tried to grasp what had happened.

Marsh ran with the army captain and the surgeon to the telegraph office where a crowd quickly gathered. The newspaper editor began to piece together the story. He handed it, paragraph by paragraph, to the telegrapher. The key began to chatter: "Bismarck, D. T., July 5, 1876: -- General Custer attacked by the Indians June 25, and he, with every officer and man in five companies, were killed. Reno with seven companies fought in intrenched position three days. The *Bismarck Tribune's* special correspondent was with the expedition and was killed."

After the bulletin was on its way, the men settled in to transmit all the detail available. They had Kellogg's notes, complete until the fatal day, descriptions by army officers, interviews with the surgeon, a scout, and with Marsh. They had lists of the dead and wounded. The telegrapher was not to leave his key for 22 hours.

But Marsh did not wait for all the news to be sent to the world. He had not yet fulfilled his mission. The wounded waited. He hurried back to the boat and swung down to Fort Abraham Lincoln.

Those at the post were waiting. They'd heard the boat whistle at Bismarck, and for two days before they'd known something was wrong. The Indian police at the post had heard rumors of a great battle; they were seen whispering together in excitement. Yet there had been no official word. Now it was here. Early on July 6 teams of officers went from one quarters to the next notifying 28 women at the post they were widows. After the announcement the post erupted. Marsh watched helplessly as frantic families mobbed the boat, begging for news, searching for their loved ones among the wounded.

When things finally quieted, and the wounded were safely in the post hospital, he received a request from Mrs. Custer. She asked him to come up and talk with the widows. He could not make himself go. He had seen enough grief. What could he say of the general, of Captain Tom, of Autie Reed, of young Boss. He thought of Charlie Reynolds. Of the hundreds of unmarked graves. "The sad and terrible blunder" had cost so many, so much. What words of comfort could he find? Besides, his work was not yet finished. On July 9 he was heading back to the Bighorn with 60 remounts for the 7th and other supplies. There was still an army in the field; the hostiles were still in the mountains.

In September General Terry praised Marsh's contributions to the campaign. "Thanks to the zeal and energy displayed by Captain Grant Marsh, the master of the Steamer, the mouth of the Little Horn was reached by her, and she was of inestimable service in bringing down our wounded."

Marsh put it in simpler terms. "I prefer that you consider my boat a soldier," he told Terry. "...send it just where you want it until you get through with it."

The Whence, the Why and the Whither

News of the battle that had stained the grass on the Little Bighorn exploded across the country. The army, defending itself against words now as well as arrows, struggled to regroup and renew its offensive. Crook's and Terry's armies pursued the Indian camp, which began to break up into smaller groups that struck wherever they found white men vulnerable, but easily eluded the large force. Miners who had coveted Black Hills gold stared at the scalpless bodies of their friends and rethought their priorities, and settlers along the upper Missouri fled to the towns and erected defenses.

Yet, as always, there were some men who would not let circumstances sway them from their intended course. Less than two months after Curly brought the shocking news to the Far West, *a man with a scholarly air and a need to know set out to seek his particular treasure along the Missouri in the wilds of Montana Territory.*

 If nothing else, naturalist Edward Drinker Cope thought ruefully as he rubbed the spot where his head had again whacked into the side of the Concord coach, this mad 600-mile ride through the August heat should prepare them for the hardships of camp life.

They were three days and nights out of Franklin, Idaho Territory, heading north toward Fort Benton in Montana Territory, and even packed in as the eight of them were, they could scarcely hold their seats. The German man with his wife and companion, the two Irishmen, and he and his two young field men were equally exhausted by the eternal jouncing. Tired as they were, longing for sleep, they could not help but nod off occasionally. Their reward was always the same -- another bruise where their unguarded heads met their dozing neighbor's or the side of the coach.

The 36-year-old Cope was just getting to know the young helpers who jiggled beside him. They'd met at the Omaha depot about the first of August, and Cope's first view of Charles H. Sternberg made him stare with astonishment. The spare, thin-faced Sternberg moved with an obvious limp. Cope had hired him on the strength of a letter that brimmed with enthusiasm for their science. Even though he knew Sternberg had spent the summer in the Smoky Hill chalk beds, he had to pull aside his other employee, J. C. Isaac, and ask if Sternberg could ride a horse.

Isaac assured him Charlie could handle the worst of mounts. He himself wasn't so sure the three of them could handle the Sioux nation. Several times that summer he and Sternberg had watched braves heading north from the Smoky Hill country. They'd tried for his scalp once before, and he didn't relish giving them another chance. Cope's expedition could have dissolved right there on the Omaha railroad platform. However he'd turned on his persuasive powers, and the reluctant Isaac's bones now vibrated with the rest.

The first two days, as they rocked and jolted along at 10 miles an hour, the scientist had enjoyed the grassy countryside. Stops to change horses every 90 minutes or so, and to gulp down bacon, biscuits and a cup of coffee at mealtime, broke the monotony. But then they'd hit a stretch of sage and sand, and now their sweaty faces were so coated with grit they all looked jaundiced. They were breathing it, eating it, bouncing along in their dust-filled cocoon, pulled by horses they could glimpse only when a breeze momentarily cleared the air.

Life in the field was harsh, Cope knew from experience, but at least there the thrill of the hunt and the joy of a find offered ample distraction from physical discomfort. He was a square-faced man, with dark, wiry hair and beard and a direct gaze. Just now, beneath the coat of dust, he was markedly pale. He'd not been in the field for nearly two years, and the 14-hour days in his Philadelphia laboratory, bent over the manuscripts, drawings and plates he was preparing for publication, had left him debilitated.

Nodding with fatigue, he was surprised when Sternberg offered to support his head so he could get some real sleep. But he was tired enough -- and practical enough -- not to let pride stand in the way. He managed to curl up and rest his head in the younger man's lap, never dreaming Sternberg questioned *his* ability not only to ride a horse but to even survive in the field.

He himself had no qualms. Though he'd never been robust, he was always at his best on a hunt. The baking sun, shimmering rocks, bad water and stony beds in flimsy tents which wore out other men invigorated him both physically and mentally. Only in the field could he really satisfy his craving for knowledge and feed the overwhelming ambition which drove him. Those twin forces had been taking him west for five years -- on his own, with Hayden's Geological Survey or the Corps of Army Engineers -- to ferret out the secrets of ages long past. Now he was headed for the badlands of the Judith River where, he hoped, he'd be able to fit some bony pieces into the puzzle of the dinosaurs.

News that the West held fantastic new fossil deposits had begun filtering east 30 years before. Cope was a child then, but he was already intrigued with the natural world. By the age of 19, without benefit of any college education, he had published a paper on his discoveries during independent study of living vertebrates.

By the time he was 21, in 1861, he had disgusted his practical Quaker father by renting out his farmland so he could pursue his true interests. He studied for three months with famed zoologist and paleontologist Joseph Leidy, and was accepted as a member of the Philadelphia Academy of Natural Sciences.

He studied geology, explored caves, examined amphibians and reptiles, aquatic mammals, insects and fish, turned out dozens of scientific papers a year. By 1870, achieving some control over his insatiable need to know everything about everything, he was focusing his remarkable analytical abilities on the field that would dominate the rest of his life -- fossil vertebrates. He'd been to the chalk beds of Kansas on the Smoky Hill, dug intensively in the Bridger Basin of Wyoming and discovered the most ancient fossil beds yet in New Mexico. And -- as he analyzed his finds and fired out papers describing them -- he'd ignited an open feud with the country's other leading fossil expert, Othniel Charles Marsh.

It was as if that flying reptile, the pterodactyl, newly discovered in the West, had come back to life to attack a plodding giant of the swamps. Marsh, with the wealth of his multi-millionaire uncle, George Peabody, and the weight of Yale University behind him, was methodically denuding the known fossil fields with teams as large as a dozen students. Collectors all over the country knew he could and would pay for their finds. His New Haven laboratory was piled with specimens he submitted to meticulous study, for the classically trained paleontologist demanded extensive documentation for every conclusion.

Cope, largely self-taught through observation, with only one three-month college course and nearly 12 years younger than Marsh, had soared easily the first time he tried his wings. While his family was comfortably fixed, he'd not had the resources to finance expeditions to the West. He'd wangled appointments with government surveys and fought the bureaucracy for time to explore and funds to publish his findings. Only his inheritance from his father had enabled him to mount this small expedition.

Analytically brilliant, he was not hesitant to leap to conclusions, his imagination afire with what might have been. The ancient world was as real, perhaps more real, to him than the sage and sand he viewed through the coach windows. As they finally lurched into Helena, he was imagining impatiently what waited him in the Judith Badlands.

What waited him, he was told, was death. Didn't he know about Custer and his men, cut to bits less than two months before?

Dramatically the hotel owner read the General's last letter, written before the battle. Hadn't he heard that Sitting Bull and his horde were still loose in the territory, eager for more white blood? The papers said his warriors had fired on one steamboat and held five others on the river. There were rumors General Crook had already been defeated. How could he think of taking four or five men down to the Judith?

Cope told them he could not only think about it, he would do it. He'd seen Indian scares before and he never took them too seriously. When a gun had been pressed on him by soldiers as he left for the field in Kansas, he'd managed to leave it behind. He was a Quaker not only by birth but by conviction. His faith was central to his life.

Besides, he was sure Sitting Bull and his warriors were involved southeast of the Judith and that left the territory clear of hostiles -- at least until the army drove them back north. He estimated he had three months to work before that happened. The weather would probably drive them out before the Sioux did. He took time to write his wife, Annie, and his daughter, Julie, who had accompanied him as far as Ogden, that Montana was beautiful, mountains and flowers everywhere, his appetite was already improving and they were about to board the stage for Fort Benton.

Before they reached Benton the stage had lost a wheel and become a springless wagon. They'd forded streams suddenly bereft of bridges, walked up mountain inclines the tired horses couldn't pull, gotten lost and several times teetered on two wheels as the wagon considered upsetting.

They found Fort Benton a lively place, the streets lined with open saloons, the grocers' shelves lined with whiskey, the main street "paved with playing cards." While he hurried around town trying out riding horses and buying a wagon and a four-horse team, Cope heard and dismissed more "cock and bull stories about the Sioux." He hired a guide and a cook whose ample girth and fat cheeks promised a satisfying table.

For nearly five days they worked their way east along the north side of the Missouri. Traveling the treeless tableland, with the river hidden beneath its cliffs, Cope thought the grasslands stretching to the end of sight "splendid." He could see the lump of the Bear Paws to the north, the snow-lit Little Belt Range to the south, and, as they neared the Judith, the tantalizing, wonderous extent of badlands about its mouth.

On August 26 the five camped in the cottonwoods on a green patch of Missouri bottom across from the mouth of the Judith. The next morning Cope perched on a five-gallon keg of pickles and, using a box of candles for a lap-desk, wrote again to Annie.

He'd held a short devotional service which advised the men to walk in love, he told her. They'd listened respectfully and he felt comforted by the small service. But it seemed much longer than three weeks since he'd seen his wife and kissed his 11-year-old daughter.

Across the river they could see a small trading post situated below the Missouri's gray, striated cliffs -- and an Indian camp with more than 100 lodges. By evening Isaac's nerves could endure it no longer. They must take turns at standing guard, he insisted.

Though no one else was particularly interested, he took the first watch. The others had no more than settled into sleep when a loud "Halt!" raised them in their bedrolls. Cope grabbed for his pants and went out to see Isaac's rifle trained on an Indian couple who, insisting they were "good Indians," continued to advance on the panicked man.

Stepping in front of Isaac to prevent disaster, Cope soon learned the Indians came searching for whiskey. He convinced them he had none but, to Isaac's consternation, invited them to spend the night under the wagon. Later, when Cope's turn came to stand guard, he mumbled that his carbine, which he'd last used to prop up his tent canvas, was clear at the bottom of his trunk. Then he rolled over and went back to sleep.

The next morning he treated the visiting pair to breakfast and showed them Annie's picture. The brave approved of her, he wrote his wife, and "the squaw suggested that thee cried when I went away." He rowed across the river to visit the camp, which contained over 1,000 Crow, met several chiefs, and won their eternal admiration by demonstrating that when he wanted to rinse his teeth he just took them out.

For several days they searched the bluffs on the north side of the Missouri. Then they crossed the river and started up the Judith. It was hardly a river by eastern terms, more a creek, really, but it provided them with good water and plenty of fish.

Then they turned east toward Dog Creek and the heart of the badlands. With every step into the desolate, eroded ravines, Cope's spirits rose. He was sure he could see several promising layers up near the 400-foot summits of the dark, steep slopes. Sternberg, riding on the scientist's right so as to hear him with his good ear, listened to a stream of description that carried him to a hardly imagined world. Almost in a trance, Cope began to talk about the fantastic animals that had populated the Missouri country before there was a river or a mountain range -- when there had been nothing but a huge sea, and later, interminable marshes and dense jungles which shook with the tread of giants. Several times Sternberg, fighting his stubborn mustang, became so engrossed in the imagined scene he forgot to curb his mount and the horse bolted to the side. When he'd return to Cope, the scientist would still be talking, vaguely surprised to see Sternberg now on his left instead of his right.

With camp established at a bend of the creek, the three bone hunters rode into the bewildering maze of ridges and gullies. Tethering their mounts on the grassy top of a likely cliff, they'd work their way down 45 degree slopes paved in broken shale, picks and collecting bags in hand, to follow the Cretaceous layer that held their quarry. Crouching, crawling, their only footholds crumbling shale, they examined it inch by inch, looking for the small streak of dust of a slightly different shade that marked a fossil. Every so often their concentration was momentarily broken when a foot dislodged a piece of shale and it clattered down the slope, fell into space and silently disappeared among the tree tops far below.

Rain, when it came, changed things from difficult to impossible. It was frustrating with time so limited. The slopes became as slippery as soap. After sliding around in the mud, unable to climb the smallest ridge, they retired to their tents in disgust to wait impatiently for a better day.

Sometimes while the rain streamed down the canvas Cope would write fondly to his daughter, describing the Indian camp, the pony he rode, urging her to collect insects, fish and prairie dogs for him to study. More often he sat hunched over his specimens, studying, speculating, turning each bone over and over again in his hands. How did this bone fit to another? Where did the muscles attach? How did they move it? What kind of creature did it support? In what kind of world did that creature thrive?

He couldn't imagine anyone not needing to know "the whence, the why and the whither of all that we see about us." Men should do something, he thought, to prove their right to be at the head of creation. "It has taken an immense period of time to develop the human brain and mind and God must expect something to come of it."

He was doing his part, for they were finding bones. A layer under the yellow sandstone just below the summit was providing tantalizing bits of teeth and bone. None of the bones was whole, and most of them lay alone, but some of them were huge -- and they were dinosaur. Whole stretches, which they examined inch by inch, were barren. Then they'd find a pocket of jewels. One piece of jaw they found contained teeth in layers, each ready to rise and replace those above when the original wore out.

Working down into the canyons was like going back in time. They crawled from the Age of the Reptiles into the age of the great sea. Between, they bent over the sands of streams from the highlands which had replaced the sea, carving out clam shells, salamanders, crocodiles and diamond-shaped scales of an ancient ancestor of the garpike. Then it was down to the marine shales to spy out delicately sculptured pieces of sea turtle shell and teeth of a strange ray-like fish whose mouth was paved with teeth like a road is paved with brick. Boiling rice to make a thick paste, they soaked strips of burlap and flour bags in it and carefully wrapped their finds.

It was fascinating, exciting, exhilarating, and the pumping adrenaline made them reckless. They worked from first light to dark, often without water, for the only available was so bitter with alkali as to be undrinkable. Dog Creek, rushing with runoff from the rains, was so opaque that a bucketful, collected and boiled in the evening and left to settle, provided only three inches of clear water the next morning.

They were all lost at one time or another in the labyrinth of gnarled black ridges and gorges. Isaac spent one night out in the rain when he couldn't find his way to camp. Sternberg, working near a summit, lost his hold and skidded so near the edge of a drop-off that he lay still for an hour before he had the courage to move again. Cope climbed a bluff near camp and found himself in such a confusion of arroyos that it cost him an hour and a half of strenuous climbing to work his way out. But he out-climbed, out-dared, out-worked them both.

At night they found their way back to their camp at the base of a bluff, congratulating themselves if they'd not chosen a ridge or ravine that necessitated a lengthy detour. One night Cope was leading the way through the dark down a buffalo trail when his horse stopped and refused to go farther. Impulsively the scientist jabbed his spurs into the animal's sides and the horse leaped. Sternberg followed. The next day they returned to the spot to find they'd jumped a gorge 10-feet across.

Finally in camp, they'd gulp the muddy water and gorge themselves with the cook's offerings. Cope had made a good choice here. The guide was keeping him supplied with young mountain sheep and they came in to sumptuous meals. Perhaps too sumptuous. Night after night Cope dreamt the bones they were finding were clothed in flesh and had come to life. He thrashed in his bed, trying to avoid their gigantic trampling feet and gaping jaws. He'd wake panting, his heart pounding, to find Sternberg's hand on his shoulder. With apologies and thanks he'd lie back for another dream.

A few days later supper became bacon and hardtack. The cook had ventured out and come back terrified. Sitting Bull's men were camped only a day down the Missouri, he claimed. He threw his belongings together and left. Cope, who'd ridden down to Cow Island to check on the steamer they hoped to ride down to Yankton, galloped into camp just in time to intercept his guide, who was about to follow the cook. Furious, he demanded the man deliver the three months work he'd been paid for. But his hot words fell on ears that were tuned for Sioux war cries. The guide also rode off for Fort Benton, and the three bone hunters were alone.

Cope did not consider abandoning the hunt. Sternberg was never ready to give up. Even Isaac, caught up in the thrill of discovery, was scornful of the cowards. There was important work to do. Cope was positive he was discovering new species of dinosaurs. He had a gift of combining reason and imagination; he was probably the best there was at creating whole creatures out of crumbs. Yet it was always nice to have more proof. Somewhere, he was convinced, with all these fragments, there had to be more complete specimens.

Climbing back up to the tableland, they moved farther up Dog Creek across an amphitheater of grassland that gladdened their dust-reddened eyes. Cope counted four herds of buffalo, 18 black-tailed deer, antelope without number, a fresh trail of elk and four grizzlies. He watched the huge sow and her three half-grown kin dig for wild artichokes. Then the breeze changed and the bears caught his scent. Rising on their hind legs they looked him over, then moved off as he marveled at a modern-day monster.

All of life fascinated him. He was in awe of creation. While he could and did lecture his helpers offhandedly with reams of technical information, placing this plant or that animal in its proper historical perspective, reeling off names and terms until they were dizzy, he could appreciate the beauty in the humblest lizard. It was a crime, he told Sternberg, to wantonly destroy any life.

They found a good campsite in the pines that topped the ridges, but the canyons were soft, black rock now, the water even more bitter, the clouds of gnats that had plagued them from the beginning impossible. They'd been bitten and chewed on until men and horses alike were covered with pus-filled sores and scabs. Desperate for relief they got out the bacon and rubbed themselves and the animals with grease. It only added stench to their misery.

Yet there, in one of the rock-hard walls, Cope found his treasure. Sweating with the effort, their hands raw and sore from weeks of abuse, he and Sternberg dug out the skull of a dinosaur with a small horn over each eye and a larger one on its nose. It was a first! They inspected, measured, gloated. Monoclonius Crassus, as Cope would call him, was a bulky plant-eater 20-feet long, with a huge skull -- and those three horns. Professor Marsh had nothing like it!

September had sped by and the last steamer would soon be heading down the Missouri. The men packed up their 1,700 pounds of specimens and turned toward the river 40 miles away. When they reached the riverside bluffs about four miles east of Cow Island they unloaded their precious cargo, and with Cope and Isaac pulling mightily on ropes from behind, inched the wagon down the cliff. When, long after midnight, they had everything on the cactus-studded bottom land, they swallowed a supper of bacon and hardtack and collapsed.

However the steamboat was not there yet, and Cope was not willing to waste a single day. He took Sternberg for one final swing through the badlands. Musing on what he'd seen and learned, picturing the country when it had supported dinosaurs instead of buffalo, Cope wandered off on his own. Engrossed in a final, hopeful search he forgot the time. Then he spotted a large mountain sheep and decided to collect a specimen that could run as well as hide....

When he found his way back to Sternberg the sun was setting and the early October dusk darkening the crevices. They were some 12 miles from the river and they knew too well the possibilities of getting lost. Cope picked a buffalo trail and set off at a gallop. For ten miles they flew over rocks and gullies, leaping whatever lay in their path. Giving their horses free rein, hurdling over cactus patches 10-feet wide, they rode blindly toward the river. Sternberg, horrified by the risk, begged Cope to give up and wait for morning. A cold, dry, supperless camp was better than being dashed to pieces on the rocks, he declared.

Cope hardly heard him. He dismounted and led his horse into a canyon. There, in black on black, he cut a stick to probe the ground in front of him. The reluctant Sternberg cut another to prod Cope's horse from behind when the sensible animal refused to budge. Down they climbed, until Cope's stick met only air. Then he'd stoop for a handful of stones and toss them into the night ahead. If the resulting rattle was a long time coming they'd trudge back to the top and try another canyon.

As they inched down a final cliff they saw lights glimmering across the water. It was the station and army camp on Cow Island, Cope was sure. What's more he was positive the steamer was in. They watered their thirsty animals, drank almost as much themselves, and started for the landing. Turning toward it they discovered a huge ridge blocked their way. Sternberg was ready to drop where he was in the dust and forget it until morning. Cope would not concede. They tried to pick their way along the muddy shoreline but that proved impossible. Up they went again, a pain-filled four miles, and slid down another ravine to the landing. Above them the sky was gray.

Cope shouted across the water for a boat. No one came. Sweat-soaked, they paced in the chill air, beating their arms to keep warm. They shouted again. The river remained empty. At last a boat appeared in the mist and they were transported across to the camp. The sergeant had feared an Indian trap, they were told, and refused to send a boat until he was sure who they were.

The pot of beans cooking for the soldiers' breakfast and raspberry jam smeared on hardtack made them forget the delay. Because the camp was full they had to sleep outside, but the sergeant lifted the tarp covering a pile of gold ore waiting shipment downstream, and the shivering scientists crawled under, not to waken until deck hands pulled it off their heads at nine in the morning.

Fossils Cope had sent down earlier from the trader's station at the Judith had arrived safely and the steamer *Josephine* was in. Their struggles seemed to be over. Cope went to the captain and asked him to pick up his wagon and gear sitting in camp four miles downstream.

The captain refused. If Cope wanted his gear on the boat Cope could bring it to the boat -- by 10 a.m. the next day. For one more day they labored. Cope bought a mackinaw which they rowed to their camp and packed. Then, with the help of two young adventurers who happened along and their strongest horse, they poled, hauled and dragged the load up to Cow Island. There, their torn clothes dripping muddy water, they at last watched the fossils safely loaded.

On board the steamer and bound down river on October 8, Cope wrote his wife a carefully understated version of his adventures in the badlands, concluding, "So all ended well and I am now going down the Missouri to Yankton to meet my missing self, who is much wanted by her husband."

Their reunion was to be delayed. At Fort Peck the *Josephine* was boarded by two army scouts who believed they'd discovered Sitting Bull's camp nearby. They rode the steamer down to Fort Buford, and the passengers were unceremoniously informed the army was commandeering their boat to transport troops back to Fort Peck to join Gen. Nelson A. Miles and follow the Sioux. Cope had disembarked and found quarters in the post when the officer in charge decided he could wait for another steamer and released the *Josephine*. A day or so later at Fort Abraham Lincoln he waited again while eight camps of replacement troops and mounts for the 7th Cavalry were transferred across the river and marched smartly off to join the campaign.

Again ostensibly underway, he wrote his

sister that he had had his fill of Missouri River travel, "direct motion being the exception and climbing over sand bars being the rule." Bored and restless, he told her he would "not trouble the navigation of this river for some time to come."

He never had much use for idle time, and his one foray for collecting was not appreciated. Wandering the shore while the crew cut wood, he came on some Sioux burial scaffolds and collected several skulls and skeletons. He boxed them up and took them on board. Always ready to teach, he was explaining characteristics of the skulls to some passengers when the deck hands raised a protest. He had jinxed them by desecrating Indian graves! They'd be attacked by the Indians, overtaken by every calamity! They wouldn't move until the bones were off the boat. Amazed, indignant, Cope argued to no avail. The Sioux bones had to go. Cope had to be content with the bones of dinosaurs. But that was not too difficult. He had 18 new species.

In 1877 the fragmentary finds of the Judith Badlands were forgotten as even larger dinosaur remains were discovered in Colorado and the public became aware of the giant beasts which had roamed the West. Cope's feud with Marsh festered for years, finally exploding in 1890 in the newspapers to the shock of the scientific world. Each had his defenders, each his detractors. Cope lost his fortune in mining ventures and had to watch his rival grow in wealth and prestige.

Still he made several more expeditions west, retaining his fascination with nature and delight in discovery. On one trip to the South Dakota Badlands he saw another dinosaur skull gleam during a lightning strike, went to bed to dream of it, and rose to dig it in the pale light of dawn.

In 1895, after several lean years, he sold his cherished collection to the American Museum of Natural History. It contained 10,000 specimens of fossil mammals, and 3,245 specimens of fish, amphibians and reptiles. He had in his lifetime identified 1,115 of the 3,200 fossil vertebrates known in North America. He'd published 1,395 papers, including "Cope's Bible," *Vertebrata of the Tertiary Formations of the West*, a 1,000-plus page account of his work with the Hayden Geological Survey. He'd made substantial contributions to man's understanding of geology, herpetology, icthyology and mammalogy. Between them, he and Marsh had made discoveries that electrified the imagination of the public and exposed an ancient world which continues to intrigue the mind of man.

When Cope died at 56 in 1897 the casket on his study table, about which his friends sat in silent remembrance, held few remains. True to his science, he had willed his brain to the Anthropometrical Society and asked that his skeleton be prepared and preserved. It should rest, he ordered, in a drawer of the anthropology laboratory for the edification of future students who also liked to read stories in bone.

The Great Spirit Looks Some Other Way

Cope had been right in assuming the army would keep Sitting Bull too busy to bother wandering scientists in the Montana badlands. While he gloated over bones from black cliffs in Montana in September 1876, Sitting Bull mourned over Sioux bodies at Slim Buttes in Dakota.

The summer's victory on the Greasy Grass had been satisfying for the Hunkpapa chief, even though he had never sought the war.

The great camp which gathered around his lodge had been a glory; his sun dance vision of soldiers falling into the camp had come true. He'd been relaxing in the council tipi when Reno's men struck the Hunkpapa camp, the farthest up the small river. He'd ridden out and led his warriors in driving the soldiers back, then turned away from the battle to see to the safety of the fleeing women and children. They had mourned their lost men, then celebrated the victory four days later in the Big Horn Mountains.

But the huge camp could not sustain itself, and the soldiers had come back to harry the scattered bands that summer and fall -- even those camped on the reservation, like the Sioux led by Iron Shield at Slim Buttes. Sitting Bull had ridden from his camp on the Grand River and tried to help, but he had been too late to do much good. He took his people back to the Yellowstone country to hunt, only to run into more soldiers and fight a general who wore a bear-trimmed coat (Col. Nelson A. Miles). In November the army destroyed Dull Knife's band of Cheyenne and by April Crazy Horse's Oglala were ready to give up the struggle.

The Hunkpapa's only hope for a peaceful life seemed to lie north of the Milk River in the land of the Grandmother. While many of the Sioux accepted the inevitable and gave up their guns and horses for life on the reservation, Sitting Bull took those who still chose to follow him across the border to Canada in the spring of 1877.

That summer a tribe of peaceful farmers from where the sun sets on the far side of the Rockies came to the same conclusion and tried to make a similar escape to the Old Woman's Country.

The Crows had refused them sanctuary. It took some time for the news to sink into the Nez Perce leaders seated in council, and the depth of the silence signaled their disheartenment. They were to be denied even this last hope. Looking Glass had met with Crow warriors and brought back the news. He knew the Crows, had often crossed the Bitterroots to hunt buffalo with them on the plains, had fought beside them against the Sioux. He'd exerted every effort to plead their cause, to gain sanctuary for the wounded, weary people who no longer had a home.

But the Crows wanted no part of their troubles. They would rather fight for the white man than against him. The Mountain Crows promised at least to remain neutral, but the River Crows were ready to sell their skills to the army which pursued the Nez Perce. Some of the Crows expressed friendship, and said they'd shoot in the air if the two tribes met in battle, but that was the most they'd promise. Perhaps, with the Flathead, the Shoshoni, and even some of their own relatives already aligned against them, the people from the Snake River country had been foolish to expect anything else.

Thunder Traveling to Loftier Mountain Heights couldn't blame the Crows. He, himself, had no wish to fight the white man. His people had been friendly with the Whites since before he was born, 37 snows before. Although in recent years, as white settlers crowded onto their land, it had become harder and harder to keep friendly feelings, he knew fighting the army would only bring more grief. There was no winning such a war. The last thing he wanted to do was fight the white man.

Yet here he was on the yellow plains 350 miles east of his beloved Valley of the Winding Waters (Wallowa River in eastern Oregon), and the trail behind them was spotted with dead. There were more dead with white skins than red, but that was no comfort. He wanted only to go home in peace, and every long-knife's body made that more unlikely.

He'd kept hoping, in spite of all doubts, that once they reached the buffalo country they'd be all right. That the Crows would welcome them and offer succor. That they could stay until the trouble with the army was smoothed out and they could go back home. It was not to be. The leaders of the five bands of non-treaty Nez Perce sat in this latest of many councils to decide what to do.

There seemed to be only one option. As some had already predicted, they'd have to keep going north to the Old Woman's Country. She'd let Sitting Bull and his people stay. Perhaps she had room for them also. The council sent out the word for the people to cross the Yellowstone and move on north.

Bending their heads against the cold drizzle, the people packed what was left of their belongings and moved toward the crossing. They had been prosperous once, known for their herds of carefully bred horses, their fat cattle, the artistic beading they lavished on everything from moccasins to cradle boards, from bridles to war clubs. But they'd had to abandon so much as they fled the soldiers -- cattle, lame ponies, cooking pots, robes, pack saddles -- that now they felt lucky to have a lodgeskin to shelter them at night.

Working for hours in the icy water to make sure the 700 people crossed the river safely, Thunder Traveling to Loftier Mountain Heights realized he had known for years this day might come. He'd been to the missionary school as a boy, learned about the white god and, like his father, grown accustomed to answering to the name of Joseph. He'd never wished the Whites harm, but he could see that they were many and the Indians few. We are like the deer, he thought, and they are like the grizzly. We would leave things as the Great Spirit Chief made them. They would change the rivers and mountains if they did not suit.

Why anyone would ever want to change their valley at the northern edge of the Wallowa Mountains was impossible to imagine. Nowhere was there richer grass for livestock, a bluer lake with fatter salmon and trout, better hunting in the fall, more beautiful deep, dark canyons to give shelter in the winter. The land was both their sustenance and their joy.

As he grew he watched the older Joseph dealing with the Whites, refusing time after time -- despite threats and promises -- to give up their land. When some other bands had signed a treaty at the council at Lapwai

(1863) and agreed to move to the reservation, he'd helped his furious father set poles in piles of rock to mark the Wallowa Valley as their own. "Inside this boundary all our people were born," the older Joseph had said. "It circles around the graves of our fathers, and we will never give up these graves to any man."

For a time they had seemed secure in their secluded valley, not bothered by the men who swarmed over the reservation land of the treaty bands, digging in the earth for gold. Yet later, as he lay dying, the blind, old chief warned his son again. "You must stop your ears," when the Whites talk treaty, he'd said, gripping Young Joseph's hand. "This country holds your father's body. Never sell the bones of your father and mother."

The horse they'd slung on a pole over his father's grave had hardly had time to dry when settlers began crowding through his poles, and Atin Keunin (Gen. O. O. Howard), who at first had seemed to understand, changed his words and ordered them to leave their homes and move to the reservation.

Joseph had not sold the land. One cannot sell what belongs to the Great Spirit Chief. But he had given it up, finally, given up his father's grave and agreed to move up to the reservation, deciding he could bear anything except seeing his people killed, except watching them die with blood on their hands.

The sacrifice came too late. Even as he coaxed his people across the angry spring current of the Snake and through camus-blue meadows toward the reservation, three of their young braves erupted in violence. Provoked by the swelling tide of theft, insult and abuse inflicted by the white settlers, furious at being ordered to the reservation, they'd sought revenge for an Indian death by killing four white men. Joseph would have given his own life if it could have undone the killings, but some things were beyond even the Great Spirit Chief. Once the irretrievable deed was done, the young men fueled their hatred with whiskey and hunted more victims. Soon it was too late for words; they could only flee.

So many were dead now, and more had stained their hands. Their trail east from Idaho was scarred with bloody ground. At White Bird Canyon, on the Camus Prairie, on the Clearwater, and in the Big Hole Valley they'd left their dead. Joseph knew it could have been much worse. The army chasing them had no squaws and no old people, no children like his daughters -- one a dozen snows and one born just two moons before -- no herd of 2,000 horses, no need to carry along everything they owned. The soldiers had cannons that blew the lodges to bits, whirling guns that spit bullets in a fiery stream, many times the Nez Perces' 300 warriors, and one army to replace another when the first wore out. Yet time after time his people had beaten the soldiers back, kept them on the defensive, evaded their traps, sent them on a false trail and made them pay at least one life for every Indian's.

His people did not have one war leader, like the soldiers. Many voices spoke in council, each free to offer his ideas, and whether an idea was suggested by the confident Looking Glass, who had battle experience and knew the buffalo country, or him as the guardian of those who could not fight, by fiery, old Toohoolhoolzote, Red Owl or another warrior of the five bands was of little matter. If it was a good idea, most chose to follow it and so far the Great Spirit Chief or their desperation, or both, had inspired a strategy which preserved them.

He knew many of the young braves gloried in their success. It was gratifying to thwart the powerful white men. He admired the skill and courage of men like his younger brother, Ollokot, who led the Wallowa warriors. Ollokot and most of the others had kept the tribe's pledge to fight only the soldiers who were trying to capture them, to attack no innocent Whites. But some of the young men, ranging wide to guard the line of march, left smoldering ranches in their wake.

They'd done well. Yet they'd left 12 of their best warriors in the ground of the Big Hole Valley, in hastily scooped graves no one would watch over. Rainbow and Five Wounds were gone, along with heart-tearing dozens of women, children and old ones. The white men had shown little mercy in their dawn attack on the sleeping camp in the Big Hole Valley. Barefoot and half-dressed, Joseph had shielded his tiny, new daughter with his own body as he tried to help her wounded mother, Toma Alwawonmi. Then he'd bundled the injured onto travois and hurried the shocked and grieving people away from the battle, caring for both his own bleeding wife and Ollokot's, while he stayed to protect the retreat.

Ollokot, his laughing, carefree right hand, who was everybody's friend, had learned quickly how to be an enemy. His brother's beloved young wife, also recently a mother, had not survived to benefit from further lessons.

They'd all come a long and weary way in these two moons. Over the slippery, precipitous Lolo Pass, south along the Bitterroots to the Camus Meadows, east through the country of smoking waters (Yellowstone Park) and north again, through canyons that nearly closed above their heads, to the open plains. They'd urged their loaded ponies up mountains, around boulders, through prickly pear, across small creeks and rushing rivers. Grass which had been sweet and green when they'd been driven from their valley was now brown and crisp beneath their feet, and the wind pulled yellowed leaves from the brush along the draws as they moved north. They were all relieved when march leader Lean Elk called a halt and the women could build their fires.

Lean Elk would much rather be back in his village, playing poker and telling stories, Joseph knew. He hadn't even intended to join the exodus, until a wound he suffered accidentally had convinced the Whites he was one of the rebels, and he'd had to join them in self-defense. The poisonous trouble had spread so fast and caught so many. Even the aggressive Looking Glass had counciled peace until the cavalry came to arrest him and -- failing to find him -- destroyed his village. Once angered, he'd remembered his warrior heritage, and he'd led them much of the way.

They hadn't seen anything of General Howard for several days. Probably the one-armed soldier chief was still waiting for new mules to replace those Ollokot and others had whisked away from his camp. That, at least, had given them something to laugh about.

And they'd left the soldiers who came at them from the east far behind in the smoking water country, searching vainly for their circuitous trail. They camped that night on the west side of the Yellowstone (near present Billings, Montana) and laughed again the next morning as they took the trail, when some of the roving braves appeared with a captured stagecoach and careened through the sagebrush in a spirited show. In a relaxed and cheerful mood, they were still stringing out of camp when scouts came galloping to wave the red blanket in warning. Troops on horseback were coming and coming fast!

At once they were on the run again. Mothers frantically snatching up their children, the able-bodied straining to help the old, horses neighing and jostling under the whip, they fled headlong across the prairie, while the warriors rode out to protect their flight. A wash (Canyon Creek) three or four miles away offered shelter, and they sped toward the sanctuary of its rock-rimmed valley. But the soldiers saw where they were headed and whipped their horses to get there first.

Just when the racing people were beginning to despair, the soldiers' line wavered and began to slow. Their braves were on the canyon ridges, pouring fire on the troops. The startled soldiers slowed and dismounted to follow on foot, and most of the tribe swept in between the low bluffs. The main herd of ponies thundered in after them and the sharpshooters on the ridges kept the troops at bay while the people threaded swiftly up the dry gulley. They didn't all make it unscathed. Three were wounded and numbers of worn-out horses could not keep up the pace and had to be left behind.

Sheltered in the gullies, they curled up for

a few hours rest on the cold, wet ground that night. At first light they were on their way again, but they had hardly cleared the canyon when a new peril galloped down on them. The River Crows, riding for the army, seemed perfectly willing to aim true when horses were the prize.

With bitter hearts the Nez Perce raced frantically before the painted, screaming Crows while, again, their men fought a delaying action. This time they lost 500 ponies. Nearly half their herd was gone. Still neither the soldiers nor the Crows had stopped them.

For six days they hurried on north, across the Musselshell, through a gap (Judith Gap) between mountain ranges which already wore a dusting of snow, along a creek (Dog Creek) that threaded dark, eroded ravines to the bank of the big river the white men called the Missouri. There, below the ford of the river on the bottomland, sat three or four tents, a huge mound of boxes and a handful of soldiers.

For a few moments the two forces eyed each other cautiously while the chiefs conferred. This time the odds were on their side and many braves were eager for revenge. They needed bullets; the families needed food and clothing. But the council passed the word: they must cross here, and they would not fire unless the soldiers fired on them. For two or three hours, guarded by a line of warriors, the long procession of families, followed by the herd, picked their way across the river and went into camp two miles up Cow Creek.

However, pushed as they'd been, they'd had little to eat for days. Children stared into empty pots, if there was still a pot in the lodge. The soldiers seemed to have piles of food. The chiefs sent two emissaries to buy some.

The soldier chief shook hands, but he said he could not sell them anything. Twice again they asked, showing him a handful of white man's money. Finally he offered them a slab of salt meat and a half sack of biscuits. It was enough to feed only a few families when hundreds were hungry, but they thanked him and took it back to camp.

Still it was hard to remain grateful with empty bellies. Although the council continued to speak for peace, some of the young braves, angry at the soldiers' refusal to share, crept to the edge of the bluffs above the post and began to shoot at the troops as they prepared their supper. It didn't take many guns to keep them corralled near their tents, and as darkness fell the Indians began to explore the pile of crates and barrels back under the river bank. Here was sugar, and flour, and beans, and coffee. Here were kettles and pots to cook in. There were enough boxes to fill a half-dozen lodges clear to the smoke hole.

The hungry men helped themselves and sent word for their wives to come get food for the families. They took out their pique by torching the pile of freight at the post. It made a grand and satisfying blaze.

After a late start the next morning they moved on up the narrow bottom of Cow Creek. The country was looking a little more like home, with pine-dark slopes of a small mountain range to the east (the Little Rockies) and the rocky ridges of another (the Bear Paw Mountains) looming ahead. They'd put about 10 miles between themselves and the river post -- and had stopped to dicker with some freighters on the trail -- when a bunch of foot soldiers was suddenly on their heels.

Again Joseph had to rush the people out of danger while the braves fired the freight wagons and fought a delaying action. However it was not a large group of soldiers, and the mounted braves easily drove them back while Joseph hurried the people on. Before long the soldiers turned tail and headed back toward the Missouri.

Another group of soldiers had failed to stop them. Perhaps no more would try. As they worked their way north toward the canyons of the Bear Paw Mountains, the column began to waver. They'd come so far, propelled by fear, stiffened by anger, summoning energy they never knew they had. Now that they felt safe they wilted.

Suddenly they felt every ache in their legs, every muscle in their backs, every stone bruise on their battered feet. The old people longed for time to get warm. The children wanted only to eat and sleep. The wounded only to lie blessedly still.

It hurt to see their favorite mounts lame, back-sore and gaunt. The hungry horses were snatching mouthfuls at every opportunity, but it would be weeks before they were sleek and fat again. Each sun they left a few dead in their trail.

More haunting were the empty places around the breakfast fires, places that belonged to the old and ill. Unable to keep up, unwilling to slow the flight, they faded into the hills along the march.

One after another the people asked to rest. Looking Glass listened to their pleas and agreed that Lean Elk had been pushing them too hard. They'd seen no soldiers for several days and none of those they'd fought had been able to stop them. Scouts were watching the trail behind. If they didn't stop to hunt they'd have no food for the winter. He could see no harm in a rest. In council the other headmen agreed to let Looking Glass direct the march again. Although some of the warriors objected that it would not be safe, he said they could sleep late in the morning; camp early in the evening. It was so good not to hurry any longer.

As they moved through the Bear Paws Joseph admired the countryside. Even though it was swept by a chill north wind, it seemed fat and beautiful to him, with cottonwoods along the creeks and plenty of bunch grass for the ponies. When they emerged on the northern edge of the mountains he looked on towards the Old Woman's Country. The soldiers had been left far behind and the sage-dotted hills seemed to stretch on forever. Another long day's march, two at the most, would put them in the land of the Old Woman. Surely there his people could live in peace. At last, he thought, we have won our freedom.

With eroded bluffs protecting them on the east and south, they set up camp along a creek which curled north toward safety and a new life.

The women and children hurried about collecting buffalo dung for fires, which they built in the lodges or in the shelter of gullies that cut their campground. The hunters had discovered a small herd of buffalo, and before long the fires flared and smoked with dripping fat from spitted steaks. It was warm by the fires out of the sharp wind. Their bellies were full. Their journey was almost over. They pulled their robes and blankets around them and fell into sleep.

The sky was light the next morning before they stirred again and slowly gathered their energies to continue the trek. Some families lingered over breakfast, and a bunch of boys got up a game of stickball; other women began striking their lodges and packing to move on. One by one the men went out to gather the horses and mules which were grazing on a meadow across the creek and bring them in for loading.

Off to the east there was dust from a buffalo herd stampeding and some of the braves were uneasy. Perhaps the soldiers were coming? But Looking Glass was in charge of the march and he refused to worry. He rode through camp assuring them there was plenty of time. "Let the children eat all they want," he said. The leisurely preparations continued.

Then a scout circled his horse on a ridge, waving his blanket wildly. They knew the sign all too well. Soldiers were right on the camp! A young boy came galloping back from the herd, screaming a warning. Cheyenne soldier-scouts were already in the gully! Yet another tribe aligned against them. The camp boiled in panic.

Joseph, who had picked up his family's bridle ropes and walked out with his daughter, Hophoponmi, and other braves to catch their mounts, sprang into action. "Horses! Horses! Save the horses!" he yelled as he sprinted toward the herd. He had just reached his mount and thrown the rope around his head when earth and air vibrated with a deadly beat -- the hooves of hundreds of horses. Two lines of horse soldiers were charging, one for the horse herd, one from behind a bluff toward the middle of the camp. In spite of fire from the warriors who'd had time to grab their guns and sprint up the bluffs above the village, the troops galloped into the frightened herd and began pushing it away from the stream.

Joseph and his daughter were cut off from camp. He threw a rope to Hophoponmi and yelled for her to catch a horse if she could and join the six dozen others who were also cut off. Toma Alwawonmi and his other children were still in camp and it was now under fire from all sides. He could not leave them. With a prayer to the Great Spirit Chief on his lips he raced through the rearing, plunging horses and the soldiers' fire.

Guns cracked. Bullets whizzed past, ripping his shirt and blanket. He could scarcely see for the smoke and dust, could hear only the roar of the guns. Suddenly his horse took a hit and stumbled. But he did not go down. In another moment he was inside the camp. His wife was waiting at the door of their lodge.

"Here's your gun. Fight!" she yelled.

Warriors, women and children threw themselves into the gullies to escape the raking fire. Joseph, shooting as fast as he could reload saw one brave fall beside him, then another, until there were six bodies within reach. However their own withering fire had stemmed the charge. The soldiers galloped back out of range.

The respite was brief. Again the blue line charged, and there were hundreds of them, Joseph knew now. The Nez Perce must make every bullet count. Holding their fire until they were sure of their targets, directing the aim at any soldier shouting commands, they sent another charge reeling back.

But the troops came galloping in again, this time even closer. Lodgepoles splintered and tipis collapsed. Then, through the black smoke, Joseph saw a dozen soldiers take two lodges at the edge of his camp. He called his men to help and charged their position.

For several minutes they fought at point-blank range. Finally the troops pulled back, leaving their dead on the ground. The Wallowa braves quickly gathered guns and ammunition from the three bodies, but did not otherwise molest them.

A few cannon balls exploded harmlessly beyond the camp, but before the gun crew could take better aim the fire of the warriors drove them away from their position. Then quiet fell, except for the occasional bark of a rifle. The troops were apparently unwilling to pay the cost of another charge. They were digging in around the camp's perimeter and the gunfire was reduced to a duel between sharpshooters from both sides.

Surrounded, the horse herd all but gone, the Nez Perce had little choice. As dusk approached, both women and men fell to work to deepen and improve their defenses. Scraping away at the cold ground with knives, camus hooks, frying pans -- whatever they could find -- the people carved into the sides of the coulees for shelter and dug out trenches to connect them, while the warriors scraped rifle pits in the bluff tops.

Joseph and the other chiefs listened as old Alahoos called out the toll of the battle. It took some time, for the list was long. Some were missing, having run before the soldiers across the prairie. Many were wounded. Twenty-two were dead -- some women, some children, some fighting men. Among these were strong, old Toohoolhoolzote, who'd spoken up so bravely to General Howard in the council of Lapwai; talkative Lean Elk, who'd led the caravan so many miles; Ollokot, his brother.

Numb with grief, Joseph mourned the tall, cheerful Ollokot who'd learned to be such an implacable warrior. Of his daughter and the group who'd fled before the Cheyenne scouts when the attack began, he could learn nothing.

Crouched in a gully, while the people wailed their sorrow and tried to bury their dead, Joseph, White Bird and Looking Glass, the three remaining chiefs, held a council. There seemed only one hope. If they could hold out for a few days, perhaps Sitting Bull would come to their aid. Charged to find him and deliver the tribe's plea for help, six of their best warriors crept away in the darkness.

As the others huddled together for warmth the wind picked up and snow began to streak through the air. Mothers, unable to light a fire, tried to comfort their shaking children. Scouting the camp, braves discovered a few wounded soldiers who'd fallen behind in the retreat. They disarmed the troopers and gave them water. Snow swirled into the gullies and piled on the buffalo robes protecting the wounded. On the bluffs the near-naked warriors crouched in their shallow pits. The icy, black night was endless.

The next morning a messenger waving a white flag picked his way through the drifts toward the camp and yelled that the soldier chief wanted to see Joseph. Should the chief go? The leaders counciled. Finally they sent a half-blood who could speak some English to talk first. When the soldier chief, who was named Miles, agreed to meet Joseph halfway, it was agreed he should go.

The man Joseph met on the whitened hillside was about his own age, with a strong, straight nose, a dark swoop of hair on his upper lip and a scar -- perhaps of battle? -- across his throat. He asked Joseph to consider his people's plight and quit the fight.

The Wallowa would be glad to quit the fight, Joseph told the general, if they could go back home. He could not speak for the other chiefs, but he was willing to talk. Beside the fire in Miles' tent, his insides warmed with hot coffee, he listened as the soldier chief seemed to say they could go home if they gave up their guns. Did this unknown general (colonel) talk straight, he wondered. Could they safely surrender their guns? Was it time to quit fighting? Or was there a chance Sitting Bull would come?

At first the soldier seemed a reasonable man, urging the Nez Perce leader to give up the fight and save lives, promising him his people could go back to their own country in the spring. It was all Joseph wanted, but he hesitated. He'd heard white mens' promises before. Did he dare deliver them, defenseless, to this man's care? Joseph pondered and tried to bargain. They would give up some guns, but they must keep some for hunting or they could starve. Miles, pacing impatiently, refused to hear him. Convinced further talk was hopeless Joseph rose to leave. But at a word from Miles, soldiers blocked his path. Before he knew it he'd been tied hand and foot and left rolled in a double blanket like a baby on a cradle board.

That night he could only lie in anguish, hearing, at dusk, shells of a bigger gun exploding in the camp, thinking of where his people might be if they hadn't stopped to rest, how they might have escaped Miles' army if they'd kept better watch. Why hadn't he done a better job of protecting his people?

In the morning Joseph's friend Yellow Bull came over to see why Joseph had not returned. Miles let him talk to his friend, but refused to leave them alone.

Yellow Bull was worried. He feared Joseph would never be let go. But an officer had come into the Nez Perce camp while Joseph met with Miles. Worried about what was happening to Joseph, Yellow Bull had pulled the soldier from his horse and kept him under guard that night in the Indian camp. Perhaps they could exchange his life for Joseph's.

"I don't know what they mean to do to me," Joseph told him with resignation, "but if they kill me you must not kill the officer. It will do no good to avenge my death by killing him."

Yellow Bull was allowed to leave and Joseph heard the sound of the siege resume. The day dragged on, as gray and chill as the last. He worried about how the fight was going, how many more were dead or wounded, whether his people could still get to the creek for water, what, if anything, they could find to eat. Yet there was still hope the messengers would reach Sitting Bull and bring help. He refused to surrender.

Later that afternoon Miles bent under the pressure and exchanged Joseph for his officer. Greeted with joy back in camp, Joseph huddled with what was left of the war council and they debated what to do. There was no sign of help from the north; no way of knowing if any would come. The strong and able probably could slip away in the night, but that meant leaving the weak and wounded behind. Some of the young men wanted to put an end to it, to charge the soldiers and earn either freedom or death. But if they were all killed, the old people, the little ones, the wounded would be left without protection. And when had white men ever shown mercy to the defenseless?

In the grim, frigid prairie the siege went on. For another night children whimpered with cold and hunger while their parents softly keened their grief, or tried to sleep sitting up against the dirt walls of their shelters. The old people sat numbly, enduring. Again the shrieking wind was filled with snow.

The fourth day of battle firing began at first light, but neither side had ammunition to waste so the shots were sporadic. Their hopes peopled the northern horizon with galloping Sioux, but the crusted snow remained without tracks.

About noon of the fifth day the soldiers lobbed in more cannon shells, but this time their aim was more deadly. One burst collapsed a shelter pit, burying four women, a boy and a girl of 12 snows. Frantically others dug through the dirt and pulled three women and the little boy to light. The girl and her grandmother were dead. They were left in what was now their grave.

As the sixth day dawned two new messengers came from the soldiers' camp with the white flag. They were in uniforms, but they wore feathers in their hats. It was Jokais and Meopkowit, Nez Perce who'd signed the treaty and lived on the reservation. They were scouting for General Howard; Cut-off Arm had caught up with them the afternoon before and now they faced two armies.

The Nez Perce scouts were helping the enemy, and there were hard words said against them, but they were brothers. Both had daughters in the Nez Perce camp. At least here was someone they could talk to and understand. The treaty Nez Perce urged the chiefs to open their ears to their words, assuring them both the generals' hearts were good. The generals promised if the Nez Perce came out and gave up their guns they would not be killed; that they could go back to the Lapwai reservation. Their message delivered, the scouts returned to Howard's camp while the leaders counciled.

Again the promise. This time from a general Joseph knew, who had seemed to understand their problems before he quit listening in council and instead 'showed them the rifle'. Facing both armies, Joseph decided their only choice was to give up the fight. He could not leave the old people, the little ones, the wounded.

Looking Glass, White Bird and some of the braves insisted that to surrender was to be hung. Whites had been killed and the Nez Perce would be held responsible. Angrily, Looking Glass recounted what had happened to his village. The Whites could not be trusted, he warned. If Joseph trusted them he would pay the price.

But Joseph looked around the camp, hearing the moans of the wounded, the cries of the hungry children. Apprehensive as he was, he could make only one decision. "For myself I do not care." he said. "It is for them I am going to surrender."

The talk was long, and Jokais and Meopkowit returned to urge surrender. Finally the headmen came to an agreement. Joseph and the Wallowa could do as they wished. Looking Glass and White Bird would try to escape north with all who did not wish to give up their guns.

However Looking Glass was never to see the north country. When the council ended he went back to his rifle pit and was relaxing with a smoke when a warrior sang out that an Indian was riding in.

It must be the Sioux coming to help! Eagerly Looking Glass jumped up to see. An instant later he lay at their feet, the top of his head shot away. The rider was not Sioux, but one of the Cheyenne scouts.

While the stunned people absorbed this latest tragedy, Joseph turned to Jokais. "Tell General Howard I know his heart. What he told me before I have it in my heart. I am tired of fighting. Our chiefs are killed. Looking Glass is dead. Toohoolhoolzote is dead. The old men are all dead. It is the young men who say yes or no.

"He who led on the young men is dead. It is cold and we have no blankets. The little children are freezing to death. My people, some of them, have run away to the hills, and have no blankets, no food; no one knows where they are -- perhaps freezing to death. I want to have time to look for my children and see how many of them I can find. Maybe I shall find them among the dead.

"Hear me, my chiefs. I am tired; my heart is sick and sad." He raised his arm toward the brightest spot in the clouds. "From where the sun now stands I will fight no more forever." He watched the two scouts ride off to the army camp and turned to prepare his people for the surrender.

Gradually the guns fell silent, and as the late afternoon sun shone feebly through the overcast he picked up his rifle, mounted his horse and rode from the blue shadows of the coulee. The raw wind caught at his bullet-pierced blanket, ruffled his top knot and whipped his braids back from his broad face, bit at the raw creases in his forehead and wrist where the soldiers' shots had nearly found their mark. He stared at his hands as they held his rifle across the saddle, scarcely aware of the soft voice of Husishusis Kute, who walked beside him, or the murmur of the four other braves of his escort.

Then he was halfway up the hill and the two generals stood before him. So much had happened since he'd last seen Atin Keunim. The bearded long-knife looked thinner and weary, but he stood straight as ever. Joseph swung down from his pony in front of the one-armed general and held out his rifle.

Howard motioned for him to give the gun to Miles. It was done.

Behind him his people straggled from the gullies. The soldiers would count 87 warriors, 40 of them wounded; 184 women and 147 children, many of them bleeding and pale, all of them gaunt, half-frozen, frightened. Thirty Nez Perce and 32 soldiers had not lived to see the surrender.

White Bird and what was left of his braves were not there. Joseph's older wife and Hophoponmi were not there. He wondered if they'd find help in the cold expanse of the Old Woman's Country.

His brother Ollokot would never ride at his side again. But Toma Alwawonmi and the new baby were still alive and with him. In the spring, the generals said, they could go home.

That spring never came for Joseph. Over Miles' protests, the Nez Perce were shipped down the Missouri to Fort Leavenworth. There, cooped on a miasmal piece of river bottom, with only its muddy water to drink, they began to die. One victim was the baby Toma Alwawonmi had nursed through the long retreat.

"The Great Spirit Chief who rules above seemed to be looking some other way and did not see what was being done to my people," Joseph said later.

Those who'd survived a 1,700-mile marathon, held off a total of 2,000 soldiers in four major battles and numerous skirmishes and kept Miles' superior force at bay for five days, could not combat bureaucracy. Their agent and the settlers in the Wallowa Valley adamantly opposed their return, and in four years one-quarter of the prisoners were dead. Joseph worked unceasingly for their return to their homeland and gained the support of many Whites who believed the terms of the surrender should be honored.

Finally in 1885 the Nez Perce were allowed to leave Indian Territory (present Oklahoma). One hundred eighty-eight of them were given permission to settle on the Lapwai reservation, but Joseph and his band of 150 were sent to the Colville reservation in Washington. Here, at least, he was reunited with his daughter Hophoponmi who had lived through the journey to Canada and returned to Lapwai with a remnant of White Bird's band in 1878. She was his only surviving child, but he outlived her also.

He was allowed to visit his beloved Valley of the Winding Waters in 1900, and stood looking at the grave of his father with tear-brimmed eyes. Never, until he died by his lodge fire in 1904, did he quit grieving for his homeland.

Even an Indian

In 1879, even as Joseph pleaded from Indian Territory for the right of his people to return to Idaho, he did not imagine they could return to their old ways. "I know that my race must change," he told a reporter.... "We only ask an even chance to live as other men live. We ask to be recognized as men. We ask that the same law shall work alike on all men.... Let me be a free man -- free to travel, free to stop, free to work, free to trade where I choose, free to choose my own teachers, free to follow the religion of my fathers, free to think and talk and act for myself -- and I will obey every law, or submit to the penalty.

"Whenever the white man treats the Indian as they treat each other, then we shall have no more wars. We shall be all alike -- brothers of one father and one mother, with one sky above us and one country around us, and one government for all. Then the Great Spirit Chief who rules above will smile upon this land, and send rain to wash out the bloody spots made by brothers' hands upon the face of the earth."

The spring of that same year another chief -- torn from his home without reason -- his people dying in Indian Territory -- raised the same plea. But this time a judge in Nebraska was listening.

 Susette LaFlesche, 25-year-old daughter of Omaha Chief Joseph LaFlesche, leaned over the paper with pen in hand and thought about what she should write. Tell him all you know, the missionary had said.

She could write easily in English, having been schooled at her father's insistence in the large, white mission school on the reservation. Later her teacher, impressed with the abilities of the slight girl with the arresting black eyes, managed to find funds to give her two years at a girls' school in New Jersey. She was a teacher herself now, returned to the reservation to help other Omaha children walk the bridge to the white man's world.

For years her family had been convinced that survival for the Omaha lay only across that bridge. Both her father and mother had white fathers and Omaha mothers, but both had chosen a life among their mothers' people, and Joseph had convinced other young men of the tribe that the future lay in farm fields, sawmills, blacksmith shops and wooden houses. Some scornfully called Joseph's cluster of houses the Village of Make-Believe White Men, but for more than 20 years he had worked to remain friends with the Whites and pull the Omaha into the world which was engulfing them. His family had given up their grandfathers' ways for white ways, given up the prairie for the schoolhouse, given up the Omaha gods for the white god. Had it all been futile, as it seemed with the Ponca?

Susette's hand hesitated over the page. Tell him all you know.

All she knew about her relatives the Ponca and their troubles with the government... What she knew would fill pages -- books. All she knew about hardship, suffering and loss. About betrayal. About uncaring, unreasoning officialdom. About being treated like animals. Worse than animals; the Whites at least provided food for their stock.

Where should she begin? In 1865, when most of the Ponca's land along the Missouri north of the Niobrara had been given to the Sioux? Or the next decade, when Sioux depredations of the passive farmers had gone unchecked and unpunished? Or with the 1875 treaty, which her uncle, White Swan, Standing Bear and the other Ponca chiefs had signed, believing it granted them land with their relatives, the Omaha, only to be told suddenly by the white men that the paper put them in the land Toward the Heat. Or in January 1877, when their agent left the Ponca chiefs stranded 500 miles away in Indian Territory, with no money, no interpreter, no horses, no way home, when they would not do as he ordered.

She remembered how the eight chiefs had looked by the time they'd made their way home as far as the Omaha Reservation that March two years before. She could hardly recognize the haggard face of her uncle or the hunched bulk of Standing Bear beside him.

It had been Standing Bear who'd told their story.

They'd been weeks on the way through intense cold; eating raw corn scavenged from fields, sleeping in haystacks when they were lucky, their feet tingeing the snow with blood through their worn-out moccasins. All because they refused to do what the white man wanted: to give up their homes and farms on the Niobrara and choose land in Indian Territory.

Should she write that in their innocence -- with her assistance and the missionary's -- they'd wired their Great Father in Washington for help, unable to believe he would sanction the agent's actions? Unwilling to believe he'd allow their peaceful tribe to be driven from their homes with bayonets. "Please answer, as we are in trouble," they'd said in their wire, "...tired, hungry, shoeless and footsore, and with heart and spirit broken and sad."

Should she write that the only answer had been silence? That the agent and the soldiers with their bayonets were waiting when the chiefs finally got home. That they had locked Standing Bear and his brother, Big Snake, away while they broke into the Ponca's houses, confiscated all their furniture and farm machinery and threw their personal belongings into wagons. That then, their bayonets ready, they'd started the 700 Ponca south through bottomless sloughs and across chill streams swollen with spring rains. As if, the Ponca said later, they were driving a herd of ponies.

Susette and her father had gone to say goodbye to their relatives as they passed through Columbus, Nebraska eight days later. By then two children already were dead, and there were several people sick, one of them Prairie Flower, Standing Bear's daughter, whose consumption-racked body suffered with every jolt of the wagon. Should she write of Standing Bear's helpless concern? Or of the way he spoke of the home he'd been forced to leave, built with his own hands, and the list of crops, chickens, plows, chairs, beds, lamps, washtubs, crockery, knives and forks this savage once counted valued possessions? Or of the cries of mourning that haunted the lodges that night? Of course, that had been only the beginning. Before the 500-mile journey was over many more were worn and ill; seven more were dead, one of them Prairie Flower.

Susette had wondered and worried about her uncle's family and the rest of the Ponca as the months went by, but the agents allowed no uncensored letters to pass between the tribes. However, even dependent on bits of rumor or what they could read between the lines, they knew it was not good with the Ponca. The rock-strewn land Toward the Heat (Indian Territory) was baked by a relentless sun. It seemed good only for graves for the scores who were falling to malaria.

Just eight weeks before, on the morning of March 4, 1879, Susette had been amazed to learn that several Ponca families were secreted in her father's village. As soon as she could do so without raising suspicion, she left her classroom near the agency and hurried to Joseph's house. There were about 30 of them, she discovered, of all ages, all of them half-starved and travel-worn, several too ill to walk. It was part of Standing Bear's band, including his wife and his two orphaned grandchildren and a half-dozen other families. The aging chief warmed himself by her father's stove.

He was going home, he said, taking his wife and his one living child to a place where they had a chance of surviving. The Ponca had tried to live in the new place -- others of the tribe were still there trying to start their lives over again. But they had dug so many, many graves in that hard ground. And when the time had come, in early January, that there was again keening in Standing Bear's lodge, he could not bring himself to put his only son in that ground. He'd comforted the sick boy by promising him a resting place on the Swift Running Water (Niobrara) where his grandmother lay. Standing Bear and his band were on the way to keep that promise; the boy's remains lay in a box in a wagon hidden near Joseph's house. They did not intend to go back to the hot land.

After dark, when they could move about without being observed, the Ponca and Omaha chiefs gathered for a council circle in her father's house. She'd listened to the speeches. Standing Bear, nearing 60 but still straight and tall, could easily command attention. He was anxious to go on to their old home. However Joseph had persuaded the weary Ponca -- without money or means to plant crops -- to stay with the Omaha until they could grow food to sustain themselves. He gave them seed, tools and land to plant wheat, urging them to stay on until its harvest, assuring them the agent would never notice 30 strange Indians among the 1,100 Omaha.

He'd been wrong about that. Susette watched the soldiers come that Sunday morning in late March, watched them pass Joseph's house to a cluster of tents beyond, which housed some of the Ponca. She'd grabbed up her skirts and run to the missionary for help. But in spite of all their pleas, and Standing Bear's protests that they had committed no crime, she'd had to watch again as the tearful band was marched away, to be imprisoned at Fort Omaha until they could be returned to Indian Territory.

The Ponca were not hostiles, like some Sioux, or even the Nez Perce. They had not fought soldiers. They had not robbed or killed settlers. They had fields of corn and potatoes, barns and wooden houses like the Whites. Like the Omaha. If the government could do this to the Ponca, what of her people? Could not they also be driven from their land? The frightening question had hung over the Omaha for two years. Did Indians have no rights at all?

Even on the reservation they were at the mercy of the agent. Susette had spent two years fighting him for the privilege of teaching her own people, first going over his head to write to the Indian Commissioner and insist her qualifications be considered, then stealing off the reservation to take the Nebraska teachers' examination. She taught at half the salary paid the white teacher, in an old house that leaked rain and snow on her barefoot pupils, without books or supplies. Still, she was teaching, and the children willingly endured difficult journeys to reach the school, and that was what mattered most.

It would have been easy to hate all white men, but Susette could not. The missionaries had given her the joy of books, her teachers at the Elizabeth Institute in New Jersey had stretched her mind and given her the weapons to fight for her people. She had never considered any other life. She was Susette LaFlesche, honor graduate of Elizabeth Institute for Young Ladies. But she was also Inshtat-heamba, Bright Eyes, daughter of Chief Inshtamaza, granddaughter of Nicomi and Watunna. She was shy by nature, always hesitant to speak out in a group. But she could not tolerate injustice, and she quickly put her writing skills to work defending her people. As her reputation grew she'd written numerous letters -- to the commissioner, the secretary of the interior, the President -- for other Omaha who refused to bear oppressive treatment in silence. Now she had a chance to write to a white man she knew would listen, one who had actually asked about the treatment of Indians, one who was trying to help the Ponca.

They hadn't known who he was when they saw the first newspaper article calling the Ponca's imprisonment "criminal cruelty." Or when the second article appeared, telling how the churches of Omaha had petitioned Secretary of Interior Carl Schurz to free them. Or when the incredible news came that because Secretary Schurz refused to act, someone had brought suit against Army Gen. George Crook for depriving Standing Bear and his band of their rights.

Rights! Did Standing Bear have rights? Could it be they all had rights? Someone thought so. Someone thought the 14th Amendment to the U.S. Constitution, which provided that a person born in the United States could not be imprisoned or detained without good reason and due process of law, should apply to all persons; that Indians were persons. He'd persuaded two lawyers to volunteer their services and they'd filed a writ of habeas corpus in the U.S. Circuit Court for the District of Nebraska to free the Ponca.

Now this man had written the Omaha and asked for information to prepare the Ponca's case. His name was T. H. Tibbles and he was an assistant editor at the *Omaha Daily Herald*. Susette concentrated, trying to condense all she knew, all she felt, into a concise statement of fact.

She did not write of her childhood memories of visiting the Ponca, of giggling with the dainty Prairie Flower and her cousins, of listening to the impressive oratory of Standing Bear.

She couldn't describe the weary defeat in her uncle's face two years before as they left Columbus for Indian Territory, or the fear in her grown cousin's embrace. Nor the flame of promise she'd seen in the alert eyes of Standing Bear's now-dead young son. She did not include a litany of the flagrant crimes white settlers had committed on and off the reservation.

Instead she let the Ponca speak for themselves. Leafing surely through her papers she pulled out the story the chiefs had told on their return from Indian Territory in 1877 and the text of the telegram they had sent to the President with such hope. Then, in a brief unemotional statement, she told of her relationship to the tribe and how she and Joseph had witnessed their departure at Columbus; of her uncle's protests that they had never agreed to leave their land; of the Ponca's willingness to live with the Omaha -- or even the Sioux; of the futility of their objections to the move.

"The statement shows how much they trusted in the justice of the white people," she closed, "believing that the wrong done them had been done only by a few, and without authority. I do hope some action will be taken in the matter soon."

For their part, the Omaha chiefs wrote out a petition asking that the Ponca be given part of the Omaha lands. "They are our brothers and our sisters, our uncles and our cousins," they wrote. "And although we are called savages we feel that sympathy for our persecuted brethren that should characterize Christians, and are willing to share what we possess with them if they can only be allowed to return..."

The trial began in Omaha May 1. Susette and her father had ridden into town the day before with the missionary and the Omaha's storekeeper, the son of another clergyman who'd long served the tribe. They'd met with the Ponca's champion and the committee of Omaha ministers who'd taken up the Ponca cause.

Susette would have been hard pressed to decide which experience was more overpowering -- being asked to tell the Ponca's story to a roomful of white men, or meeting Thomas Henry Tibbles. The editor, about 40, was a large man with a great mane of black hair, but it was his confidence and energy that engulfed her. He'd been crusading for one cause or another since he took part in the border wars of Kansas. The rights of Blacks, religion and the plight of Nebraska settlers suffering starvation after the 1874 grasshopper plague had engaged his attention in turn. Now he was determined to free the Ponca.

Their freedom, if it were granted, would come at an ironic price, Susette discovered. The Ponca's lawyers, Omaha residents John L. Webster and Andrew J. Poppleton, would have to prove Standing Bear and his followers had permanently severed their relations with their tribe in favor of civilization. Thus -- no longer wards of the government -- they could become persons in the eyes of the law. In order to merit the protection of the Constitution, the peaceful Ponca had to renounce their heritage.

The next morning Susette, Joseph and the missionary crowded with the concerned clergymen and curious townspeople into the packed courtroom. General Crook was there, looking formidable in his full dress uniform and bristling, black beard, but Tibbles had explained that he openly sympathized with the Ponca and hoped the court would void his orders to transport them to Indian Territory.

U.S. District Judge Elmer Dundy was on the bench, a figure of power in his black robe.

So, too, in one corner, was Standing Bear, in his council attire, a red and blue blanket around his shoulders, an impressive necklace of grizzly claws curving across his blue shirt front. His brother was seated beside him, as was his wife, who cuddled their grandson in her lap. Susette recognized Lieutenant Carpenter, who'd led the arresting party, and their storekeeper, Willie Hamilton, who were to be witnesses for the Ponca.

Hamilton was first to give his testimony, but the questions put to him seemed to do little but establish that the Ponca had appeared at the Omaha reservation in poor health, been invited to stay and had begun to plant wheat as soon as they were physically able. The attorneys sparred about whether the men worked on Sunday, whether their tents and clothes were their own or government's, whether the chiefs controlled the people. Lieutenant Carpenter's testimony, while friendly, seemed no more definitive.

But then Attorney Webster proposed to question Standing Bear.

Immediately the government's attorney rose to protest. "Does this court think an Indian a competent witness?" Could a non-person testify in his own behalf? Susette waited the important answer.

"They are competent for every purpose in both civil and criminal courts," Judge Dundy stated with finality. "The law makes no distinction on account of race, color, or previous condition."

Perhaps there was hope.

With Willie Hamilton as interpreter, attention focused on Standing Bear. Slowly -- questions arcing through the warm May air from Webster to Hamilton to Standing Bear to Hamilton to Webster and the court -- the chief told his story. How good it had been in Dakota with their cropland and a school for the children. How bad it was in the south, with 158 dead before he left. How he had asked and asked the agent to let them go home, and finally left on his own in hopes of saving his last child. How all he wanted to do was work and make his own living like the white men.

Mostly he answered patiently the endless questions about how many of his people had come with him, how many had stayed in the south, where they wanted to live and why.

But when Webster asked him to tell the court about his son, the chief's voice was charged with emotion. The boy had been his hope for the future. He'd sent him to school so that he could be a link with civilization; so that someone with Ponca blood could deal with the white men and protect their people. The hot country had killed his son and his hope, but he would not abandon his mission to bury the boy's bones where he was born. At one time the chief's powerful voice rose with his frustration. "It seems as though I haven't a place in the world, no place to go, and no home to go to, but when I see your faces here, I think some of you are trying to help me, so that I can get a place sometime to live in, and when it comes my time to die, to die peacefully and happy."

The first day of testimony drew to a close and the next morning the Ponca's attorney took the floor. At first it was encouraging to hear Webster arguing that the United States had no right to Ponca lands, no authority to move them to Indian Territory, no justification in making them go back. "They are born on our soil," he said. "What are they? Are they wild animals to be chased by every hound?" No! They were men, asking only to go home.

However, after noon recess the government's lawyer had his turn. In a courtroom thronged with army officers, their wives, lawyers, reporters and prominent Nebraska residents, he declared the Ponca were not even entitled to trial in a federal court: that there was no precedent allowing an Indian access to the courts; that only citizens were entitled to the writ of habeas corpus. Indians, he said, committed atrocities which proved they could not be part of a civilized system. They were "outside" the system and were not entitled to the rights of citizens under the law.

That there were precedents for that belief Susette knew only too well. Subdued and tense, the Indians filed out for the supper hour.

Yet that evening the rustle of the crowd settling into their seats was quickly hushed as Poppleton began his argument for justice. The Ponca had a right to habeas corpus: the weakest, poorest human being had such a right, he declared. Minors and insane people were protected by it. Ethiopians, Chinese, and Frenchmen could enjoy its benefits. Every human being had such a right.

The Ponca had committed no crime; they did not know why they'd been arrested and imprisoned. Their treatment was an outrage; an infamy! And Standing Bear's Ponca, the lawyer noted, were no longer part of the Ponca tribe. They asked for no annuities. They chose to live civilized lives as individuals, and as such were entitled to the protection of the Constitution.

Finally, late in the evening, the lawyers had exhausted both their voices and their arguments. The Ponca's fate was in the hands of the judge. White men had determined their strategy and decided the questions Standing Bear was asked. In two long days they had been able to understand only those questions. White men had argued their place in a legal system that stretched back across an ocean most of them had never seen, to a country they'd never heard of; a white judge would determine their fate.

Still, to Susette's surprise, Judge Dundy seemed to appreciate the isolation the Ponca felt in the courtroom. Standing Bear had asked to speak to the court, he said. It was unprecedented, but he would allow it.

The chief rose slowly and extended his hand toward the judge until all attention in the courtroom was focused upon it. For a long moment he said nothing. Then he spoke in the forceful language Susette knew so well, pausing to let Willie Hamilton interpret his words for the court.

His hand was not the color of the judge's, he said quietly, yet if he pierced it, he would feel pain. He waited for Hamilton to interpret his words. Then he raised his eyes to Dundy. "If you pierce your hand," he said with quiet logic, "you also feel pain.

"The blood that will flow from mine will be the same color as yours. I am a man. The same God made us both.

"Where do you think I come from?" he asked. "From the water, the woods or where? God made me, and he put me on my land.

"But I was ordered to stand up and leave my land. Who the man was I don't know. He told me to leave and I had to go. It was hard for me to go. I objected to going. I looked around me for someone to help me but I found none...

"My friends and brothers: I am now with the soldiers and officers. I want to go back to my old place up north. I want to save myself and my tribe.

"My brothers, it seems to me as if I stood in front of a great prairie fire. I would take up my babies and run to save their lives; or as if I stood on the bank of an overflowing river, and I would take my people and fly to higher ground. Oh! my brothers, the Almighty looks down on me, and knows what I am, and hears my words. May the Almighty send a good spirit to brood over you, my brothers, to move you to help me."

And he was not a savage. He had never tried to hurt a white man. God made him, but he didn't know how to write or read. God made the white people to teach him. One time he had given shelter to a half-frozen soldier whom he found on the prairie; he had rescued another starving white man and guided him to safety. Had he been a savage, he reminded the judge, he would have cut off the man's head and taken his scalp.

"Look on me. Take pity on me, and help me to save the lives of the women and children. My brothers, a power which I cannot resist crowds me down to the ground. I need help. I have done."

For a moment the stunned audience remained quiet, some of the women wiping away tears. Then the crowd burst into applause and pushed forward to shake the chief's hand.

For 10 anxious days the Indians swung between hope and pessimism before they were called back to the courtroom to hear the judge's decision. Squeezed again into the crowded room, Susette felt her heart jump at the first words Judge Dundy read from the bench.

"During the 15 years in which I have been engaged in administering the laws of my country, I have never been called upon to hear or decide a case that appealed so strongly to my sympathy as the one now under consideration," he was saying. Based on sympathy, the judge said, he would have released the Ponca at the close of arguments 10 days before.

It seemed too good to be true. She waited for the "but," and it came. Sympathy notwithstanding, the case must be decided on principles of law, the judge went on. Unless the Ponca could claim protection under the law, they must be returned to Indian Territory. He began a summary of the facts of the case and then proceeded to discuss the basic question of jurisdiction. Did the Indians even have a place in court, were they persons with the right to habeas corpus? Susette tensed as Dundy related his deliberations.

"Webster describes a person as 'a living soul; a self-conscious being; a moral agent; especially a living human being, a man, woman or child; an individual of the human race,'" the judge said. "This is comprehensive enough, it would seem," he remarked dryly, "to include even an Indian."

Even an Indian? Could it be?

"I must hold, then," the judge went on, "that Indians, and consequently the relators, are persons."

They had a right to their day in court! But Susette had little time to savor that fact. The judge went on to explore the government's right to tell Standing Bear's band where to live.

Again she listened to the story she knew so well of the Ponca's past two years, this time with all its legal ramifications. Yet the judge was not ignoring the human factor. Susette heard phrases such as "the love of home and native land," "parental affection," "Christian in principal."

Then Dundy was saying Standing Bear's Ponca had a right to withdraw from their tribe if they wished. The United States had freely received immigrants from all nations, he said, why not Indian nations? And once they'd severed tribal ties, the government held no arbitrary authority to control their place of residence.

The judge's summation rang through the courtroom. An Indian is a person, with rights, including the inalienable right to life, liberty and the pursuit of happiness as long as he obeys the laws. The army has no authority to return the Ponca to Indian Territory. He ordered Standing Bear's band released from custody.

The victory was complete. Savoring the success, hopeful for its implications, Susette and her father returned home to the Omaha reservation, and Standing Bear and his band settled temporarily on land just beyond its border.

However Susette's uncle, White Swan, and his family were still down in Indian Territory. Tibbles came to the reservation and asked the young teacher and her father to go see how the tribe in the south was faring. They found the Ponca, who had left 236 substantial homes on the Niobrara, housed in canvas tents and six leaky shanties. The despair in her cousin's face told the story.

"All we think of is sickness and death," the young mother said.

When they left, Susette packed another letter written in her careful hand, this one dictated by Chief White Eagle.

"When people lose what they hold dear to them the heart cries all the time," the chief said. "I speak now to you lawyers who have helped Standing Bear, and to those of you who profess to be God's people. We had thought that there were none to take pity on us and none to help us. We thought all the white men hated us, but now we have seen you take pity on Standing Bear when you heard his story... I thank you in the name of our people for what you have done for us through your kindness to Standing Bear, and I ask of you to go still further in your kindness and help us to regain our land and rights. You cannot bring our dead back to life, but you can yet save the living."

Susette delivered the letter to Tibbles, believing her task was over.

However her fight for the Indian cause was to control her life for the next ten years. Before she knew what was happening she'd been pushed into the limelight to tell the Ponca's story, first in an Omaha church, then -- terrifyingly -- during a lecture tour Tibbles arranged to Chicago, Boston and other eastern cities that fall. Nearly paralyzed with shyness, she would have refused, had not the Omaha's titles to their land also been challenged. The Standing Bear decision meant nothing to the Department of the Interior. The department was determinedly pursuing its goal of placing all Indians, regardless of treaties, in Indian Territory.

When a bill was introduced in Congress to move her people from Nebraska to Indian Territory, Susette could not refuse Tibbles' request that she go with him and Standing Bear to act as interpreter. With her 22-year-old brother Frank as her escort, the four headed east to tell their story and plead for money to fight the government.

On platform after platform, in churches, meeting houses and private homes, Susette stood dwarfed by the huge chief, he dressed for the occasion in the ceremonial clothes he'd worn at his trial, she wearing as usual a simple dark dress, her hair pulled into a neat coil behind her head, her hands often buried in the folds of her skirt to hide their trembling. She met mayors and governors, read her speeches on the same dais as Oliver Wendell Holmes and Wendell Phillips, heard Henry Wadsworth Longfellow call her his Hiawatha. Actually she was Bright Eyes to the easterners. The press and society found her Omaha name more romantic and appealing than Susette LaFlesche. Frank, even dressed in his walking suit and with his hair parted fashionably on the right, was known as Woodworker.

Susette was willing to tolerate much more than that if it helped her people. The urgency of the need was impressed on them all when they learned in late October that Standing Bear's brother, Big Snake, had been killed "resisting" arrest in Indian Territory. The same day Tibbles received word that his wife had died in Omaha. However, both men put their private grief away and continued to work for the cause. Tibbles compiled a book detailing the Standing Bear case, and they provided author Helen Hunt Jackson with inspiration and material for a book she would call *A Century of Dishonor*.

Refusing to give in to the strain of appearing in public, Susette gave speeches, shook hands at receptions and granted interviews until close to exhaustion. Finally, in February 1880, the four were called to testify before a Senate committee in Washington. With the weight of the Interior

Department and Indian Commissioner aligned against her, she tried to tell the wrongs the Ponca and Omaha had suffered.

The Omaha agent called her a liar. The commissioner claimed the Ponca were perfectly happy in Indian Territory. And even though Massachusetts Sen. Henry L. Dawes introduced legislation to return the tribe to its Dakota reservation, the bill languished in committee for months. Discouraged and nearing collapse, Susette and the three men went home to Nebraska.

During the summer she developed her own literary and artistic talents by writing a story for children about her great-great grandmother and Omaha life in the old days. She wanted to preserve and share the humanness of the tribal legacy which was being systematically destroyed. Tibbles was at work on another book and Susette expressed her thoughts in an introduction she wrote for it.

"Allow an Indian to suggest that the solution of the vexed 'Indian Question' is citizenship," she wrote, "with all its attending duties and responsibilities, as well as the privileges of protection under the law." The Indian was not an extraordinary being, she said. He was, like others, a creature of his surroundings. But, "The huge plow of the 'Indian system' has run for a hundred years, beam down, turning down into the darkness of the earth every hope and aspiration which we have cherished...," she wrote. "What sort of harvest will it yield to the nation whose hand has guided the plow?"

Standing Bear's band had been granted an unclaimed island in the Niobrara, and with his son's bones finally laid to rest, the Ponca chief was again becoming a farmer. But her uncle and the rest of the tribe were still in Indian Territory and legislation still threatened the Omaha, Santee Sioux and other peaceful tribes; in the fall she was back on the lecture circuit.

The battle for the Ponca ended in March 1881 when Congress passed legislation providing 160 acres for every Ponca, either on their old reservation or in Indian Territory. By that time those in the south had adjusted to the climate, made homes and were too weary of the struggle to move again. "We waited for three years to get our own (land) back again, but it was like climbing a wall," one said. "There is nothing to take hold of."

"We decided finally it was impossible," said another. "Impossible. Impossible. Impossible."

With the Ponca question settled -- however unsatisfactorily -- Susette and Tibbles returned to Nebraska. They were married that July, and continued to work to see the Omaha's land grant confirmed. Legislation granting the Omaha title to their land in severalty was passed August 7, 1882. The threat of being driven to Indian Territory at last was gone. So was, finally and forever, their old free way of life. With relief Susette watched the people sign the allotment papers. But remembering her childhood nights on the wide prairie, listening to stories in her grandmother's arms, secure in her family's love, she wondered whether there was anything in civilization which could make good to them what they had lost.

In the ensuing years, Susette and her family, especially her brother Frank, helped ethnologist Alice Fletcher preserve and record the culture of the Omaha. He earned a law degree and became known for his ethnological work for the Indian Bureau. Two of her sisters, Rosalie and Marguerite, also became teachers and mentors to their people on the reservation. The third and youngest, Susan, became the first Indian woman physician in 1889. She also worked tirelessly for her people in Nebraska.

Susette and T.H. continued to lecture, traveling as far as England in 1887. Tibbles eventually went back to the newspaper business and the couple lived in Omaha and Lincoln, framed pictures crowding the top of a reed organ in one corner of Susette's parlor, a buffalo robe, quill embroideries and bead work displayed in the other. He became involved in the Populist cause.

Susette continued to write and illustrated a book of Omaha history in 1898. Later they returned to Susette's farm (near Bancroft) where she died in 1903 at the age of 49, a troubled woman who watched her people struggle with the curse of alcohol and wondered if, after all, the Omaha had taken the right path.

Standing Bear, The Person, lived in contented, if not always compliant, obscurity on his land in Dakota until his death in

1908. His dignified yet implacable determination to resist injustice had changed lives far beyond the shores of the Swift Running Water.

Beyond the Stone Heaps

While some Whites came to consider Indians human beings in 1879, there were many who would have argued the definition. They looked at results rather than causes, and identified with pain inflicted on their own kind more easily than wrongs visited on people they could not understand. They had sons who died on the Rosebud, brothers who lay stripped and mutilated on the Little Bighorn, husbands who marched away to deal with the savages. They were grateful the army had harried most of the renegade Sioux and Cheyenne onto their reservations, glad that Iron Shield and Crazy Horse were dead, that Sitting Bull had been chased across the border into Canada. Their sympathies lay with the settlers trying to carve out a life in a dangerous land and the troopers who were trying to protect them.

As *Chicago Times* war correspondent John F. Finerty watched the 100 raw recruits tramp off the steamer *Josephine* at old Fort Peck on July 2, 1879, he had more than a twinge of sympathy for the latest batch of soldiers who'd been sent to hunt for Sitting Bull. He'd spent the summer of 1876 with Crook's army while they chased after the Hunkpapa chief, and had come close to losing his life in the process. Luckily the bean-pole Irishman had not had his choice of assignments in the campaign against the Sioux. He was with Crook instead of Custer, so his red scalplock still clung tight to his head.

However it was not because he avoided action. When he rode with troops, he rode with them -- whatever the risk -- and soldiers had followed his skinny back in more than one charge. He had no patience with journalists who tried to remain safely in the rear. For one thing, in fights with the Indians he'd found there usually was no rear; the reserves were invariably called into action. But more important, he believed he had no right to criticize unless he shared the hardship and danger.

Whether this batch of troopers would see any real battles was uncertain, but they'd been ordered to chase Sitting Bull back up to Canada and see that he stayed there. There were too many reports of stolen horses and frightened settlers between the Missouri and the Canadian line. Rumors had the hostiles on Frenchman's Creek, a little way north, or on the Milk River, closer to the border. Some said the trouble was caused by small war parties; others thought Sitting Bull's whole camp was on the American side. Whatever the situation, Col. Nelson A. Miles was ordered to see that the Sioux caused no more trouble in Montana.

While the troops awaited the arrival of their commander, they hurried to fortify their position on the river bottom of the Missouri's north bank by dragging in dead trees. Finerty thought the greenhorns made an incredible racket while they worked, but they got the job done. They all knew Sitting Bull might be only 40 miles away.

Finerty was familiar with the mix of men that made up the frontier armies. Three years before, in the field with Crook, he'd made friends with British and German officers who'd trained on the fields of Europe, Civil War veterans, city boys from the east, and other Irish immigrants who needed a job and were always ready for a scrap. He got on well with the men, always ready for a drink or a laugh, especially if it was on himself. The troops called him Jack, or Long John, and kidded him that his legs were so long that if he ever forgot and straightened them while on horseback, his mount would just walk out from under him.

His own immigration in 1864 had not been entirely voluntary. At 17 he was fighting for Ireland's freedom, and by the time he was 18 he'd become such a thorn in the British paw that he had to flee the country to avoid arrest. Landing in New York, he'd enlisted in a Yankee regiment to fight for another cause, but he hadn't forgotten the chains on Ireland, and he continued to work to break them.

Immigrants or native born, most of the enlisted men who faced the Indians were capable and loyal, he'd decided, in spite of the fact they were often sent into the field without even a manual of arms or time to learn the drill calls. Once there, they learned on the job, spending so much time in such labors as making roads, digging rifle pits and building camps that their knowledge of guard duty, picket duty and Indian tactics had to be absorbed on a catch-as-catch-can basis. They might not be as polished as European soldiers, Finerty thought, but combining the ardor of the Irish, the stolid courage of the Germans and the coolness of the Yankees in one unit made an outfit equal to any in the world.

Now, in the July heat of the Missouri bottoms, this latest batch of soldiers began their lessons. The songs that had risen as they worked the first day deteriorated to curses the next when clouds of mosquitoes darkened the air. Desperate for relief, they started smudge fires of damp sagebrush, then worked teary-eyed and coughing in the smoke. The weeds they waded through gave off poison that raised a firey itch on their legs and arms. They fell exhausted into their tents at night, only to have a storm tear the shelter from over their heads and drench them with such torrents that they were forced to cover their faces to breathe. When it was over they rolled in their wet blankets and went back to sleep.

"When a man goes into the Indian expedition business, he must never make himself unhappy about trifles," Finerty explained to his readers.

He knew from experience what trifles they'd face. In the summer of '76, after the Rosebud, they'd all been weeks without a change of clothes. Like the rest he'd washed his shirt when he could, in a creek, without benefit of soap, and sat his horse in nearly seatless trousers. Between creeks he'd done the best he could to depopulate his clothes of crawling things by hand. He took comfort in reflecting "that probably Julius Caesar, Pompey, and Mark Anthony picked 'gray-backs' off their togas in olden times." But he wondered what romantic young ladies would think to see their dashing soldiers engrossed in such a project.

Learning to sleep in mud puddles was only the beginning. They'd have to ride 40 or 50 miles a day, bed down without tents or fires, and live by crunching on hardtack and chewing raw bacon, feeling lucky if they had a cup of coffee to wash it down. He'd worn his boots for two weeks straight, afraid if he took them off he'd never get the weather-shrunken things back on again. "The wild freedom of the plains sounds well in a comfortable parlor," he told his readers, "but does not feel quite as nice when your hide is wet and clammy with rain, like the skin of a frog, and when you have as much mud on your person as would disgrace a stockyard's pig." As for the romance of soldiering, he found, "The rays of the star of glory are made up of filth, hardship and disappointments. Fighting is the least of the evils attendant on a military career."

With the arrival of Miles and the rest of the force on July 11, the recruits added another ray to the star of glory. Horses.

This expedition would be mounted -- even the infantry -- and those who could not ride would learn. As Finerty grinned at the show, city boys were tossed through the air "like so many footballs." Some clung to the pommel like a drowning man to a reed. Others readily parted company with their mounts at every sharp turn, "flying like spread eagles through the air." On July 15, nursing their bruises, they marched out to face the finest light cavalry in the world.

The Sioux up north are like the grass, the Assiniboin had warned Miles. "And like the grass, we shall burn them up," Miles replied. Finerty noticed that the lines in Miles' face had deepened in the three years since he'd seen him, and the colonel's close-cut hair was beginning to gray. But he seemed the same energetic commander he'd met before. If Sitting Bull was looking for a fight, Miles was more than ready to give him one. He'd subdued the Nez Perce, and his cannon were always ready for more action.

The newspaperman had mixed feelings about the Indians. Three years before, after his unit's first brush with hostiles, he had not hesitated to call the average Indian a "mysterious, untameable, barbaric, unreasonable, childish, superstitious, treacherous, thievish, murderous creature." Yet a few days later he was moved to awe at the wild beauty of the painted Crow and Shoshoni scouts who raced alongside the column. He had watched them cry in anguish over their dead; then he'd been forced to turn away as they mutilated and degraded the body of a fallen enemy.

Before they left the Missouri, Finerty noted how Miles' Cheyenne and Sioux scouts had sent their pay back to their wives, children, mothers, fathers and other relatives. The savages had some of the finer feelings of humanity, after all.

Now, as the force moved northwest along the Milk River, through rain-drenched prairie redolent with sage, he could understand why Sitting Bull wanted the country for his people. It was among the best buffalo ranges in North America. But he did not question that the Hunkpapa must be humbled so that settlers would feel safe along the Milk. Miles had a sizeable force to challenge the Hunkpapa. Nearly 700 officers and men, plus 150 Indian scouts, took the muddy road north, the wheels of supply wagons and gun carriages marking their wake.

Finerty was intrigued that Miles had adopted one of the Indians' methods to his own use. About a dozen miles north of Fort Peck, he sent a man up Tiger Butte with a small mirror contraption on a tripod and orders to telegraph messages between forces.

Angling the mirror toward the sun, the men had learned to flash dots and dashes by covering and uncovering it rapidly in turn. The heliograph was a good system, the reporter thought, the flashes from the mirror's surface, as bright as lightning, could relay messages from hilltop to hilltop for 25 miles or more. But when the sun disappeared it was useless, and unfortunately they often rode under clouds that belched real lightning. With Lt. Philo Clark, about 100 men and some 50 scouts probing ahead up Beaver Creek, the waterlogged column squished along the south side of the Milk River, running swift and cream-colored between high banks.

Then suddenly on July 17 there was news. Clark had found the Sioux father up the Beaver. He needed help! At the word, the column stirred into motion. Miles ordered every available man into the saddle. In moments they were galloping over the prairie. Now, when they would have welcomed the clouds, the sky burned bright blue. Sweat foamed under the bridle lines on the horses' necks and ran in rivulets down the men's chests. Alternately trotting and galloping, only occasionally slowing to a walk, they rode with dreadful possibilities swirling in their minds.

Sitting Bull's camp was said to be huge -- as many as 2,000 warriors. Finerty and some of the men of the 2nd Cavalry had helped bury the blackened bodies after the Rosebud fight three years before -- had been close enough to the Little Bighorn to see the smoke of battle, had known men at Slim Buttes who were maimed for life. Clark had only 150 men; the whole force was just over 800 strong, and 150 of those were Indians.

As they rode 10 miles, then 15, they began to meet Indian scouts -- Assiniboin and Bannock who'd abandoned the battle. But Clark seemed to be pushing the Sioux north, and as the relief force approached the banks of the Milk five miles farther on, they saw his small force had caught up to the main Sioux camp. It could have been a disastrous discovery. The balance of power was suddenly in the Sioux camp, and Clark's force, including his Cheyenne and Crow scouts, who were fighting loyally, were caught in the river's ravine. Through the black smoke of battle Finerty could see warriors riding to surround the soldiers.

They'd found him just in time. Immediately Miles ordered the Hotchkiss guns to the front, and they began throwing shells over Clark's troops and into the Sioux on the far bank. The troopers deployed in two skirmish lines along the small bluffs that formed the south bank, but it was the artillery that made the difference.

As shells exploded with deadly effect in their midst, the main body of warriors began to wheel and gallop away. As always there were those who stayed to protect the retreat. In the face of the soldiers' fire, Finerty saw one brave cooly lead his pony down the opposite bluff and take aim on Colonel Miles and his officers where they stood grouped across the water. He fired, without apparent effect, then mounted his horse and deliberately rode away. The retreat of the main party was not so deliberate. The Indians had been hunting, and most of their kill lay abandoned on the prairie, with saddles and other camp goods strewn around.

However, it was sunset, and the nightly thunderheads loomed dark in the west. They were miles ahead of their supply train. The colonel turned the column around and began a march south to find it. As the first huge drops hit, Finerty knew this would be another miserable night march. He knew too well the awful feeling of riding through a black night, aware that you were part of a darker shadow that pushed forward, but able only to feel the presence of those closest to you, listening to the thud of horses hoofs, the repressed jingle of guns and tack, wondering where your mount's next step would fall. Wondering where the hostiles were.

This march was not to be totally dark. Soon lightning was stabbing out of the black sky, and then rain pelted them with astonishing force. Whipped by a violent wind, shaken by thunder, they strained to keep close to the horse ahead, guided after each shower of lightning by an eerie phosphorescent glow on the animal's ears. A rivulet streamed from Finerty's broad-brimmed hat and water ran into his boots. They slid blindly down the sides of Beaver Creek and clung to the saddle as their mounts lurched and stumbled through the boulders in the stream. At last they heard sweet music -- the braying of mules with the supply train -- and tumbled from their horses, grateful for any bed, however sodden.

Water continued to plague their steps when they rode north again toward Frenchman's Creek to follow the Sioux trail. It was not difficult to follow, stinking as it did with heaps of abandoned buffalo meat. The rain had turned every crossing into a challenge, and while the Indian scouts easily swam across, two soldiers nearly drowned when they lost control of their horses.

But they were nearly at the border, and after much searching on July 24 they found a small pile of rocks with a trench around its base. Looking east and west they picked out other piles about two miles distant. Across this line was Europe, the soldiers said, though neither the grass nor sky appeared to change color at the boundary.

With the Woody Mountains which held Sitting Bull's camp in sight, they bivouaced and waited for the Queen's representative, a Major Walsh, to come to call. Finerty, prickly at the British presence, appreciated the major's decision to wear a buckskin suit instead of his official red coat, and was pleased to hear his Irish accent. Invited to Miles' tent for the conference, Finerty listened to Walsh talk and realized the major actually loved Sitting Bull and his people. The Canadian praised the character of the tribe he'd dealt with for two years, and raised Miles' hackles by declaring they could out-fight any like number of white soldiers brought against them; that they were better horsemen and shots than the finest British cavalry. However, they hated and feared the artillery Miles had brought to bear, and did not want to fight white men any more.

Miles informed the Canadian officer he had orders to drive all hostiles north of the line. The United States would not tolerate any more Sioux raids in American territory.

Raids? Walsh acknowledged he was under orders to report any hostile Sioux actions to the Americans. But was going on a buffalo hunt a hostile act? The people were hungry. If they were to eat, they had to go where the buffalo were, and the shrinking herds did not seem to care whether they were north or south of small piles of stones.

Even with Miles' force camped on the border, a few Sioux probed south on July 23 and clashed with the army scouts. There were a few dead and wounded on both sides, but Finerty sensed a new caution in the attacking braves. They seemed less dashing and reckless than they were in '76, and he mused that starvation would tame even the boldest warriors.

What was Sitting Bull like now, this bold savage who had kept so much of the West in turmoil the past three years? The reporter could not bear to be so close without trying to see his fabled camp. Walsh said the chief had been in the fight at the Milk. Could he have seen him? Did he hate white men as fiercely as they said? Could his camp actually number in the thousands?

On July 29 he set out with Walsh, four red-coated Mounties and two Sioux scouts to see for himself. They rode into the grass-topped bluffs that formed the Woody Mountains and camped on the creek where the Sioux often held their Sun Dances. Gazing up at the poles silhouetted against the sunset sky, the reporter pictured the barbaric ceremonies, the whooping warriors and their trampling horses. The Sioux had been here just a few nights ago, Walsh said, until he had persuaded them to move farther north at Miles' approach. The next afternoon they topped a divide and Finerty sighted "the village so many American generals had looked for in vain."

Queer sensations stirred in him as he surveyed the white tipis covering the valley of Mushroom Creek five miles away. It was even stranger to ride toward the thump of drums and rising chants; stranger yet to follow as Walsh pushed through the throng of armed and painted braves until they could see the center of a large ring of Sioux. There about 50 warriors of an Oglala band wove and bobbed in dance around a Cheyenne scalp still fresh from the recent battle.

It seemed to him grotesque and wild, the noise satanic, and dressed as he was, in the blue shirt of the American army, he was conscious of many hostile glances. However with Walsh to vouch for him, he was not molested. When the dance wound down and the Mountie told him all the chiefs were about to gather in council, he felt a thrill. At last, he would see Sitting Bull! Yet after the people were gathered in a great semicircle in front of Walsh's quarters, he asked in vain for the famous chief.

"He is not among them," Walsh said. "He will not speak in council where Americans are present." But, at the crestfallen expression on Finerty's face, he reassured him, "You will see him, however, before very long."

A short time later an Indian spurred his horse to a stop behind the chiefs. He was plainly dressed, without paint on his broad face, his hair without a feather. He carried only a portion of eagle's wing, which he used as a fan as he stared at Finerty with what seemed to the reporter to be a mix of insolence and curiosity. Then he dismounted and limped over to take a seat in a shady spot. Finerty did not need to ask his name. "He will hear everything but say nothing," Walsh explained, unless he felt a need.

Walsh helped him identify some of the other warriors: Sitting Bull's adopted Assiniboin brother Jumping Bull, carrying a wound in his thigh from the scrap with Miles; Lone Bull, the chief's nephew; Bad Soup, his brother-in-law, whom Finerty thought looked as hungry as Cassius; Little Knife, Clouded Horn, Rain-in-the-Face; the Oglala Broad Trail, the Sans Arc Spotted Eagle, the Assiniboin Little Mountain, the Miniconjou Big Necklace. It was obvious people of many bands had been attracted to Sitting Bull's camp.

Walsh began relaying Miles' message that the Sioux must not cross the border to hunt; they must wait for the herds to cross the line. Walsh could not permit them to violate the laws or protect them if they did.

As if to reinforce his warning a Hunkpapa galloped up to the circle with a message. Two young men who crossed the border at Timber Buttes to push a herd over the line had been attacked by Miles' Cheyennes. One was dead, the other wounded.

There was a stir in the circle as Walsh pointed out the hard truth of Miles' orders. Then Bad Soup demanded to know who the man in the soldier shirt was. Assured that he was Walsh's friend, a man who writes for white men's newspapers and could tell their story, Bad Soup asked again for reassurance. "He is not a head soldier?"

"He is not," Walsh answered firmly. "It is enough that he is a friend of mine. He has no bad heart against the Sioux."

At that an Oglala chief named Hero sprang up to shake Finerty's hand and begin to pour out his frustration. Quickly the interpreter translated for the reporter. "When my young men go hunting over there," he said, sweeping his arm toward the south, "they are met with fire. My women are killed and my children starve. My Grandmother says I must not go to war, and I obey her.

"I see my people starving, and I go to kill the buffalo. The Great Spirit made no lines. The buffalo tastes the same on both sides of the stone heaps. I can find no change. Why then do the Americans meet us with fire when we only wish to feed ourselves and our women and children?

"The Great Spirit has given me a stomach -- he has given me the buffalo. I see the buffalo near the stone heaps and I must not shoot him, even while my children cry for his meat. The Great Spirit never meant to tempt me with the buffalo so near while my people are hungry. This strange white man hears me. Will he put my words straight before the people of his nation?"

At Finerty's nod, Hero asked the tall Irishman to respond.

Terribly conscious of his audience, he began to speak. "I cannot rival the eloquence of your chiefs," he said. "The Sioux are renowned in oratory as well as in war, but I will speak with an honest heart. My business is to write what my people may read. I have not come to fight you or to spy upon you, but to see how you live and to talk with your wise men."

Encouraged by a chorus of "Hau's" that followed the interpreter's version of his words, he continued. "All white men have not bad hearts for the Indian. Were I your enemy I could not sleep in the tipi of the White Sioux (Major Walsh); he would cast me out." Then, realizing the need to distance himself from the army, he said he would not try to explain why the Sioux were fired at across the border. "I am not an agent of the American Government, nor am I a soldier in its pay," he explained. "I can do no more than a simple citizen of the United States -- hear what you say and put it before my people." Americans did not wish to starve their families, he assured them, if they would cease to war. And, like them, Americans did not always hear the truth.

Bad Soup was not noticeably impressed. Few Americans spoke the truth, he said. He hoped this one was different. "The Americans have taught the Sioux how to break their promises," he said. "They took our land, piece by piece, until everything was gone, and we had to take refuge in the country of our White Grandmother....They send Bear's Coat and his soldiers to shoot us down. They arm the Crow and Cheyenne, the Bannock and the Assiniboin, to murder our young men."

Walsh reiterated that the Sioux were not to cross the line, and the council wound down. Finerty bought tobacco for a smoke with the chiefs -- Sitting Bull remained aloof, amusing himself by breaking horses -- and then retired to muse on what he thought would probably be the most singular experience of his life.

Whatever he was, the reporter had to admit, Sitting Bull was not a beggar.

The next day he climbed a butte and was overwhelmed at the size of the village. There must be at least 1,000 lodges, he thought, ranged along the green serpentine of Mushroom Creek. That meant about 2,500 fighting men. Their horses grazed in every direction -- 15,000 was his guess -- supporting a barbaric chivalry against which the hand of civilization had been raised since the days of Columbus. Strange, he thought, that "after centuries of relentless war so large a body, flushed with the memory of more than one gallant victory, should still exist." Much as he admired the abilities of Miles and his men, he was grateful he had not had to join them in a charge meant to humble this "nest of hornets."

Sitting Bull remained unapproachable, telling the interpreter he wanted nothing to do with Americans who had taken his country.

Finerty, his Irish dander up, said the interpreter could return the compliment to the chief. Tell him, the reporter said, that I have no wish to talk to a chief who has long since been wrung dry about his hatred of Americans and has nothing new to say. He was not about to beg for an interview. Still, he had to admit Sitting Bull, nearing 50 but looking younger, held a mysterious power over the Sioux; the high-minded and vicious alike flocked to his symbol of unbending resistance. Yet the trader's wife spoke of him as the nicest Indian around the post, with innate good manners, and he had seen the chief laugh easily and often.

The reporter wandered around the camp, admiring the people's clean habits, stopping to watch the boys race their ponies, watching the women scour the bluffs for berries to help fill their cooking pots. It was obvious they had little meat, and only Walsh's generosity kept them from having to eat their horses.

White Eagle and other chiefs who would talk with him insisted they'd never give up their guns and horses so they could be accepted on an American reservation. To do so would be to become beggars, they said. Yet Finerty could see no other end for their story.

Back in the army camp on August 4, he stood with Miles' staff on a bluff overlooking the Milk River and watched the great northern herd of buffalo pass muster. However there were thousands, now, instead of millions. In a few years they will be gone, he thought, and with them the Indian problem.

Finerty hardly had time to be bored, back in his Chicago offices, when he was again on his way west to accompany troops hurrying to relieve a unit surrounded by suddenly hostile Ute in Colorado. In 1881 he reported the campaign against the Apache in Arizona, filing, as usual, his lively, accurate, eyewitness accounts. Then it was back to Chicago to found a weekly newspaper and serve a term in Congress. But he did not forget the life of misery, tedium and terror which was the lot of soldiers who fought the Indian wars, and in 1890 he gathered his reports as a correspondent into a book, *War-path and Bivouac*, which he dedicated to the American army.

The men he accompanied returned the affection, citing him repeatedly for bravery and urging him to join their ranks. He "seeks his items on the skirmish line, and uses pencil and carbine with equal facility," one wrote. When the Irish immigrant laid down his pencil for good in 1908, the mayor of Chicago, six judges and other leading citizens were his honorary pallbearers. Probably he would have been more proud that in the mile-long procession which escorted his coffin from his home to Holy Angels Church marched several hundred of the veterans whose campfires he had shared and whose story he had done his best to tell.

Abode of Iron

John Finerty foresaw the end of the northern buffalo herds in 1879, but even he probably was surprised at the speed with which their numbers melted away. In 1880 the Northern Pacific Railroad cut its way through the heart of the herd's last sanctuary.

Numerous cars full of hides had been rolling east from Bismarck since 1876, but when the railroad crossed the Little Missouri badlands into Montana in 1880, the work of the hunters became shockingly easy. They could ride the rails by the carload; sometimes they did not even need to dismount the car before they had their quarry in their sights. In 1881 hides which had covered 50,000 bison were loaded at Bismarck. In 1882, 5,000 hunters garnered 200,000 hides -- one hunter claiming a personal kill of 5,000.

The Sioux were allowed to participate in the extermination. In September 1883, 1,000 braves -- among them the finally humbled Sitting Bull -- took part in the hunt. The bitter and disillusioned chief had held out until July 1881, but starvation had proved too strong an enemy. The Canadian government would not feed his people; they could not feed themselves. His camp had dwindled away as band after band gave up the struggle and crossed the border to live on the reservation. In the summer of 1881 he and the 186 old followers who remained loyal had returned to the United States and surrendered their guns and horses at Fort Buford. The Hunkpapa had been ordered to the Standing Rock reservation to sustain themselves by farming, but Sitting Bull himself had been confined at Fort Randall for nearly two years before he was released to join the others at Standing Rock. The 1883 hunt was a welcome release from handling a hoe, but the plains were already so emptied of the brown beasts that hunters found only 40,000 to eliminate. In 1884, hunters could manage only one carload of hides to ship east from Dickinson.

There were no more shipments of woolly brown hides. Railroad cars which had held skins soon began to fill with the final remains -- the bleached white bones and skulls of the prairie monarch. They glared from the streambeds, humped under the sagebrush and scattered along the hilltops, markers for bodies valued only by wolves and coyotes, for graves dug only by the wind.

Yet the great expanses could not remain empty. Vacant prairies west of Bismarck were almost immediately cut by other hooves as the grasses became fodder for the bisons' southern cousins. They had tamer ways, longer horns and scarcely any wool at all.

The young man working his way north down the bottom of the Little Missouri canyon in mid-November 1884 reined in his horse and bared his teeth in a squint as he tried to pick the trail out of the gloom. They had a dozen miles to go yet, and he was as anxious as the pony to get out of the bitter cold. However, the river ice was not hard-frozen and he had to be sure of his choice of crossings. The weak sun had long since abandoned the fissured bluffs to darkness; his thick spectacles seemed almost to reduce what light the stars provided. Yet the instant he was sure of the trail he prodded the pony forward, unconcerned as the groaning, cracking surface gave way and his mount lunged and pawed on through icy water to the far shore.

Again and again as they picked their way north through the canyon, they splashed across the winding river. And now it began to snow, dry pellets dropping through the sub-zero cold to obscure the trail even more and muffle the pony's hoofbeats. Nothing else moved or made a sound. Then a wolf howled out of the blackness nearby. It was a spare, cruel, dangerous land, and it was where he needed to be.

It was a long way yet to the ranch. Farther still to the halls of the New York legislature and the machinations of Republican politics. Not far enough from his young wife's grave. Twenty-six-year-old Theodore Roosevelt had every intention of reaching the ranch, but the other destinations were part of a past he had put behind him. The ranch was both his future and his salvation.

The past nine months had been a nightmare of heartbreak and disappointment. First the unbelievable February day when he'd gone from his mother's deathbed to that of his wife. Then the career-killing necessity of supporting a Presidential candidate he deplored in a losing campaign. He was certain the surprising amount of influence he'd built as a state assemblyman in the four years since his graduation from Harvard was destroyed. He did not expect ever to be active in politics again.

Alice's death left a darker shadow, one which even the newborn daughter who survived her could not lift. He'd fled to his newly discovered haven of the Dakota badlands as soon as practicable after her death, and there, seated at a rough-hewn ranch table, allowed himself to write his final expression of grief. "She was beautiful in face and form, and lovelier still in spirit," he wrote. "...And when my heart's dearest died, the light went from my life for ever." He never spoke of her again.

Instead, he'd sought peace through the physical activity he always craved. Leaving the months-old settlement of Medora and riding 33 miles up the wild canyon of the Little Missouri, he'd chosen the site for the ranch which would now be his career. If he found it before he froze.

With the snow increasing, the pony stumbled along an invisible trail and Roosevelt had to face the fact he might not make the ranch. Still, he was sure he was close to a squatter's shack which sat in a grove of cottonwoods three or four miles nearer. He strained to see a light through the storm. Minutes followed long minutes but the darkness remained unbroken.

When he finally stumbled into the cabin it was deserted and empty. There was no light, no fire, no food to welcome him. He was able to get a fire going, but his eager search uncovered nothing to eat. Disappointed and weary, he tramped down to the river, broke ice to get water and made a cup of tea from a packet he carried in his pocket. That was supper. Belly growling, he rolled in his blankets and tried to sleep.

He awoke in the gray dawn to hear sharp-tailed grouse calling and was quickly out with his rifle. The birds made fine targets in the bare trees and he shot the heads off five in succession. Some speedy work with his knife, some salt from his saddle bags, and two of them were roasting by the fire.

There was nothing he liked better than hunting, but he'd not always been able to shoot so accurately. His first gun had proved a frustration when his 14-year-old friends could shoot things he couldn't even see. He'd puzzled about that until they also read a billboard that was just a blur to him. The subsequently purchased spectacles opened a world of wonderful, undreamed clarity.

The eyeglasses had been a problem on his first trip to Dakota the year before to hunt buffalo. They were the finishing touch the skinny, sickly-looking young easterner needed to convince Dakota cowboys he was, indeed, a dude. They were right. He'd spent half his life in a sickbed while his wealthy family paid for private tutors. He'd toured Europe, twice. His manner was affected, his voice squeaky, and he was accustomed to cutaways and canes. He was also unsure of himself -- afraid of the mean horses, grizzly bears and gunfighters the West contained -- wondering if he could survive the challenge he'd chosen.

He had never let the cowboys see the fear. For a week he'd ridden one of their toughest comrades into the cold, rain-soaked ground, and he had shot his bull. Since then he'd added numerous deer, elk, antelope -- even grizzlies -- to his list, and his treasured, custom-made buckskin suit brought fewer and fewer snickers.

Still, he could not make a living hunting. He had to learn the cattle business, and he'd made a good start at that, too. Buoyed by the optimistic talk of the settlers near the Little Missouri, he had invested $14,000 in part ownership of a ranch called the Maltese Cross, ordered $26,000 more in cattle to stock his new Elkhorn Ranch and hired two acquaintances from Maine to run the operation.

He was investing fairly heavily -- to his family's dismay -- but the talk both around the town of Little Missouri and in the east foresaw ready profits of 20 percent or more for cattle ranches on the plains. The buffalo were gone; the incredibly nutritious grass was there for the taking; the Northern Pacific Railroad would provide transportation to market.

What's more, a French nobleman had just founded a town on the opposite side of the river. The Marquis de Mores named the village for his wife, Medora, and began building a livestock and slaughterhouse enterprise he promised would revolutionize the industry. Instead of shipping cattle on the hoof, he'd dress them at Medora and ship the meat in refrigerated cars. That would result in even higher profits, he predicted, and Medora would soon be as large as Omaha.

In 1883 most of the Little Missouri Valley was available and it seemed tailor-made for an energetic, optimistic man. Entranced with the rugged beauty of the area and eager to get in on the ground floor of the business, Roosevelt had bought into the Maltese Cross even as he stalked the handful of surviving buffalo.

His life had experienced vast changes in the year since then, but the changes had only made the ranch he approached more important. Having filled his stomach with the grouse, he rode on to find his two New Englanders felling logs for his ranch house.

The point on the river's west side had been a green haven when he last saw it, deep in grass and shaded by arching cottonwoods, the verdant bottom stretching west for 300 yards to the base of colorful cliffs. He had pictured the cabin -- to be one of the largest in the badlands -- looking out across the river to the carved and fissured faces of the cliffs which hemmed the stream's east side.

Now the scene was white and hard and cold, the trees gray sentinels over the frozen river. It matched his mood, but he was not one to brood. He picked up an ax and attacked one of the large cottonwoods at the base of the cliff. In the next two days he downed 17 trees. It was only about a third as many as the Maine woodsmen cut, but his methods were more determined than systematic; he had to grin when he heard one describe his trees as "beavered down."

However his mind needed something to chew on, also, and he talked with the men about a lawless element that seemed intent on intimidating him and other ranchers. Since the county was not yet organized, Roosevelt could see the ranchers would have to maintain their own order. He knew Montana had a successful stockmen's association (which encompassed a picked group of vigilantes to enforce the law) but efforts to begin an organization in Dakota had failed. He was determined to change that. In late November, ignoring blizzards and temperatures ranging to 20 degrees below zero, he headed upriver, visiting each ranch and asking the men to meet in Medora on December 19. Then he settled in at the Maltese Cross and devoted himself to challenging the badlands.

Day after day he went out after game through country frozen hard as granite. The cold, so intense it was another presence, stealing the breath, wrapping the forehead in pain, seemed to him "to brood over the earth like the shadow of silent death." The temperature plunged to 50 below; refused to climb past -10 for two weeks at a stretch. The trees groaned and cracked through the long nights, while the river lay "fixed and immovable as a bar of bent steel." In spite of fur cap and gloves he came home with frozen cheeks, frostbitten fingers. The world was of iron, and he loved it. He set himself to be its match.

When he wasn't hunting for grouse, black-tailed deer, antelope or bighorn sheep, he helped the men chop wood or took the wagon to fetch coal from a vein in Chimney Butte. Or clamped his legs around his share of his 52 new horses until they learned to tolerate a man in a saddle. He'd begun deliberately at the age of 12 to create the healthy body he was born without, forcing his asthmatic lungs and delicate stomach to endure weight lifting, gymnastics, walking, boxing, rowing and camping trips. He still accomplished most of what he did through dogged determination, but his chest was beginning to look less concave and his shoulders were starting to broaden.

The 10 other stockmen who gathered in Medora the week before Christmas evidently sensed his growth. He was younger than most of them, new to the country and less experienced, but he was direct and honest and by now they knew he never bowed to fear. They elected him chairman and asked him to draw up bylaws for the Little Missouri Stockmen's Association. Hereafter when they faced problems, they could present a united front.

Back East for a subdued Christmas with his little daughter Alice, Roosevelt spent the rest of the winter pouring out his impressions and experiences involving the West. By early March 1885 he had written 95,000 lyrical words about the *Hunting Trips of a Ranchman*. He was always writing. Family and friends had been well supplied with letters from the badlands, and he had earlier published a history of the naval war of 1812. However this book about wildlife and hunting captured the public. It radiated vitality and enthusiasm while providing accurate, comprehensive information about the western animals. He had begun observing wildlife as a boy, and the book reflected his deep, scientific interest.

Still, writing about his experiences exhausted the author as the trips themselves had not. The words usually came quickly, but he worried and stewed over the revisions, writing and rewriting and never satisfied with what he produced. In mid-April he arrived back at the Elkhorn looking as pale and drawn as on his first trip west.

Yet, when his 1,000 head of Shorthorn cattle arrived at Medora on May 5, the politician-turned-cowboy found himself in charge of getting them to the Elkhorn. He and four men were faced with a daunting prospect; the canyon was blocked by floodwaters and they would have to herd the thousand head of beef on a circuitous 50-mile route along the divide west of the river.

As they headed north the line of beeves seemed to stretch almost that long, the stronger cattle quickly outdistancing the weaker. Roosevelt put two men at the head, two at the rear and tried to keep the flanks intact. They could not make their pace match the water holes. The third day they watered the beasts at noon, but night found them long miles from the nearest water. They were forced to circle the restless herd in a dry camp. As dusk gathered, Roosevelt shared the first watch with one of his cowboys. The herd bedded down and the riders prepared for a long night. Then, just when darkness was complete, the animals heaved to their feet. Faster than one could think they charged toward freedom. A night stampede! There was nothing worse.

Reacting instantly, Roosevelt spurred his horse alongside the herd. If they scattered into the scores of hills, he would have no herd. He whipped his horse to keep close, just able to see the darker outline of the galloping animals. No time to think about treacherous gopher holes and hidden gullies. Time only to head for each breach in the bellowing mass, turn it back and head for the next. His horse somersaulted into a gorge and he was pitched to the ground. He grabbed a handful of mane and threw himself back on. Off they went, to tumble into another hollow. Dazed, he had a flash of gratitude that he'd not fallen under the galloping hooves, and was off again.

An hour later, bruised and dripping with sweat, he sat on his trembling pony and knew they had won. This part of his investment was safe for the moment. Three days later they trailed into the Elkhorn, and he changed his clothes for the second time that week.

However, he had little leisure to savor his accomplishment. It was time for the general spring roundup, and he rode out with about a dozen of his men to learn the routine and do his part. With their chuck wagon and herd of remounts -- each man took 10 horses for his own use -- he joined one of the institutions of the plains cattle business.

This year the Little Missouri ranchers met at the mouth of Box Elder Creek to begin the giant sweep for cattle that had roamed free since the previous fall. Without fences to limit their wanderings, the herds scattered before storms, drifted as they grazed and mixed until a man's cows might be anywhere in the country. Now, with new calves tailing their mothers, it was time to gather them in and mark each with the appropriate brand.

Seeking cows and calves out of numberless canyons and hollows, herding them into camp, cutting out and branding the newcomers and controlling the huge herds meant five weeks of strenuous but essential work, and Roosevelt was determined to carry his weight.

The distances would have appalled the average New Yorker. The ranchers planned to cover more than 200 miles along the Little Missouri and west into Montana, and the circle riders would cover that five times over while combing every pocket and ravine along the way. Often they rode 100 miles a day, up and down, in and out of streams, through brush and cactus, pushing cows who made every attempt to go the other way.

That took from 3 a.m. until noon. Then dust rose from every quarter as the teams of riders drove in their reluctant quarry.

While a couple of men kept the herd corralled, the others grabbed a quick dinner and a new horse for the afternoon's work. By turn, each rancher sent a man or two into the herd to sort out the cows with his brand and work each gently to the edge of the herd. Now the cows which had resisted the gathering refused to leave it. It became a contest between horse and cow, the cow plunging, twisting and wheeling back toward the herd; the small, lithe cutting pony matching it stride for stride, anticipating, blocking, thwarting its moves with grace that was a joy to watch.

Roosevelt readily admitted he was not much with a rope, and his eyes were not sharp enough to pick out the brands, but once the calf was cut out he was quick to wrestle it to the branding fire and hold the struggling animal until the brand was burned into its hide. Then he loosed that squalling creature and went after the next. It was sweaty, dirty, exhausting work.

He was aware he had to prove himself to the men who did not know him. He'd grown to expect jokes about "Four-eyes" the first day or two with a new group -- was conscious of the audience which gathered around as he mounted his horse each morning, hoping for a show. They often got it, because four of his string of ponies were scarcely broken broncos. They fought the rope, the hackamore, the saddle and any man's touch. One had to be blindfolded before Roosevelt could get near him, and when the bandana was released he went into a continuous series of stiff-legged jumps, reversing ends with each jump. Whirling around and around, the dizzy rider finally had to grab the saddle front and back while his hat, glasses and gun flew off in different directions. But he hung on.

Finally other cowboys whipped the horse into a gallop and the dude rode him the rest of the morning. Another horse threw him repeatedly, until a sympathetic cowboy offered his help in quieting the animal. Roosevelt refused his offer and, nose bleeding, kept climbing back aboard until the pony gave up the battle. Jokes about "Four-eyes" became things of the past.

It was a huge horse he'd named Ben Butler that nearly did him in. On a cold, rainy morning two weeks into the roundup he was assigned to ride the outer circle and decided he needed Ben Butler's stamina. The mean-eyed outlaw had a reputation for a special trick; he liked to fall backward on his rider. Roosevelt had hardly pushed his foot in the stirrup when the horse reared and fell backward on him. Smashed beneath the great weight, Roosevelt felt a sharp pain in his shoulder. But when freed he remounted and tried to get the horse to move. When not even being dragged with ropes could make the stubborn horse move his feet, Roosevelt chose another mount and got on with his work. For two more weeks he worked with the point of his shoulder broken, wincing with pain every time he tried to raise his arm past a certain point.

On they searched, past the Big Ox Bow, through Tipi Bottom to the base of Chimney Butte. Rain continually plagued them and before they made their beds at night they had to wring out their blankets. On June 2 Roosevelt had just pulled his tarpaulin over him for what sleep he could get in the downpour when the call rang out for help with the herd. He sprinted to his horse and just reached the milling animals when there was a stab of lightning, a crack of thunder and the herd was tails up and on the run. He spurred his pony and rode to help head off his second stampede.

One moment he was galloping alongside the cattle, catching glimpses of their tossing horns and rolling eyes with each lightning flash. The next moment they disappeared and he and his horse were airborne over the river bank. They plunged into the water with the herd, fought for balance, sloshed across and ran on. By now the bunch he chased had begun to dwindle, and he finally halted them in a grove of trees. Three times they bolted again and three times he brought them to a halt. Satisfied they would finally stay put, he swung off his exhausted horse and leaned against a tree until dawn. Then he worked his way back toward camp, gathering up strays as he went.

In camp, breakfast was over and the men were starting out to ride the circle. Roosevelt swallowed a few bites of biscuit and coffee, mounted another horse and went off to ride the hills another 10 hours. Then he changed horses again and worked the herd until sunset. After 40 hours in the saddle he fell asleep when his body touched the blankets, but he was up as usual at 4 a.m. for another day. He was thin to the point of gauntness, bleached white with alkali, but he had the respect of every man.

He respected them in turn. Gone was any hint of eastern snobbery or elitism. He could appreciate self-reliance, endurance, perseverance, courage and a hard morality -- "the stern, manly qualities that are invaluable to a nation."

Evidently he needed only a few square meals back at the ranch to repair the ravages of the roundup, for reporters who interviewed him on his next trip east saw him as "rugged, bronzed and in the prime of health," his New York accent replaced with a confident western twang, his walk sturdy, his bearing firm and his voice "strong enough to drive oxen." The dude had become "a thorough Westerner."

Just how thoroughly he'd absorbed the Western ethic would probably have astounded the reporter. After an idyllic autumn on the ranch and another winter in the east, Roosevelt returned to the Elkhorn again on March 19, 1886. He was just in time to watch the Little Missouri acting like its namesake. The river had thawed in February that year, but it had since refrozen. A day after his arrival Roosevelt was conscious of a distant rumble that gradually became a low roar. Finally, around the bend above the ranch house, they could see the cause: a gigantic ice jam had formed upriver and was on its way to the Missouri.

They watched it crest like an ocean wave, pour jagged blocks of ice over the crest, and plow its way down the riverbed. It was frightening to see it come relentlessly on, propelled by the water behind it, piling up in mid-river and spilling out along both shores. It ground and tore the cottonwoods along the bank, and for a few moments, when it attacked the trees in front of his porch, Roosevelt feared for the ranch house itself. That danger passed, but the river he looked on was so changed he hardly knew it. Huge piles of ice edged its bed and stretched from each side nearly to midstream; there a channel of black water raced furiously between sheer ice walls.

That night he thought the ice masses glittered like crystal in the moonlight, but the enchantment soon vanished as the ice blackened and shrunk and became an ugly obstacle. They needed to cross the river to care for the horses they pastured on the other side and to hunt, and they kept a small boat for the purpose. By the time they had clambered over the ice, heaving the boat along as they climbed, Roosevelt felt like an arctic explorer.

However he never recognized obstacles when game was in the offing, and one morning he was about to embark to track down a pair of cougars on the river's east side when they discovered the boat was gone. A cut tether rope and a red woolen mitten left on the ice told them it had been stolen.

They knew immediately who must have taken it. The only other boat on the Little Missouri belonged to suspected cattle-and-horse-thief Mike Finnegan, who lived some 20 miles above the Elkhorn. The mean-tempered Finnegan, who lived with two other shady characters, had managed to escape the vigilantes the previous fall, and they knew he was anxious to leave the country.

A check of his littered shack proved their theory; it was deserted. With travel impossible for horses, the three had taken the Elkhorn's boat to make sure no one could follow them.

Furious at the deed, and unable to follow the thieves any other way, Roosevelt set his men to building a flat-bottomed scow. However, he felt more than anger at the theft. He was certain if the thieves were not pursued and brought to justice he would be taken for an easy mark, and the Elkhorn would become the target of every lawbreaker in the territory. Despite the 60 outlaws Montana vigilantes had disposed of the preceding fall, there were other men as trigger-ready as Finnegan who would be quick to take advantage. He could not and would not submit meekly to any injustice.

For three long days the two New Englanders toiled on the boat while their quarry widened their lead. Then for three more days a blizzard rattled the windows. Incapable of doing nothing, Roosevelt kept his mind occupied by beginning to write a biography of Sen. Thomas Hart Benton which he had promised a publisher, and on March 30, when the three of them finally were able to load their two weeks' supplies, he tucked a book by English poet and critic Mathew Arnold in with the pistols, rifles and ammunition they would need on their manhunt.

The river they poled and paddled twisted in every direction between cliffs of clay and sandstone that were brown one moment, yellow the next, purple, then red. Black bands of coal streaked across the faces of points eroded into shapes that reminded Roosevelt of crouching goblins. In narrow reaches they floated through ice walls ten feet high and the cottonwood trunks glared white, shredded of bark. Miniature icebergs splashed noisily from the frozen walls, and now and again they were startled as loosened chunks of cliff face plunged into the stream.

By noon the next day they were farther north than Roosevelt had ever been. There was no law -- scarcely a settler -- in the badlands between them and the Missouri. If and when they caught up with Finnegan -- or if he surprised them with an ambush -- the three easterners would be on their own.

The raw wind conspired to blow in their faces no matter how the channel twisted; in spite of the current they had to labor with paddles to make any progress. Long before they stopped for the night the grips of the oars were coated with ice.

The third day began fortunately when they were able to shoot three deer to replenish their supplies. They pushed off again with glad hearts, but as the hours wore on the intense cold numbed both their bodies and spirits. Then, nearly 100 miles north of the ranch, they rounded a bend and saw the Elkhorn's boat. A few yards back from shore a spiral of smoke curled up from a patch of brush.

They had caught up with the thieves. Finnegan, who had once laid siege to the whole town of Medora with his rifle; burly half-breed Ed Burnsted, and drink-dulled Chris Pfaffenbach were someplace on shore.

Quickly they held a whispered conference as they stripped off their heavy coats and pulled for the bank. Roosevelt buckled on his pistol and leapt out to provide cover as they beached the boat. Finnegan was a good shot and he had no scruples. If he saw them first they were easy targets. Hearts racing, they crept toward the campfire.

Only one figure sat by the fire, relaxed and unaware, his weapons on the ground beside him. When the three ranchmen stepped into view with leveled guns he made no move to resist. It was the old German, Pfaffenbach, who without his friends had neither the wit nor the will to challenge them. The other two thieves were out hunting, he said. Quickly they secured his guns and ordered him to sit silent where he was on threat of death. Then they crouched behind a bank and waited for the hunters to return.

For more than an hour they knelt in the cold quiet. Then they heard voices and looked up to see Finnegan and Burnsted approaching through the sagebrush, the sun glinting off the barrels of their shouldered rifles. On they came, confident and unaware, Finnegan's red hair and beard bobbing, a bright spot in the dull landscape. When they were within 20 yards the impromptu lawmen stood up and Roosevelt shouted for the thieves to put up their hands.

Covered by three guns, the half-breed Burnsted obeyed at once, dropping his gun. Red Finnegan hesitated. His grip tightened on his rifle as he glanced around to gauge his chances. But Roosevelt stepped toward him, centered his rifle on his chest and repeated the command. Finnegan muttered an oath and dropped his gun.

They had their thieves. But how to keep them? In this cold, if they were tied hand and foot they'd be frozen by morning. There was nothing to do but keep guard through the night. After searching the three carefully, tying their weapons in a bedroll and making them take off their boots, the ranchers bedded the outlaws down in buffalo robes by the fire. They decided each of them would stand watch half the night for two nights, then sleep the third. Roosevelt loaded a double-barreled shotgun with buckshot and took the first watch.

When dawn broke on April 2 they divided their prisoners (and the loot they had collected on their trip downriver) between the two boats and headed for a ranch about 30 miles farther on where they hoped to find help. However before dark they were staring at another ice jam. It was black and solid, filling the channel for several miles. They could not go upstream against the current; they could either abandon their boats and goods and walk, or wait for a thaw. They decided to wait.

"Hung up by ice," Roosevelt wrote in his diary on April 3. He repeated the entry on April 4. On April 5 they worked downstream a couple of miles. On April 6 they crept one or two more, only to be stopped again. At night the water in the pail froze solid. Scarcely any melting took place before noon. One of them had to watch the prisoners every minute, day and night. And they were near the Killdeer Mountains now, so they were watching for Indians also. Small bands of braves often roamed from the Sioux reservation, sometimes doing harm to settlers who looked vulnerable.

That Indians had been around recently was certain; there was no game to be had. As their supplies dwindled to nothing but flour, two of the cattlemen hunted while the third stood guard.

Their hunts were fruitless. As they moved from one grove of barren cottonwoods to another, or climbed the bluffs to stare across the empty prairie, Roosevelt was struck with the bleak, brown lifelessness of the scene. The only thing that moved was the river, and unleavened bread made with its yellowed water was their only food.

Still, he'd come prepared with food for his mind and in spite of hunting, fighting the river ice and sleep-short nights he retained the energy to read. As the days dragged on he devoured *Anna Karenina* from start to finish, thrilling over Tolstoy's words. He finished his volume of Mathew Arnold and borrowed the *History of the James Brothers* from his captives, surprised to find they also carried several "silly society novels." The outlaws, assured repeatedly they would be shot, made no attempt to escape, but the ranchers began to feel the strain of being constantly alert.

On April 8, Roosevelt was about to concede defeat and release the captives he could not feed when he made one last hike on the prairie in hopes of finding a ranch. He came on an outlying cow camp. The ranch -- and help -- was still 15 miles away in the foothills of the Killdeer Mountains, but the cowpuncher lent him a bronco and the next day he was back at the river with the news that he'd hired a wagon, a team of horses and a driver. They marched their captives to the ranch.

Then, reluctant to abandon their boats and gear, and sure the jam was about to break, Roosevelt instructed his men to return to the river and take their belongings on down to Mandan. Meanwhile, driven by a bewildered settler who could not understand why he didn't just hang the robbers, he started the prisoners south for the nearest town, Dickinson, 40 miles away.

Only the prisoners and the driver rode. Roosevelt walked behind, his Winchester ready. He knew nothing about the settler, he reasoned, and the prairie soil was too wet and heavy, the team too small to allow a runaway escape. He could watch them more safely from a distance than in the close confines of the wagon.

It took him two days and a night to complete his mission. Trudging through ankle-deep mud and a cold misty rain, conscious of the odds against him, he carefully kept his distance from the thieves. As darkness closed down the first day, he was relieved to come on a settler's cabin where they could take shelter. But exhausted as he was he resolved not to sleep; the closer the jail, the more chance his prisoners would make a break for it. He ordered all three captives onto an upper bunk bed and spent the night sitting with his back against the cabin door, his gun across his knees, grimly forbidding himself to sleep. When he limped down Dickinson's main street the next afternoon and turned his prisoners over to the sheriff, he'd not slept for 36 hours.

Yet the doctor he sought out to care for his blistered feet did not think he looked unduly tired. "He was all teeth and eyes, but even so he seemed a man unusually wide awake," the doctor recalled later. "...He impressed me and he puzzled me, and when I went home to lunch, an hour later, I told my wife that I had met the most peculiar and at the same time the most wonderful man I had ever come to know. I could not understand why he was out there on the frontier.... it seemed to me that he belonged...in the East, in the turmoil of large affairs."

Others came to the same conclusion. On July 4 Roosevelt was a featured speaker at the Dickinson Independence Day celebration, and a reporter who listened to the speech and later visited with the speaker was so impressed with his consecration to high ideals of citizenship and service that he came to the conclusion Roosevelt would one day be president of the nation.

The rancher expressed no surprise at the idea. "If your prophecy comes true," he said, "I will do my part to make a good one." He was 28 years old. He returned east to re-enter politics, and 14 years later he was elected Vice-President under William McKinley. In 1901 McKinley's assassination moved the rancher to the White House, where he served seven years.

Remarried, father of six children, author of two more books on hunting, a four-volume history of the West and several other books, hero of the Spanish-American War, winner of the Nobel Peace Prize, he gave his years on the Little Missouri much credit for his achievements. There in the badlands he found not only physical well-being but strength of purpose, appreciation and respect for the individual, and the will to try to shape his country's future.

"I have always said I would not have been President if it had not been for my experience in North Dakota," he said in later years. "(It was) the most important educational asset of all my life."

Yet his feelings for the West were deeper than that. He remembered riding through air "fresh and sweet and odorous" with scents of springtime, galloping "for miles at a stretch with his horse's hooves sinking at every stride into the carpet of prairie roses," while the meadowlark "found a rich, strong voice." He remembered the pealing notes of a rutting elk's call echoing "through the dark valleys as if from silver bugles," and how it felt to come home from a frigid winter hunt and see "the red gleam of the firelight as it shines through the ranch window and flickers over the trunks of the cottonwoods." He remembered the hard outlines of the cliffs "gradually growing soft and purple as the flaming sunset" faded and died away, to leave the Little Missouri gleaming "like running quicksilver in the moonlight." He never forgot the feeling of absolute freedom he had out on a solitary hunt; the total satisfaction of finally knowing he could cope.

Roosevelt returned many times to find release in the West's pleasures and renew lasting friendships. Once, considering which chapter of his life he would choose to retain if only one could remain in his memory, he said, "I would take the memory of my life on the ranch with its experiences close to nature and among the men who lived nearest her."

A Conquerer With a Coupling Pin

When Roosevelt made his 4th of July speech in Dickinson in 1886, grass which should have been soft and green was already crisping for lack of rain. The rancher-politician looked out over a countryside that cracked and dried in the shimmering heat. The only clouds rained grasshoppers which raced the cattle for the scanty grass. There were too many cattle, Roosevelt knew, too many mouths scouring the ground for another bite. Ranchers eager for profits had not stopped to consider whether there was grass enough to support their ambitions.

Had the grass been plentiful it might not have mattered.

When winter came that year it brought the precipitation which summer denied. Blizzard followed blizzard, whipping granules of ice into the cattle's hides, burying the canyons and gullies in ice-crusted shrouds. The herds, unable to find either shelter or food, were driven by the wind until they dropped of exhaustion on the frozen prairie or piled atop one another in a draw. When Roosevelt returned to the Elkhorn in April 1887 he counted 23 corpses in one brush patch. Only a few hundred of his steers survived. There were not enough cattle left alive on the Little Missouri to justify a roundup.

Roosevelt hung on to his cherished Elkhorn ranch house, but after 1887 it was a hunting lodge instead of a home. Eastern and European capitalists who had financed many of the ranches retreated to lick their wounds, and most of the residents of Medora and Little Missouri moved on in search of better fortune.

However there were others who still considered the unsettled West a cornucopia of opportunities. One Minnesota man looked across the arc of the upper Missouri and saw wheat fields and grain elevators, fields of potatoes, stockyards, coal mines and copper smelters. He had used his expertise to populate much of the Red River valley and had already probed west to Devil's Lake in Dakota. He had been to the Missouri's Great Falls to assess their power and carefully studied all the land along the river between. In the spring of 1887, undeterred by the lesson dealt the livestock industry, he was ready to make his move.

On April 1, 1887, the new settlement of Minot began to stir long before it was light. Actually, it had been weeks since the nights had known much quiet. With a huge camp of 10,000 men just west of town and trains thundering in at all hours, no one had been getting much sleep. The St. Paul, Minneapolis and Manitoba Railroad had given birth to the town just the summer before -- already five hotels, 12 saloons, three general stores and a laundry kept the new depot company -- and no one was about to object if Jim Hill's engines made a little noise.

They made more than a little. As soon as harvest was over the previous fall the materials trains had begun chugging in, loaded to capacity with scrapers, long, thick timbers, pilings, logs for ties, kegs of spikes and 50-pound rails. Switch engines worked in 12-hour shifts to organize and deposit the cargo. The stacks at track's end grew to enormous proportions, until it looked like enough equipment to lay track to the ends of the earth.

Engineers, bridge-building gangs, 3,000 grading crews with their hefty teams, and steel gangs piled into town with every cowhand, immigrant and drifter in the territory in need of a job. Some of them had worked on the 117-mile stretch from Devil's Lake to Minot, but the job they faced now was almost six times that long.

They weren't heading for the ends of the earth, but they were aiming for Helena, Montana Territory, and it seemed nearly that far. They'd have to take with them not only every last spike, maul, drag shovel, pick and wheelbarrow, but every bushel of grain for the teams, every can of beans, barrel of flour, blanket, every triple-decked bunk car and tent for the men.

When they moved out at first light on April 1 the frost was not yet out of the prairie. However, Jim Hill was not one to wait until things were easy. He'd begun this line, laid out hundreds of thousands of dollars for surveys and plans before he'd even known if he could legally cross the land involved. Western Dakota and northern Montana territories were reservation land. The remnants of the Mandan, Gros Ventre and Arikara tribes had just ceded most of their land west of the Missouri, but at the time he'd persuaded his stockholders to risk the new line, no white man had the right to lay one log atop another west of Fort Berthold.

Only two months before had Congress finally given permission for the Manitoba to buy the necessary right-of-way from the tribes. Hill knew the streets of Washington, D.C. almost as well as those of St. Paul, and his letter books were thick with the correspondence required to convince reluctant European capitalists they should risk money on a line some called "Hill's Folly."

But the doubters had thought he was headed for ruin before. He was sure he would reach Helena first. The bridging crews had moved ahead, to fly the track over creeks and stand trestles in the coulees, like the six-tiered wall of timber triangles they were leaving behind in Gassman Coulee just west of Minot. Hill's engines were to slow for curves and labor uphill only as much as absolutely necessary. Not one degree, not one foot more.

Largely self-educated, Hill liked to quote from Plutarch about a Roman road builder who, when he met valleys or rivers caused them to be filled up or bridged, "so well leveled that, all being of an equal height on both sides, the work presented one uniform and beautiful prospect."

The most beautiful thing about the prospect, of course, was the profit to be made from a line that could transport heavier loads. As Hill often reminded his engineers, an extra quarter of a percent in grade was equivalent "to having to lift 1,000 tons 13 feet in the air for each mile of rail traversed." They were not allowed to forget, and in case they had, Hill tromped over, measured and approved every inch of the route before the course was set.

The grading gangs swarmed west, clucking to their teams, using their own weight to force the wooden blades into the earth, scraping a six-foot scar on each side of the survey line. Behind them others cleared away the sage and brush and scooped the broken ground onto the untouched six-foot strip between, where horse-drawn drag shovels leveled and packed it until it began to resemble a roadbed two or three feet above the prairie. (Hopefully the infamous Dakota snows would blow off the track.) With some of the ground still frozen, the work was slow. Sometimes they had to call in the powder men to blow their way clear. Then for a few moments the acrid smell of black powder overpowered the scent of sage and dust and sweat.

Behind the graders came the wagons of ties, squared only on the important side, which laborers heaved into place between two ropes stretched tautly down the bed. They were scarcely set -- a stride apart -- when the iron car arrived, the team blowing with the effort of pulling the load of rails for a power that would largely replace them.

Now the specialists took over and the noises became metallic: the dull ring of a rail slid from the flat car and dropped to the ties, the clank of four rail movers clamping to the rail top so the muscular Irishmen could lift it into place, the clang of the spike mauls driving the spikes home in the ties. Three blows usually did the job; then it was on to the next tie, and the next and the next.

The workers may not have known that no gang had ever laid 643 miles of track in one season from one end of track. Jim Hill knew.

He knew everything worth knowing about the railroad business. And he knew he and the other investors in the Manitoba line stood to lose $1 million if he failed. James Jerome Hill had no intention of failing. Napoleon was one of his heroes; while still a boy in Canada he'd signaled his intent to be something more than plain Jim Hill when he took the name of the emperor's brother for a middle name. He knew the value of "having nerve." The fact that the scoffers in Europe, know-it-alls in St. Paul -- and even some of his own stockholders -- called this line another of his follies only made him more determined.

An eastern journalist had sneered that the Manitoba Road would find nothing but buffalo bones to ship east and when those ran out the country would go back to the Indians. Few people could understand why Hill and his partners would even attempt to build a line without the huge land grants every other transcontinental line had been awarded. Especially when the line they planned would roughly parallel the already established Northern Pacific, which arrowed west from Bismarck to the Yellowstone, up to Helena and on through the Rockies to the west coast.

Hill shook his head at such lack of vision. There were plenty of buffalo bones, to be sure, but he saw more life than death in the expanse which lay west. He had always been able to see beyond the next season and into the next decade. The 50-year-old entrepreneur had climbed steadily in the transportation business since beginning as a steamship company clerk in St. Paul in 1856. He had walked the Red River valley when it was the domain of fur trappers, noticed how the grass grew rich and strong where the carts of the traders cut the earth, and established a packet line to serve the wheat farms he knew would someday populate the countryside. He'd gone out searching for coal while others thought only of wood, studied it carefully, assured himself of a good supply by buying Iowa mines and begun a prosperous fuel business.

He was a river man by trade and instinct, but in 1876, watching immigrants pile out of the cars of the Northern Pacific, he'd formed a partnership with wealthy Canadian friends and risked his business and his five children's home to buy the bankrupt St. Paul and Pacific Railroad. It was no more "than two streaks of rust and a right-of-way." That was his first "folly."

Success began with knowledge, he thought, and he was never happier than when he was absorbing it. His friends were amazed at his ability to "vacuum up" the contents of a book and keep it forever in his memory. From there it required only "work, hard work, intelligent work and then some more work," he said cheerfully when pressed for the secret of success.

He might have underscored "intelligent work." The Saint Paul and Pacific had land grants worth $13 million which, wisely used, could finance construction on the line. The partners mortgaged themselves to the nth degree to raise $5.5 million and bought the road. Walking a path mined with government regulations and time limits, sabotaging rival roads and continual financial crises, Hill taught himself the railroad business on the job, learned to lay track, and proceeded to give other railroaders lessons in efficiency. By 1878 the St. Paul had a connection with Winnipeg and passenger trains moving north and west on the line were pulling a dozen cars instead of four or five. By 1879 he was buying bigger engines and firing them with coal. The rusty streaks of his first folly were turning to gold. By 1880 he'd increased the net profit by $1 million. He shoveled the profits into more track, more and better equipment. By 1883 his railroad stock was worth $14 million. He'd probed west from the Red River and had trains running to Devil's Lake in Dakota Territory. With the branch lines he'd thrown out as farm-to-market roads he was supervising 1,200 miles of track.

He knew every inch. When he traveled the road a constant stream of memos swirled in his wake. There were coal stains on the depot at Grand Forks, rough track on this section, idle cars setting on that. This depot had a damaged plank in the platform, that employee had whisky on his breath. There were neglected materials trackside here, poorly located water tanks there. Most of his employees would have been astonished to learn he spotted all these defects with only one eye; vision in the other had been destroyed by an accident when he was a boy.

In the early 1880s he kept occupied by establishing between Minneapolis and St. Paul one of the country's most efficient freight yards, by helping to plan the Canadian Pacific's transcontinental line, and by building a bridge to carry two tracks across the Mississippi just above St. Anthony's Falls. His bridge, however, would not be the creaking, wooden passageway other railroads called bridges. It would be of stone and it would curve across the water. The scoffers watched its halting progress and called it his second folly. At times he despaired that the stone arches of its sweeping curve would ever bear freight, but when it was finished in 1883 he had the satisfaction of knowing it would outlast him and probably his children.

He also bought a 3,000 acre farm outside St. Paul because he found agriculture to be of compelling interest. Unlike most railroad barons of his day, he believed the prosperity of the railroad depended on the prosperity of the communities it served.

"The railroad...is in partnership with the land," he preached to anyone who would listen. Because the success of the railway rose or fell with that of the people it served, he decided to make sure they were successful. He studied varieties of wheat and suggested better seed. The immigrants' dependence on one crop worried him and he encouraged them to diversify. He began importing the finest bulls and cows from Scotland, certain they could endure Minnesota winters. To the surprise -- and suspicion -- of the farmers, he offered free Polled Angus or Shorthorn bulls, blooded pigs and Shropshire lambs to anyone who would care for them and allow them to service his neighbors' stock.

By then he was sure he had "all and more than I can ever want and all that will be good for those who come after me." He'd built a handsome new white brick mansion which boasted two indoor bathrooms, added an art gallery to display the French moderns he'd grown fond of and installed a tutor for his brood, now increased to six.

The children his Catholic wife, Mary, had presented him were an important part of his life. He valued Sunday afternoons when they all lingered at the dinner table as the sun glowed through the stained-glass window, or gathered around the grand piano for a rousing session of the Scottish ballads and Protestant hymns of his childhood, or listened with appreciation as he recited Robert Burns' poetry by the page.

His fortune was made. Those who did not know him well expected him to sell out and retire. Earlier in life he'd anticipated the day it would be possible. He was growing stouter around the middle and his chin whiskers were streaked with gray. Neuralgia gripped him in the winter and he was surprised how often he felt fatigued at the end of his 12-hour days.

He was constantly concerned with family. Frequently away on business, he required associates at home to inform him daily about his family's welfare. They'd lost one baby; he'd nearly lost Mary to pneumonia; she usually went south for the winter now. With nine children someone was nearly always sick; he lived in dread of telegrams. He fretted about what kind of educational foundation the tutor was giving the children and planned where his sons would go to college.

Yet family, farm and wide-spreading interests were not enough to occupy his mind. He discovered he needed more than the security and comfort money brought; the life of the moneyed gentry held little appeal. He couldn't bear to abandon the young road he'd nursed into being; knew without question no one could develop its potential the way he could. And his energy demanded action, a challenge, a problem he could grasp in his teeth and worry to solution. Looking west he saw one.

He'd always been intrigued by the Far East and the trade it represented. As a boy he'd tried to ship out to the Orient. In more recent years he'd hoped the Canadian Pacific might give the Manitoba a link with the west coast and all that it promised. But if that failed...?

For years he'd watched adventurers leave St. Paul for points west, seen some of them come back with fortunes in gold or silver. Since 1880 he'd been studying western Montana. A St. Paul friend had moved to Helena and Hill questioned him closely on the resources of the area. It has range land, copper and coal, he was told, and the Great Falls would provide an ideal site for power and a city. The Manitoba could come out the north side of the Missouri to Fort Benton -- a far less expensive route than the rival Northern Pacific had found to the south -- and if he wanted to go farther yet there was said to be a pass over the Rockies at the source of the Marias River. Out the Missouri, up the Milk River, over the Rockies via the Marias -- it was the route Isaac Stevens had recommended 35 years before -- a path the Northern Pacific had ignored.

It was an exciting prospect, but Hill never did anything on impulse. He invested privately in land around the Great Falls and bided his time. In 1884 the Montana boosters persuaded him to come out to see for himself. He journeyed out to see the falls which had thrilled travelers ever since Lewis and Clark, shoot prairie chickens and sit around the campfire talking railroad. He went home to order a preliminary survey of the route between Helena and the mines of Butte and to send a geologist to study the coal fields around Sand Coulee southeast of the falls.

That fall he was back in Helena with eastern money men. On this trip he traveled west by wagon, stopping from time to time as he always did when assessing the promise of an area, to thrust a shovel into the prairie and finger the soil.

The pieces began to click into place. The coal was good quality lignite. Even more promising, the Red Mountain district seemed to contain high-grade gold and silver ore. A road between Butte and Helena, although expensive, was possible. And if someone else didn't preempt the route north from Helena to the Great Falls, the rival Northern Pacific would. Hill organized the Red Mountain Coal Mining Company, the Great Falls Water Power and Light Company, and took out a charter for the Montana Central Railway. In the spring of 1886 he ordered crews to begin preparing the roadbed north through Prickly Pear Canyon towards Great Falls, 97 miles away. When the Northern Pacific refused to transport the rails for his new line at a reasonable price, he shrugged. Soon he would have a better way to get them there.

He was convinced it was time to open the northern plains along the Missouri. Never interested in extending a line for its own sake, he was confident settlement would follow as soon as the way was opened. It was time to bring in plows to cut the virgin sod, to pasture cattle on the infinity of grassland, to plant depots and watch towns grow around them. He would throw track across the 643 miles between Minot and Helena. Beyond Helena loomed the great northwestern forests and the ocean; beyond that a continent teeming with customers. If things looked right, he might go farther.

Hill had a Scotsman's regard for the dollar. At home his children wore ready-made clothes and hand-me-down coats, and the girls got new bonnets only when the old were outgrown. In business he had found, "It pays to be where the money is spent."

As the spring days first thawed and then firmed the Dakota prairie, the work crews learned they could look up nearly any time and see his short, stocky form observing their work from buckboard or horseback as he hurried out to approve the final route. He had engineers and a contractor he respected, but he trusted his judgment above all others. His balding head often glistened in the sun as he bent over the plans and compared them to the lay of the land. He listened carefully when the engineers differed, but the Manitoba went where his stubby finger pointed.

People of the Old Missury

He also was sure only his insistent presence could goad the work along at the pace they must achieve. Winter was a short five months hence and the track was creeping away from Minot. Impatient with incompetence and never able to tolerate shirking, he expected quick obedience and a full day's work, but he knew many of the foremen by name and he was not above bending his own back if the occasion arose. He inspired terror in slackers, loyalty and belief in those willing to work.

The first day they laid 3,000 feet; the second day two miles. By the end of April they'd completed only 35 miles.

However, as May advanced the crews settled into their jobs. The grading crews stretched over dozens of miles; dust rose in a long plume above the prairie and the gangs laboring in their wake. Each would finish its job in turn and then hurry ahead to begin another section; the line was a swirling mass as crews circled constantly to the head of construction and teamsters shuttled back and forth to supply thousands of horses and men with grain and food. Materials trains puffed out the new track to crowd their heels and urge them on.

As May ended they reached the Missouri and gave birth to the tent village of Williston. One hundred eleven miles of new track shone behind them; they'd climbed nearly 300 feet.

Even as they passed, the tents of Williston were being replaced by foundations for log and lumber buildings. Saloons and boarding houses sprang from the prairie, and families swarmed off steamboats, some of them with the goods to stock new stores. Leaving the new trade center they laid track north of old Fort Union, which had served a populace with different needs.

June brought both heat and maddening mosquitoes as they worked west along the Missouri bottom. Many of the horses, unable to stand the climate and the work, collapsed in their traces. It was hard, heavy, dangerous work for man and horse alike and several times a crew had to stop to dig a shallow grave for a man who'd fallen to accident or exhaustion. They were on Indian land now, and the men could often see breech-clouted braves watching their work. Hill was scrupulous about paying the tribes the market price -- 50 cents an acre -- for the 150-foot swath his road cut across the countryside.

They bunched up at Big Muddy Creek while a homemade ferry relayed the advance teams across, then bridged the bottom and surged on past Wolf Point, where a few decades before trappers had piled so many gray hides that the steamer captains named the stop for the cargo they loaded there. Now both the predators and the great herds which provided their prey had vanished.

Twenty-five miles past Wolf Point they left the Missouri's course for that of the Milk River, slanting north along the Milk's more friendly valley. Once around the Bear Paw Mountains, they'd curve back south to reach Fort Benton.

By the first of July they'd laid 191.7 miles of track. By August another 100 stretched behind them. There was nothing in front but empty prairie, nothing behind but track and the ruins of a few abandoned trading posts. September 6 they worked their way along Bull Hook Bottoms, and on September 8 the gangs outdid themselves to lay eight miles of track and reach the most populous place they'd seen since spring. Soldiers spilled out of the brick buildings of eight-year-old Fort Assiniboine to superintend the job, while the band of the 20th Infantry urged the gangs on. At four o'clock that afternoon the grimy, slouch-hatted crews had spiked 60 feet of their ninth mile when, to their disgust, the axle on the iron car broke and ended their day. They groused that they could have done more, but posed proudly while a photographer recorded their best day's work.

Most days they laid about 3.5 miles of track and finished work to fall into their bedrolls without such adulation, thinking less of that day's 1,100 ties set and 4,400 spikes hammered home than of those they'd face in the morning. By the end of the month they had angled south again and passed Fort Benton, Hill's rails spelling the end of jobs for bullwhackers, mule skinners and river men alike. He added insult to injury by sweeping the track around the old river port when less-than-prescient city fathers refused him a right-of-way through town.

As they neared Great Falls they found no such disinterest; Hill's friend began to plan a suitable celebration. But the practical Scotsman vetoed any party until they reached Helena and the end of the job. He knew too well that celebrations would result in hangovers, and bleary-eyed workers would not be eager to swing a maul. Refusing to see two or three days wasted, he ordered the disappointed men out of Great Falls before dawn. By October 1 smoke could stream above 509 miles of track behind them as the locomotives' whistles added their song to the coyotes' chorus.

With the Montana Central's roadbed already prepared through the canyons to Helena, the work proceeded at a rapid pace, and on November 16 they entered Montana Territory's capital. Hill, who had spent the summer shuttling back and forth from St. Paul, headed west again two days later in his personal business car for the appropriate ceremonies.

In his early years he'd traveled the north country by snowshoe and dogsled, swum icy rivers when he had to, and survived one frigid night only by sleeping with his dogs. He'd begun his career as a river man and still loved the excitement of a "city of steamerboats" at the levee. But from the time he'd watched Minnesota's first locomotive, diamond-stacked and shining, arrive in St. Paul by barge 25 years before, and helped load its three freight cars for the 10-mile trip upriver to the end of track, he'd known where the future lay.

He took pride in the line he'd built -- steel rails above, sturdy white oak ties below when even Jim Hill couldn't avoid a sharp curve. His men had loaded and unloaded 16,406 carloads of materials, moved 9.7 million cubic yards of earth and 32,000 cubic yards of rock, and placed nine million feet of timber. Best of all he'd reached the Rockies and 80 percent of his road had a grade of less than 21 feet per mile. He could handle Montana's heaviest ores and still make a profit. The St. Paul, Minneapolis and Manitoba officially absorbed the Montana Central line and two years later Hill was president of a newly organized Great Northern Railway.

The new name symbolized the greater purpose he had been contemplating for years -- a connection with the Pacific ports. He had just launched a fleet of steamships on the Great Lakes that could carry the Manitoba's cargo clear to Buffalo. This final link would make his road a true transcontinental line. He poured over the 13-volume set of Isaac Stevens' 1853-54 survey and hired another Stevens, this one named John F., to find the elusive pass at the source of the Marias.

On December 11, 1889, John Stevens braved -40 degree temperatures to locate a 5,000-foot pass on a Marias River tributary (near the present Glacier National Park entrance). It was almost straight west of the line up the Milk Valley. By spring Hill was ready to tackle the Rockies, the Cascades and the 900 miles to Puget Sound.

Even though the route they mapped to Spokane had "lighter grades, less cost and shorter distances" than the competing Northern Pacific's, it was an engineering nightmare of heavy forest, deep snow, creeks and rivers to be bridged, gorges to be crossed by trestles, embankments to be built and tunnels to be drilled (by hand). Hill pushed for completion in 1892, but even his unceasing efforts and increasingly sharp tongue could not accomplish the impossible. He had to compromise his standards and accept a temporary series of switchbacks to get over the crest of the Cascades until the needed 2.6 miles of tunnel could be drilled. It was January 6, 1893, when the final spike was driven and in June the first Great Northern through passenger train left St. Paul for the coast. The city feted the reluctant Hill, who thought the money would have been better spent on a public library.

In 1901 he enjoyed another triumph when he and his partners gained control of his long-time rival, the Northern Pacific, and could add the midwestern and southern connections of the Chicago, Burlington and Quincy line to his network. Now, as he'd dreamed for years, he could ship cotton to Japan and flour to China while Pacific timber was carried east to the treeless plains. A year later he was sparring with Theodore Roosevelt's trust busters. He lost that battle, but gained Roosevelt's respect and friendship.

Hill, "The Little Giant," by now one of the best-known men in the country, finally relinquished the presidency of the Great Northern to his son in 1907, but he did not retire. He spoke out for scientific farming methods, advocating crop rotation, diversification, better methods of cultivation and improved seed, and Roosevelt invited him to the first conference on the conservation of natural resources.

By 1909 he had written a book detailing his beliefs about economics, transportation and agriculture and was actively recruiting Europeans to homestead the empty land along his line in Montana. *"Three hundred miles of railroad through the Great Reservation and 18 million acres of free government land recently opened to settlers in the Milk River Valley of Montana,"* the line trumpeted.

"Almost an empire in itself."
"Chinook Winds."
"Spring begins in February."
"Millions of acres of these lands yet in the virgin purity inviting the plowman's hand."

They came in droves, many from Scandinavia, transported for next to nothing on Hill's line, to populate the prairie, and with his help prospered -- for a few years. "He has captured more territory with a coupling pin, and made it habitable for man than did Julius Caesar with the sword," one senator said of the man many called "The Empire Builder." He had time to establish a reference library in St. Paul before he died at 77 in 1916, blissfully unaware that the final hard, dry years of the decade would turn his name into a curse on the lips of his Montana settlers.

A millionaire 60 times over, he continued to work through his final illness, ever in touch with the railroad empire he had built. "Most men who have really lived," he had written upon his retirement four years before, "have had, in some shape, their great adventure. This railway is mine."

Chasing Crane's Story

The railway which gave Jim Hill such satisfaction, which poured trainload after trainload of farmers and shopkeepers onto the plains, was only another great weight on the Indians' spirit.

The Swedes, Norwegians and Germans who gazed eagerly from trackside saw only the land's potential, not its past. They could not grieve for what was gone -- they had never galloped in the midst of stampeding buffalo, never bathed their children in a prairie stream, never echoed the call of the wolf. They knew nothing of Chief Joseph's agony, nothing of Sitting Bull's odyssey.

With his land and the buffalo gone, the Hunkpapa chief had tried to get what he could from the white man's world. In 1884 he'd traveled with Bill Cody's Wild West Show, learned white people would pay to stare at him and buy his autograph. By the time the Manitoba pushed west from Minot, he was living on the Standing Rock Reservation in a log house on the Grand River, with chickens scratching in his yard and his children attending the white man's school.

As the new settlers pressed closer to the reservation, coveting its unplowed lands, the government pressured the Sioux to sell nearly half of what they owned. Sitting Bull talked strongly against the sale and refused to yield. Even when the price was more than doubled the following year, 1889, he remained adamant.

But other leaders listened to the government's assurances that selling was in their best interests; that each family should choose a farm and the tribe sell the rest while they still had the right; that they would get the help they needed to learn to farm and still receive their rations as they always had. They heard the promises instead of Sitting Bull's warnings. They signed -- at least enough of them signed that the government considered it done -- and the lack of the old chief's signature was deemed unimportant.

The Sioux gave up all the land between the Cheyenne and White rivers plus a strip along the western edge of the reservation. The bands were divided between six smaller reserves, and by November settlers in North and South Dakota were celebrating their statehood.

Two weeks after the agreement was signed, the promises had been broken. Congress reduced the annual Sioux appropriation, and despite fields that produced dust devils instead of crops, the Sioux beef ration was cut almost in half. That winter, as hunger ate away their resistance, the weakened Indians succumbed to waves of influenza and whooping cough.

Even more deadly was despair. The buffalo, their land, life as they knew it was gone. There was no way to fight, no where to run, no one to help, no hope for tomorrow. Unless -- unless the Great Spirit again turned his ear to their prayers.

 The young woman had been so exhausted she'd fallen asleep before supper was ready. Stiff and sore from a long day on horseback, she'd been gently wakened to eat and had immediately been asleep again. But now, long before dawn would lighten the sides of the tipi, she was awake again. She sat up groggily to see Whirling Hawk's wives raking the coals of the fire and adding new wood, setting the coffee pot over the flames and putting some dried beef to toast. A visitor had appeared out of the empty darkness of the high plains, and he would be cheerfully welcomed and fed regardless of the hour. Like the others she pulled a blanket around her, for even in late July the night air of the Nebraska sand hills could be cool, and listened to what the visitor had to say.

His name was Chasing Crane, it seemed, and he was filled with a strange story, so excited that his words came spilling out in a torrent, and she had to listen intently to catch his meaning.

Elaine Goodale had been speaking Dakota for three years now, but what he was saying was so unexpected that she wondered if she could be understanding it correctly.

"God has appeared to the Crows across the Stony Mountains," he said. "They say he arrived out of nowhere and announced that he was the Savior who once before came upon earth and was killed by the white people."

Around her there were grunts of amazement.

This Messiah was beautiful to look on, Chasing Crane said. He had waving hair and was painted with a sign of power. He had told the Crows he could no longer bear to hear parents crying for their children as they died of hunger and strange diseases brought by the white men. He was going to let down the sky upon all the Whites. He was going to bring back the buffalo for the people.

The Sioux seated around Elaine listened as though spellbound. Almost under their breaths they voiced "*Ai's*" of approval. To have the buffalo again. To have the white man gone. It was too wonderful to imagine.

The men of the hunting party were so moved by Chasing Crane's message they decided to prepare a sweat bath. They filed from the tipi to erect a shelter while their wives heated stones and fixed kettles of water. Seated in the steamy chamber they sang the old songs, and when Elaine drifted off to sleep again it was to the muffled, rhythmic beat of Sioux drums.

She'd shared many new experiences with her adopted people since she'd come to southern Dakota in 1885 to see the Great Sioux Reservation and the families of her pupils at Hampton Normal and Agricultural Institute. Hampton, a boarding school established in Virginia for Blacks, had added an Indian department where she'd taught with growing satisfaction for two years.

However she'd wanted to do something more, and during the summer of 1885 she had financed a six-week tour of the Sioux agencies in southern Dakota by selling accounts of her tour to eastern newspapers. When she stood beside a government schoolhouse at the White River camp of the Brule Sioux, a paintless shack which had never been used, and looked from its broken windows to the shy faces of Indian children who had never seen a book, she knew here was the greater need. She made herself a promise to fill it.

It hadn't been easy. She was 22 and unmarried. She was a reserved, sheltered intellectual, a recognized poet who'd been publishing since she was 13, a daughter of reclusive, bookish New Englanders who'd named her for Tennyson's poetic heroine. She couldn't go alone. Her mother and friends were horrified that she would go at all. The other Hampton teacher who volunteered to go with her was also female and single; the Indian Office refused to appoint two young females to teach at White River.

However Elaine and her friend, Laura Tileston, side-stepped that barrier when Laura managed to secure an appointment as a missionary. The two had arrived to set up housekeeping in a rough board cabin beside the 300 souls in Medicine Bull's camp, eight miles from the agency and any other Whites except the housekeeper they'd hired from Chamberlain. They'd scrubbed the walls of the dilapidated school and set to work.

Elaine had been determined to "begin at the beginning...to blaze a new trail in the obscure corner of a wild land." She'd seen what boarding schools could accomplish, but she believed it "only reasonable and humane" that Indian parents have a chance to educate their children without forcing them into complete separation. She intended to establish a school these children could attend during the day and still return home at night.

In her youthful idealism, she had never imagined how far back a beginning could be.

The rough-hewn benches in her crude classroom were as far removed from the green lawns and brick towers of Hampton Institute as her grimy, frightened young students were from the relatively advanced young braves she'd taught back east. She and her friend taught hygiene along with English, cooking along with reading, the parents along with the children. They set up sewing classes so the girls could make their clothes, and helped the boys cultivate a vegetable garden. Elaine was not only a teacher, but a nurse who carried food to sick children, and an agronomist who tried to help the men with their farming. When inadequate government supplies gave out the teachers wrote to friends in the East and begged for contributions to keep them going.

Although she knew people sometimes took her to be cold, distant and grave, Elaine found herself quickly accepted by the Brule. Ignoring official frowns, she'd immediately begun to learn their language. She was not too refined to join the girls in a game of tag, too dignified to wrestle with a calf that needed feeding, nor too ladylike to adopt the Indian's sensible moccasins, in spite of raised eyebrows at the agency. She'd never had much patience with fashion, never worried much about how she looked.

The longer she knew the Brule, the more she cared for them. She'd never been happier, she realized, even though her writing had to come a poor second to her work with the Indians.

When, during rare leisurely moments or late at night, she sat down with her pen, the Sioux became her subject. She kept educational and religious journals and papers in the East well supplied with informative, sympathetic articles about reservation life.

When her colleague had to return east in 1888, Elaine was determined to stay. Bowing to social necessity, she persuaded her unmarried aunt to come live with her. Then she'd begun traveling to different parts of the 30,000-square-mile reservation so she could get to know the six separate agencies and the wilder tribes. That's how she'd come to be in Whirling Hawk's deer-hunting camp the summer night in 1889 when Chasing Crane brought the news of the Indian Messiah.

The night after Chasing Crane's strange visit the weather turned violent. Thunder cracked and a gale tore at the tipis until it was impossible to sleep. Elaine sat up with the rest, wondering if the lodge would collapse on their heads, listening to the rain and wind while Whirling Hawk's wives silently stirred the fire.

The brave smoked steadily. She wondered if the smoke was a sacrifice to the gods, or if he just did it to keep up his spirits. Whirling Hawk had not been anxious to have her company on the hunt. The 50-year-old brave was an old-fashioned man and she'd had to beg hard, and pay good money, before he allowed her to accompany the five wagons that carried his family group. His two wives, sisters whom she knew only slightly, had tried to convince her she wouldn't like the life. They'd be gone for weeks, they said. Where they went and when they returned depended entirely on where and when they found deer and antelope. It would be like the old days.

It was. Almost. She bathed with her Sioux sisters in streams and ponds, learning from them how to preserve her modesty. She ate wild berries and breathed the aromatic smoke when the men stripped red willow bark for their pipes. She was hungry when they were, and rejoiced with them when Whirling Hawk shot the first antelope. Like them she ate the liver with gusto, although she took time to broil her portion briefly.

She joined them in hysterical laughter as the men threw themselves around a pond to capture a flock of half-grown ducks. She watched a young mother give birth on the prairie with less fuss than that raised over the discovery of a beaver dam.

Yet she knew it was also different from the old days. The Brule traveled now with wagons instead of travois and had to carve a road to get down into the pine-studded Niobrara canyon. The hills around the Niobrara and from the Niobrara to the Platte held settlers instead of buffalo. South of the Niobrara they began to pass homesteads where gaunt women in faded calico stared from their soddy doors. Elaine visited with the settlers, feeling sympathy for the delicate, refined young mother who'd hung the lace curtains from her former home at her soddy windows, but who stood barefoot in the dust to greet her visitor. Elaine baked biscuits in a log cabin where a widow struggled to raise her children alone. She gently discouraged a lonely young bachelor's timid invitation to correspond.

Elaine, riding her pony sidesaddle beside the Sioux wagons, knew she herself was an object of interest. She was an attractive woman, with wide-set eyes and softly curling brown hair. Clothed like the other Indian women in a calico smock, her skin deeply tanned and her hair in a long braid down her back, she aroused curiosity, but not rancor. One budding community tried to persuade her to stay and teach their new school.

Elaine found the Indians were invariably given a friendly reception. One night, while their herd of longhorns lowed in the distance, 10 young cowboys called on the Indians' camp, good-humoredly scraping up 93 cents among them so one of their group could buy a pair of moccasins. Whenever they camped near a settlement the residents thronged to their camp at first light, anxious to trade and talk, even if they could only communicate through signs. The men shared an interest in horseflesh, and while some of the settlers tried to take advantage of supposed ignorance, she noticed the Sioux usually could take care of themselves in a trade.

Whirling Hawk, she saw with amusement, had his own private joke. He was a master at playing a destitute wanderer who'd been without food for days. The white men who offered him meals -- which were never refused -- would have been amazed to learn he sometimes consumed three breakfasts in one morning. He regularly came back to camp with another hat (which he never wore), or unneeded food, and had great fun ridiculing the gifts and the givers. He felt no guilt. Any gift from a white man, he told Elaine, was only a small installment on a debt that could never be paid.

However one night, as they wandered back toward the reservation, the group's contact with whites produced tragic results. While it was illegal to sell the Indians liquor, the men occasionally were able to buy a painkiller or a bottle of lemon extract to drink. This night one brave came back to camp with a bottle of bitters. Elaine went to sleep to the sounds of their celebration.

The next morning she woke to the screams of Whirling Hawk's young wife. The brave was dead. Amid growing hysteria, Elaine tried to question the other men. All had drunk what Whirling Hawk drank and all had been very ill. Whatever it was had come from the trader a few miles back.

Angry and suspicious, not wanting to believe the poisoning could be deliberate, the teacher insisted the Indians take her back to face the trader. She marched into his small store and demanded to know what he'd sold the brave. Intimidated by the determined white woman and frightened by the presence of the grieving Indians, he insisted the bitters he sold were harmless.

But the brave had also asked for something to doctor his horse; he'd left the store with tincture of aconite. Perhaps the men had mixed the two.

There was nothing Elaine could do but accept his explanation. She ordered the man to provide a coffin for Whirling Hawk and the sad party hurried back toward the reservation.

For five days the poet gathered or begged food and wood and tended to the grieving widows, who, according to custom, had immediately given away all their possessions. Then she stood on the bluffs above the Missouri, with the women she thought of as sisters, for Whirling Hawk's burial. The wives, with hair cropped and legs bleeding from self-inflicted wounds, wailed, she thought, as if the whole world were lost.

It was a year later, in October 1890, when Elaine Goodale again heard stories of the Indian Messiah. It had been a year of change for both her and the tribes. She was now Supervisor of Indian Education in the two Dakotas, the unprecedented appointment granted after she toured the East in the fall of 1889, speaking and writing for her cherished day schools and the Indian cause.

She was justly proud of her pupils' progress, gratified at the interest their parents took in their schools -- lacking as they were in space and materials -- and anxious to fill their requests for more classrooms. "If they can be gradually thrown more upon their own responsibility and resources," she'd written the Commissioner of Indian Affairs, "they will soon be in a position to take care of their own schools."

She'd returned to spend several productive months traveling by wagon among the reservations' 60 schools to conduct unannounced inspections, assist overwhelmed teachers and weed out incompetent ones. She was at Standing Rock Agency, home to Sitting Bull, when Chasing Crane's story surfaced again. But it was more than a story, now. It was a religion.

Intrigued by the tales they kept hearing of an Indian holy man who foresaw a wonderful new world, the Sioux at the Rosebud, Pine Ridge and Cheyenne agencies had sent seven representatives west in the fall of 1889. They had listened to the son of God, a Paiute named Wovoka, been moved by his stirring words and brought back a letter from him when they returned in the spring of 1890.

The people were to do a special ghost dance every six weeks, and sometime soon, perhaps the next spring, they would be reunited with all their dead loved ones to live forever in a beautiful world full of game and free of hunger, disease and white men.

Elaine, increasingly shocked at the half-starved appearance of the bands she visited, could understand the religion's appeal. It had been a summer of drought. Unceasing hot winds had sucked the life from the Indians' small gardens; the native hay shrank away and left nothing to harvest. With government rations reduced, people she'd thought of as lean and wiry with glowing skins now had prominent ribs and sad, dull eyes sunk in sharpened faces.

Word of the Messiah's message could not have come at a more desperate time or fallen on more fallow ground.

The driver of Elaine's wagon was a nephew of Sitting Bull, and she invited the chief to her tent, placed among the golden October foliage 30 miles up the Grand River. The chief's 17-year-old son, Crowfoot, attended the day school Elaine had come to inspect. The old man enjoyed her beef and bacon, and professed his friendship for the white man, but he graciously refused to answer her questions about the Ghost Dance religion. He seemed more interested in a church convention scheduled at nearby St. Elizabeth's mission.

However, the next school she visited was half empty. The children were out with their parents, the teacher told her, participating in a large gathering to celebrate the dance. The Standing Rock agency was abuzz with talk about the dance, but those she consulted assured her it was only a novelty and would not last long. Elaine decided to head her wagon west to visit the most remote camps on the reservation on her way back to Pine Ridge.

Several miles below the forks of the Cheyenne River, they came on Big Foot's camp of Miniconjou Sioux. There, as usual, she was greeted cheerfully and invited in to eat. They visited over beef, Indian bread and hot, black coffee, with Elaine uncomfortably aware the Miniconjou might be sharing their last supplies. Then she shook the chief's hand and was on her way again, escorted for the first mile by laughing children and barking dogs. A few miles upriver from Big Foot's camp, she chatted briefly with a small group of cavalrymen. The bored men were wondering why they had to sit out in the wilderness.

Just before reaching Pine Ridge she shared a supper with Good Thunder, one of the men who'd gone west to meet Wovoka. In a soft voice the white-haired brave related how he'd seen the Christ and how beautiful He'd been, with long yellow hair and a blue robe; how He'd spoken to them without words while an eagle, a hawk and a dove attended Him; how He'd promised He would gather the souls of all Indians to a paradise where they'd hunt the buffalo, dress in skins and live in skin tents as in the old days. Impressed with his sincerity, understanding his need to believe, Elaine rode back to the Oglala agency at Pine Ridge.

The agency was located just north of the Nebraska border and the pine-filled ravines of the ridge which gave it its name. The assemblage of buildings included a large boarding school, dispensary, hotel, store and a small Episcopal church with a Sioux pastor who was a friend of hers. She was immediately engulfed in an atmosphere of suspicion, anxiety and fear.

The new Sioux agent, Daniel Royer, was a druggist who'd just arrived at his new post. He was obviously intimidated by his charges, and the Sioux had quickly named him Young Man Afraid of Lakotah. As the bright, crisp October days chilled into the first snows of November he spent most days shut up in his house, pleading with the government to send troops to protect him.

Elaine thought his fear ridiculous. She knew only a few of the Indians had embraced the Ghost Dance faith, and that those Christianized remained loyal to their white friends. She continued to go about her work, her mind filled, as always, with the needs of her schools and her students, her notebook filling with a list that detailed each child's age, grade, years of schooling, health and any other pertinent information she could gather.

November 12 was a beef-issue day, and the agency was crowded with Sioux who'd driven in for their semi-monthly issue of meat. As Elaine crossed the wide barren square that separated the agency buildings, on her way to the Oglala Boarding School, she heard a commotion in the crowd in front of the agency office. When she heard angry shouts she hesitated and tried to see what was happening in the crush of braves surrounding a few Indian policemen.

Too far away to make out any words, she watched as an unarmed Indian came to the door of the office, called to the crowd and talked for several minutes. There was no doubt about the authority in his figure and voice. Gradually the crowd became quieter, and she turned back toward the boarding school and her work.

Later she learned that when an Indian policeman had moved through the crowd to arrest a brave for cattle stealing, he'd been surrounded by angry members of the Ghost Dancing bands. They'd held him at knifepoint, waved their guns and threatened to kill the Whites and burn down the agency. The peacemaker in the agency door had been the Oglala chief American Horse. He'd managed to make them see an attack on the Whites would be not only wrong but suicidal. By force of personality alone, he'd stilled the protest.

The agent loaded up his family and retreated in panic to Rushville, 28 miles south. He refused to return until he had troops to protect him. Elaine considered him a scaremonger and thought him below contempt. Feeling no concern for her safety, she gathered up her camping outfit, called the Sioux couple who accompanied her on her circuit and set out again. On a moon-bright November night a short time later she joined the Sioux near Porcupine Tail Butte to witness a Ghost Dance.

Sitting with a group of Indian spectators, Elaine watched a young woman in a white buckskin dress walk into a circle of a hundred Sioux who were seated around a slim, freshly cut cottonwood log. It had earlier been set upright to represent the Holy Center, and in the moonlight, she could see it dangled with streamers, eagle feathers and other tokens. The Sioux woman shot an arrow in each direction, then held a pipe toward the west, the home of the Messiah.

The people seated around the tree began to chant a prayer. Then each ate a bite of food from a bowl that was passed around. The leader of the dance rose, stretched his arms heavenward and prayed to the Great Holy. He asked that the dancers be carried to the land of the spirits where they could see their dead relatives and the wonderful life to come. When he was finished, the dancers rose, lifted their arms to the west and sang a brief opening song.

"Father, I come. Mother, I come. Brother, I come. Father, give us back our arrows." When the words had faded into the night, the dancers laced their fingers with the persons next to them and began to shuffle to the left.

Now Elaine realized there were women in the dance, something she'd never seen before. Little children were welcomed, too, and even old people with canes. There were no drums. The unaccompanied voices sounded strange to her ear.

The people circling the log's base, even the women, wore painted faces and eagle feathers in their hair. They also wore a sacred shirt or dress of fringed white muslin. A blue cross and an eagle were painted on the back and from the shoulders and sleeves more eagle feathers jiggled with their movements. The eagle, their holiest bird, was to carry them up to visit their departed loved ones. The special shirts were said to protect their wearers even from bullets.

As an hour went by the songs changed and the dancing accelerated. "Once more we shall hunt the buffalo -- Our Father has said it!" the circle cried. The leader broke in again with a prayer. The women wailed with a sound Elaine found heart-breaking and unforgettable.

Now an old woman broke from the ring and fell unconscious at Elaine's feet. She lay motionless for a few moments; then rose to cry her vision. "My children, I have seen those dear ones we lost long ago!" she declared.

The circle responded "*Ah! He-ye-ye!*"

"They are living in a most beautiful country covered with buffalo!"

"*He-ye-ye!* Our Father has said it!"

"Their tipis are of skins. They are feasting and playing. They are perfectly happy!"

"*He-ye-ye!*"

"Here everything looks hateful to me -- how can I bear it?"

The circle responded with groans and cries.

The priest repeated the Messiah's promise. They would all see their departed loved ones "with the new grass" in the spring. They had only to believe. Other dancers fell into trances and related their visions. There were other songs, other prayers. Finally the people sang their dream:

Over the whole earth they are coming.
The buffalo are coming.
The Eagle has brought the message to the tribe.
The Father says so, the Father says so.

Elaine listened for half the night, shivering with cold but unable to pull herself away. Finally she retreated to her tent -- exhausted, yet exhilarated -- strangely moved. Outside the dancing continued until dawn.

She moved on to Medicine Root, and Day School #8. On November 19 a local chief confronted the teachers and demanded to know why soldiers had arrived at Rushville, 70 miles away. "We have done nothing wrong," he said. "If the Messiah does not come in the spring, as promised, we shall stop dancing."

Elaine, who'd heard nothing of troops arriving, could neither answer nor reassure him.

The next day the other government employees received orders to come in to the agency. The teacher Elaine was observing taught until noon at her insistence; then she set out on horseback for safety. Elaine, having received no orders, stayed another night, sleeping within sound of another Ghost Dance.

The next morning, however, her breakfast was interrupted by a native policeman with word she was wanted at the agency. She soon discovered the Indians had also received word they all must go in to the agency or lose their rations. Traveling on roads jammed with hundreds of anxious Sioux and their possessions, she was in Pine Ridge by sunset.

It was a Pine Ridge she had never seen before. Tall white tents stood in strict rows, instead of circles. The earth was cut in trenches and piled into breastworks. Armed sentinels in buffalo coats manned every corner and bugles sounded regularly. Many of the Sioux were there, too. Hundreds of tents, wagons and horses filled the area. But many had fled to the Bad Lands in fear. Those who'd come in, she learned, were now known as "the friendlies;" those who'd done nothing but flee were called "the hostiles."

The Oglala Boarding School was fenced with barbed wire; armed guards patrolled its boundary. Inside the students were virtually hostages. In classrooms filled with unease, the teachers tried to teach the restless children, feed them and keep order.

As November ended and Christmas neared, Elaine felt as if she were waiting helplessly for a catastrophe. Hoping there might still be a peaceful solution, she took solace in helping to prepare the Christmas the children had come to expect.

One other element brightened her days. A new doctor had arrived at the agency. He was a 32-year-old Sioux from Minnesota, a recent graduate of Boston University, named Charles Eastman. He immediately set about reorganizing his office, requested more medical supplies and bought a horse so that he could visit sick people in their camps. She was impressed at his energy and was deeply touched when she learned he had sat up all night with a sick baby. He began to visit her temporary home at the Episcopal rectory; she went with him on calls, carrying food to the sick. As their friendship deepened he told her his story.

He'd begun life in a Sioux village in Minnesota but, separated from his father in the turmoil of the Santee uprising in 1862, he had spent his childhood in the wilds of Manitoba with his uncle.

He had not seen a school nor heard English until he was 15 and his father, who'd converted to Christianity and broken tribal ties to become a farmer, had sought him out and brought him back to the United States for schooling. He, like Elaine, was dedicated to helping the Sioux survive in a changing world.

By the time the Christmas tree was hung with small gifts for the children, they were engaged. Her world cushioned with the sweetness of new love, the scent of cedar garlands in the little brown chapel on the hill, and the sounds of nightly Christmas carol practice, Elaine was unprepared for news that came December 15. Sitting Bull had been shot to death!

But it was true. The chief she had visited only weeks before was dead. His 17-year-old son Crowfoot and his adopted brother Jumping Bull had died in the hail of fire that brought him down.

So had five other Hunkpapa supporters and six of the Indian police who'd been trying to arrest him. His terrified people had fled, and some were reported to be at Big Foot's camp near the forks of the Cheyenne, although the stories that whirled through the agency changed with every telling.

Nearly every Sioux family had someone among the hostiles, for the order to come in to a camp thronged with soldiers had deeply divided the Sioux. The same lodge might shelter both Christians and Ghost Dancers, and families broke apart as they tried to decide what to do and where they would be most safe. Elaine's driver, with relatives among the refugees in the Bad Lands, visited them secretly at night and kept her informed on the state of affairs.

Even the friendly Sioux were restless and unhappy at the agency. Their ponies were half-starved for lack of grazing and they longed to go home. The missionaries and teachers begged that the people be allowed to return to their normal lives, but no one listened. As news of the tense situation reached eastern journalists, they crowded into Rushville and Pine Ridge to cover the story. Some, like the *Omaha World-Herald's* Thomas Tibbles and his wife, Susette, could find little on the reservation worth writing about. Others, when they found no war to report, felt obliged to invent one.

Still, on Christmas Eve the church was a haven of peace and beauty. The huge cedar tree, almost touching the ceiling, draped with strings of popcorn, sacks of fruit and candy, and glowing with candles, thrilled the first contingent of children. After the Christmas story was read in Dakota, Elaine took pleasure in each beaming face as the children received their gifts from the tree and clothing from boxes sent by eastern donors. The chapel was not big enough to hold them all at once, so the celebration was to be repeated for a new group seven more nights.

About 10 o'clock on the morning of the 29th, Elaine walked to the chapel through sunshine surprisingly warm for December. She was filling bags with candy and marking gifts for the sixth party when she heard a rumble in the distance. She knew at once nothing natural had made that noise, and a chill of dread went down her spine. By noon Indian runners had brought the news.

Soldiers at Wounded Knee Creek, 18 miles northeast of the agency, had rounded up Big Foot and his Miniconjou, confiscated the Indians' guns and shot them! Scores were dead. Women and children as well as braves had been raked by rifle fire and shrapnel from Hotchkiss guns.

The Indians at the agency went wild with fear. As Elaine watched, hills that had been white with their tipis melted back to brown. Everywhere she looked the Indians were catching their horses, piling their children in wagons and racing away. The Whites were equally terrified. They heard the cavalry had been cut off from the agency and a horde of savages was already riding to kill all the Whites they could find.

Suddenly a line of mounted warriors appeared on the ridge above the agency. A ghost-shirted brave rode provocatively across the square, shouting, "Prepare to fight! We are going to shoot into the agency." Dr. Eastman, busy at the dispensary but fearing for Elaine's safety, sent a saddled horse to the church and asked her to ride to Rushville. Although touched by his concern, she refused to leave her adopted people.

The mission house and church filled with terrified, sobbing women and children of mixed blood. As the shutters were slammed and a thin line of available infantrymen and Sioux police established a perimeter, Elaine, the minister's wife, two missionary women and Susette Tibbles lit the oil lamps and tried to ease the tension with coffee and sandwiches.

In the late afternoon panic flared again as shots began to rain on the outlying buildings. They tensed for an all-out attack.

However, as the early dusk fell, the line of warriors disappeared and it was quiet once more. Through it all Elaine could not forget that those on the other side of the walls, those fleeing through the cold night, those lying dead at Wounded Knee Creek were also her friends.

Long after dark the wagons of the 7th Cavalry pulled in with their pitiful cargo of wounded. Now, at least, there was something to do. The soldiers rushed about, transferring their 30-some wounded and a few wounded braves into the hospital, carrying their dead into a makeshift morgue. The horses were unhitched and taken to the stable, but there was not room for all of the wounded Indians. The minister discovered them lying quietly in their bloody rags in the cold darkness. It seemed a fitting end to a day of horror.

Quickly he moved the crowd in the church to another cabin and every able-bodied person available worked to pull the pews from the church and spread the floor with hay. Elaine and the other women yanked quilts from their beds and spread them to receive 33 torn and wounded Sioux. Only six were men; the rest were women and children.

Elaine found the next few days even more nightmarish. While Dr. Eastman and an army surgeon worked night and day to save as many as possible, she and the other women nursed, cooked and comforted as well as they could. Most of the wounds were severe, and despite their best efforts one after another of their patients were carried out for burial. The tree had been dragged out, Christmas carols had given way to the subdued moans of the wounded, gifts to bloody bandages. Only the cedar garlanding the windows reminded her of the world that was.

The third day after the fight her fiance recruited a party to search the battlefield for survivors. Under a blanket of new snow they found seven still breathing, including one baby. After the shaken doctor returned to the agency, he and Elaine began to question survivors. Gradually they pieced together what had happened. How Big Foot's people had been intercepted on their way to the agency and surrounded by a square of soldiers. How the soldiers had demanded their guns and they had begun to surrender them. How their tipis, wagons and even their women had been searched -- their cooking knives and sewing awls taken away. How one troublesome, hot-blooded brave, pushed past his limit, raised his gun. How that wild shot had turned a peaceful surrender into a slaughter.

Twenty-five soldiers had died, many the victims of their comrades' bullets. Another 37 were wounded. The bodies of 84 Sioux braves, 44 Sioux women, and 18 Sioux children lay in a grotesque frozen pattern on the battlefield, their ghost shirts pierced with the same finality as the soldiers' tunics. Another two to four dozen died later. With them died the last, desperate hope of the Sioux. The buffalo were not coming back. The white men would not disappear. The old life was gone.

The teacher wrote an account of the battle as she saw it -- "a general and indiscriminate slaughter of the unarmed and the helpless" -- which was published in eastern papers. The government censured her for her efforts. Two weeks later she watched "a forlorn and weary cavalcade" of some 2,000 Sioux trail over the snow-covered ridges into the agency. The last frightened bands had finally been convinced they would not be disarmed and massacred if they surrendered. Elaine and the missionaries began the task of mending the Indians' shattered faith in the white man.

Elaine married Charles Eastman in 1891 and they returned east in 1892. With marriage, she gave up her career and devoted herself to promoting her husband's writing and raising their six children.

She admitted frustration in the secondary role -- housebound while he traveled widely to lecture and meet stimulating people -- but she remained devoted to helping him express himself and interpret his people. She continued writing all her life, collaborating on nine books with her husband, writing seven of her own, and continuing to translate her experiences into poetry. When she died in 1953 she was still vitally concerned with the lives of her adopted people.

Traveling the New Way

In the late 1880s all the Indians on the Upper Missouri were reeling before the relentless press of white society, but not all of them found themselves crucified on the cross of progress.

Waheenee's family and the other Hidatsa, Mandan and Arikara people at Like-a-Fishhook Village had bent before white pressure for as long as they could remember. Like the other tribes, they sorrowed for the old days, but they could see more hope in the new. The agricultural lifestyle the Whites were demanding did not seem so impossibly strange to them; they could accommodate without surrendering everything, bend instead of break.

In 1876 a missionary had come to live near the village, bringing his wife with him, and opening a school where English was taught. The next year a government school was opened, and by 1879 the agency was like a small town. While Waheenee and Son of a Star made sure their son learned all the skills of hunting and warfare, they also wanted him to learn English, and he began school when he was eight. Not all the Hidatsa were willing to send their children to school, and many of those who started became discouraged and dropped out. However, Goodbird's grandfather, Small Ankle, encouraged his studies. "It is their books that make white people strong," he would say, and before long Goodbird was answering the call of the school bell in the mornings to learn to read and fighting sham battles with mud balls in the afternoon to develop his courage.

The missionary's religion was another matter. While neither Small Ankle nor Son of a Star opposed what he taught, they were not ready to change their beliefs. "The old gods are best for me," Small Ankle told his son. Yet he did not discourage Goodbird if he wanted to attend services in the mission. It was the Hidatsa way. Goodbird must decide for himself which spirits he would honor.

In the year the Whites would call 1887, Waheenee's son, Goodbird, stared down at the Missouri's waters as they rounded a sharp curve and swirled and tore against a high bluff. The water was swift and deep here, full of angry whirlpools. The river had eaten away at the bank until it rose steep and stark, denuded of any protection, yet it continued to resist the water's grinding force. When he pulled his attention away from the river to study the bluff that stretched far above the bank, he could see only grass and the wind that moved it -- above its crest, an empty sky.

His people called it Awatahesh, "the Hill that is by Itself," and it had often been the destination of young men seeking visions. It was a wild, lonely place, untouched by men, eerie as the cry of the owl in the night. In such a place one might find his god, Goodbird thought. Long ago he had made a promise to his father. He was now 17 winters. It was time he made his promise good.

He moved on down the river to a thicket of brush and found a Juneberry bush. He searched out a sturdy branch and began to carve it with his knife. When he was finished he had two pieces as thick as his thumb and a little longer than his fist, each with one end sharpened to a fine, white point. He pressed the points against his skin. Satisfied they would do their job, he rose and went home to tell his father his decision.

The home he approached was no longer the rounded, brown lodge he'd known as a child. There, like his mother before him, he'd been awakened in the morning by Grandfather Small Ankle's call to be up and down to the river for his bath, and he'd raced his cousins and young uncles through the doorway.

But there were no tall poles with tributes to Above Woman, Sacred Woman and the birds flanking this log doorway. Nor were there throngs of noisy children and dogs underfoot, smoke spirals from many fires, voices calling, laughing or complaining, neighbors' greetings as he neared his door. Home now was the log cabin he had helped his father build. The roof and floor were still dirt, to be sure, but the lines were square instead of circular, and instead of standing in the midst of a village, it stood virtually alone. Only the homes of his closest relatives were nearby, for each family lived in its own lodge now, and Like-a-Fishhook Village was no more.

It had been difficult to leave the village two years before, especially for his mother and the older people, hard to turn their backs on the homes they'd known all their lives and the scaffolds of those who'd gone to the ghost village. Yet they realized it had to be. The buffalo were all but gone; the timber was used up; their fields had been farmed until they produced smaller and smaller ears of corn, fewer and fewer melons, in spite of the women's best efforts.

And the agent kept talking about allotments. The government wanted each Indian to choose his own land, to put his name on a piece that was measured off. Then that land would be his alone and he would take his family to live on it and farm. The government would give each family 160 acres, he said, and plows and cattle. "The big game is being killed off and you must plant bigger fields or starve," he warned them.

They could not deny the truth of what he said. It made their hearts heavy, but it was so. Little by little the lodges had emptied, most of the Arikara moving east, the Mandan south and the Hidatsa north. Small Ankle and his family had decided to move north, to the vicinity of Awatahesh, about 40 miles above Like-a-Fishhook, and the agent had nodded and said he would call their settlement Independence. They'd packed their belongings as they had so many times before, but this time they'd loaded the medicine bundles, the bags and parfleches, the mortar and pestle, the lodge skins and poles, into a wagon. It carried more goods, but it had no facility for crossing rivers, and when it was time to cross to the south side of the Missouri, Son of a Star had had to use a wrench to unbolt the pieces so they could ferry them over in a bullboat, one by one.

The tipi, too, had come in handy, for they'd lived in it for a month while he and his father built the cabin. As Goodbird approached it he could see the result of their labors and remember sweating over the 40 logs they'd cut on the bottom land and dragged up to the cabin with the team. His mother had helped them notch the corners, but he and his father had cut the sod for the roof with a plow, not having or needing Waheenee's team of eight strong women to dig the sod, 20 young ones to carry it in and six old matrons to tamp it down. His mother had mixed clay and hay to plaster the cracks, but she had not set in the glass windows or placed the iron stove in the center of the dirt floor.

It had seemed a foreign place, at first, with its square corners, and the roof almost within arm's reach overhead. The sunshine came in through the window now, instead of marking the day by tracking its bright path across the floor, as in the old days. His parents' bed was on one side, his on the other, and there was not room for four or five families. His bed was made of lumber, more like a white man's, and he slept on a straw mattress and used a quilt and blankets along with his buffalo robe; his mother's and father's bed of boards atop logs reminded him more of the way things used to be when he was still small enough to cuddle beside them on cold winter nights.

However he did not plan to spend this night in bed. He intended to seek dreams one did not experience in a comfortable bed. He showed Son of a Star the Juneberry pieces, and receiving his father's warm approval, stripped to his breech clout and moccasins and began coating his body with white clay. Red was the color of rejoicing; one wore black when he celebrated the joy of a dead enemy; white would show the spirits he had no deeds to celebrate, no reason to rejoice, that he needed their comfort.

His father left to ask a man named Crow to assist them, and Goodbird got a rawhide rope, an ax and a post and walked back to wait them at his chosen spot on the top of the bank beneath Awatahesh. He waited in the fading light, tense, excited, fearful, determined, thinking of the time when he was a child and had stood with the crowd to watch Turtle-no-Head perform his dance. The rapid "Ah-la-la-la-la-la!" of the women's song, the calls of encouragement and praise from the old men had stirred his blood, and he decided at that moment that someday he would do the same dance.

Crow and his father came at last and Goodbird knelt at their feet. Son of a Star pinched the skin on one side of his chest and held it while Crow wet an arrowhead and pushed the arrow through the fold. Goodbird, his heart racing, watched the trickle of blood down his chest, surprised at how little it hurt. In a moment the other breast was slashed and one of his Juneberry skewers was pushed through each cut. Then, as his father used the ax to pound the post into the edge of the bank, thongs on one end of the rope were looped around each skewer and secured. Son of a Star fastened the other end of the rope around the post and said, "Now, my son, slide down the rope."

Holding the rope, Goodbird backed down the bank until it was tight. Then he loosened his grip, clasped his hands behind his back and hung over the water, his weight suspended from the skewers in his chest, his body at an angle so that his feet were just able to touch the pale clay of undercut bank. He could hear the voice of his father above. "Stay here as long as you can," he said. "But when you cannot stand the suffering any longer, take off the rope and come home." Then the men's steps faded and he was alone.

He knew his father did not wish him pain except as it was necessary for him to find his god. Son of a Star's chest bore the same scars, as did his grandfather Small Ankle's and every respected man in the village. Each went through his ordeal to seek a vision and so gain protection from the gods. A poor man who came to beg might be fed, but afterward the men would say, "See, his body is just like a woman's. He never cut himself and suffered. If he had, he would be welcome everywhere and have plenty to eat and not be poor, because his gods would take care of him."

How many times he had heard Son of a Star explain how the gods would see that a man who made himself suffer struck many enemies and earned many honors, that when he was old he would have a good house and many horses. Goodbird had drawn the honor charts for many men, depicting their brave deeds, and all of them bore the marks of their vision quests.

The twilight deepened and stars appeared in the early summer sky. The night was quiet, except for an occasional cry from some hunting creature or its prey. The river washed and swirled below him. Everything in the prairie had a spirit -- sky, cloud, stone, water, bird, beast. Were the spirits watching? Would they reward his sacrifice with a vision, give him a special animal spirit to watch over him? His uncle had heard a spirit address him as Strong Bull during a vision, and so earned himself a new name. Small Ankle told of a man who sought a vision from the buffalo god, and who was rewarded when the four buffalo skulls he dragged into the river came to life and pulled him out of the dangerous current.

Could he endure long enough to fall into the dream state? He began to pray, "O, gods, I am poor...."

The hours dragged on as the stars wheeled in the sky. Were the gods there? He'd believed in the spirits all his life. His mother and father, his grandfather, his aunts and uncles said it was so.

Each warrior had his bundle of medicine that protected him in battle, and he kept it on a medicine post in his lodge. Small Ankle's sacred bundle of the Waterbuster clan had such an honored place in the lodge where Goodbird grew up that no one walked between it and the fire. The two skulls and carved wooden pipe the skins contained, stored in a special stand at one side of the lodge, were the most powerful medicine in the tribe and made Small Ankle's lodge a holy place where none presumed to lounge or play on the roof as they did on other lodges.

Small Ankle told him how his great-grandfather, Missouri River, had used the bundle to decide the plan of the village and the location of their lodge when they built Like-a-Fishhook Village seven winters after the smallpox. The *maa-duush* required special rituals and songs, and only one man was trained to ask its blessings. He'd seen his father pray to it and bring the rain, or cure a sick person, or attract the buffalo. No one knew how long it had been passed from one generation in the clan to the next.

Suspended between black water and black sky, he felt only a dull throb of pain that beat under his thoughts and pulsated his prayers. His great-grandfather Old Yellow Elk's special god was an otter. He had died in the smallpox winter and been laid out on a hill with an otter skin for his pillow. With so many dying in those terrible weeks there had not been time nor strength to honor him with a scaffold grave, so the family had piled logs over his body to keep off the wolves. But that night he'd called from the hill for the family to come get him, and when they'd pulled off the logs he stood up and walked home. He'd been to the ghost village, he said, and it was a fine place, but his god, the otter, had brought him back under the water of the Missouri....

The sky showed the faintest tinge of gray. His grandfather Big Cloud's gods were the thunder eagles which came from the west. He'd seen one once in a vision, and it had a forked tail and wings that spread from bluff to bluff across the big river. Lightning was the flash of his eye; thunder his scream. Goodbird's very name was a prayer to those gods. Would they hear him? A terrible weariness ate at his back and legs and sapped his strength.

He'd grown up with stories like the one about the Sun and Itsikamahidish: How the Sun charmed the blanket of sky into coming down near enough to the flat plane of earth that he could mount it for his daily arc, and the Hidatsa god had learned the same song, also mounted to the sky and chased the Sun across his path. The Sun was a man, his body painted glowing red like fire, and Itsikamahidish had found the place where the Sun stops every noon for a moment to smoke. The Sun had become angry and had blinded the trickster and hurled him to earth, but the god had caught the Sun in a snare and pulled him from the sky, where he remained until the moon came looking. Other tales told of buffalo that lived under the waters of the Missouri; his father liked to tell how he'd heard their hooves on the river rocks one quiet night.

All this Goodbird had believed, implicitly, until he was about 12 winters. Then one day, walking home from the many-windowed "House with Eyes," where the missionaries taught English in Like-a-Fishhook, he'd realized he could not believe both his people and the white man. He enjoyed school and liked to learn, although he found English a difficult language. He'd even taken what the teacher called a Christian name, Edward, to be said before Goodbird. He liked the missionary's songs about Jesus and tried to follow his laws. But his teacher said the earth was round; that the sun was a ball of fire. If she spoke the truth, and Goodbird believed she did, for every day he learned something new that told him it was so, the adventures of Itsikamahidish could not have happened! He argued loudly with his scornful older cousin in defense of his new knowledge and the white man's wisdom, but beneath the bluster there was the quivery feeling of walking on Missouri ice that had rotted in the sun.

The missionary's voice was far away now and no one was challenging his gods, but he realized he'd reached the end of his endurance. He grasped the rope and began to haul himself painfully up over the crest of the bank, where he pulled out the skewers and walked slowly home. Perhaps the dream would come in his bed, after all.

Evidently he slept too soundly, for he had no message when he awoke. He was disappointed, but not without hope. He knew of other men who'd had to seek their god more than once, and he had many others things to occupy his mind.

Since they'd been at Awatahesh Goodbird's life had focused on hunting. His parents were busy trying to develop the farm, and the rations the family received twice a moon from the agent were not enough to live on. He hunted from necessity, but it also was his joy. He rose nearly every morning to steal from the cabin in the dark and creep through the timber before the deer returned from feeding on the upland hills. He knew that a whitetail would immediately bound away, but that a blacktail would pause one instant for a backward look. Crouched in the chill air he'd watch their forms materialize in the soft light and work around until the breeze was in his face. He was a good shot with the Winchester he'd traded for when he was 14, and liked to remember the time he'd instinctively swung up the barrel and squeezed off a shot that killed a buck and a doe with one bullet. He had killed his first buffalo calf when he was 12 winters. It had taken two shots, but the second was a shot straight into the heart.

Often he hunted alone, but one day he left the cabin on horseback about noon, intent on catching up with four friends who'd already started for a hunt in the Little Missouri badlands.

Dressed in the yellow buckskin coat his mother had made him and black cloth leggings, he delayed to stalk an antelope herd. Wrapping a buff-colored handkerchief around his head to be less conspicuous, he crept to a hilltop, thrust his cleaning rods in the earth at an angle so they crossed to form a rest for his gun, and sighted on a young animal. In a moment he had the satisfaction of seeing it fall, but by the time he retrieved it and dressed it out, he'd lost the trail of his friends.

Sunset found him on Blue Berry Tree Creek and he decided to make a solitary camp. He busied himself with gathering wood, starting a fire and putting a side of the antelope to roast. When it began to brown and drip, he opened the sack of flour he carried and scooped out a hollow in the top. Fetching water from the creek, he poured it into the hollow and stirred it into a ball that filled both his hands. Then he flattened the dough and spread it on the coals to bake, his sack of flour as dry as when he'd begun.

Only after he'd eaten and the hills had receded into darkness did he began to feel uneasy. He'd heard stories of the Sioux from the days his mother had handed him his first quiver of prairie dog skin and he'd filled it with grass-stem arrows. Nearly every winter count listed some Hidatsa lost to their hands. His grandfather told of an attack on the old village, and the boy had easily imagined a wounded woman huddling under her bed while a Sioux stalked the roof of her lodge. Small Ankle had himself killed one of these enemies, and Son of a Star had bled from one of their bullets.

When Goodbird was 14 he'd ridden with Son of a Star and a war party after Sioux who'd been lurking around the horse herd in spite of supposed peace between the two peoples. Those thieves had melted away in the dark, depriving him of his chance to face the enemy, but no one knew when or where they might decide to strike. He rechecked the hobbles that held his horse and lay down with his rifle at his right hand.

Just as he was getting drowsy the horse stirred. Goodbird got up again and checked the perimeters of his camp. Then he studied the faint mark of the horizon around him, watching for a dark shape against the stars. There was movement on the crest of one hill. Carefully he crawled up to peer over the crest. It was only a bunch of cattle the white men were now grazing on the Little Missouri bottom. Feeling foolish, he walked back to his camp and a sound sleep.

The next morning he caught up with his friends and had a satisfying hunt, killing a whitetail and two blacktail deer. With more than enough dried meat to load his horse, he headed home, again alone.

This time his lonely campfire was approached by two Indians and he reached for his rifle. But one man waved his hands like wings, then swept his right hand to the right with palm down. It was the sign for Goodbird's name; they were friends. They'd used signs rather than calling out, as a precaution against attracting Sioux, they said. Perhaps his moment of panic over the cows hadn't been so foolish after all.

Still feeling the need to seek his god, Goodbird tried again late that fall to have a vision. This time he chose the windswept top of a lonely hill and his father attached him to a post he could circle. Around and around he ran, determined to exhaust himself, pulling back against the skewers while light snow spit from the black sky and he shivered and shook with cold. Feeling so alone he would have welcomed ghosts for company, he again beseeched the gods to hear him. Again he went home to a dreamless sleep.

He expected to try again, but before he could the government forbid the Indians to use the ceremony. Son of a Star was angry they should be forbidden to seek their gods. He did not accept Christianity, but he did not interfere with their practices. Why should they prevent the Hidatsa from worshipping the way they wished?

Goodbird discovered he was rather relieved; the Indian way was a hard one for a young man to travel. Yet he was not ready to cut his hair and give up all their songs, dances, ceremonies and skin clothes to be come a Christian, as the missionary demanded. No Christian would honor a medicine bundle, the preacher said. They should all be burned. Burned! Small Ankle did not even consider such a sacrilege; the *maa-duush* was still in its place of honor in his new earth lodge.

Still Goodbird's thoughts were turning to other ways of life. His ability with languages (he could speak four Indian tongues as well as English), and industrious ways attracted the attention of the agent. The government established a depot at Independence so the families would not have to trek 40 miles to pick up their rations, and Goodbird was asked to take charge of distribution. He found himself doling out seven pounds of beef and flour, four ounces of coffee, a half-pound of sugar, a pound of bacon, salt and soap to each of 200 people and marking out the appropriate number on their cardboard tickets. Once a year there were clothes, vested suits and hats for the men, but also more useful quilts and blankets.

He and his father broke their land with the plow the government gave them and planted wheat and oats. Their harvest that fall was a good one and he found surprising satisfaction in hauling their four loads of grain to Hebron and heading home with $80.

As their reservation became part of the state of North Dakota, and the Sioux made their own desperate search for salvation to the south, Goodbird took more and more pleasure in working the land near the river which was suitable for crops, in sowing seed and watching the green shoots appear, in learning to use the machinery to plant and harvest.

His mother loved growing things, as she always had, but she preferred the old ways.

Industrious as ever, Waheenee continued to plant her own garden. She accepted the plow as an easier way to break the ground and used the white man's hoe, but she cut its awkward long handle off short. She tried, but subsequently rejected, most of the seed the agent provided. They were using wheat flour now, but the white man's potatoes the agent had made them plant were smelly and spoiled when she tried to store them in the cache pits. She preferred the Mandan squash to the white man's, the Arikara melons, the yellow hard corn and pole beans her mothers and grandmothers had planted. And she knew a garden belonged on bottom land, not on the dry sandy bench land as the Whites imagined, where the plants soon withered in the hot wind.

Waheenee still used her stone mallet and anvil when there were choke cherries to crush or bones to break for marrow and the ash-trunk mortar and pestle her father had made for pounding corn. However some of the white man's ways were finding a welcome in their cabin. Their pails were of metal now, not buffalo heart skin. They usually drank coffee instead of broth, and Goodbird had learned to prefer it with cream from their milk cow.

But the agent couldn't seem to understand that pigs were more trouble than they were worth. Any self-respecting Hidatsa gave his relatives generous portions of meat whenever he slaughtered, and with a pig there wasn't enough left to bother with. It was also difficult, when the agent told Goodbird to become a policeman, to make him realize a 19-year-old did not have the maturity and stature to tell his elders what to do.

However Goodbird was anxious to help his people, and when the agent asked him to take the job of assistant farmer in 1895, he was happy to try. He helped each man mark off a ten-acre plot -- after the government farmer explained what an acre was -- advised them on plowing and seeding and sent the plow shares for sharpening when they needed it. When it was time to cut hay in the meadows, he saw that the mowing machine several shared was properly oiled and passed on to the next man. He went from cabin to cabin telling the agent's orders, counting the stacks of wild hay to make sure each family had gathered its quota. He advised them on their gardens and the importance of keeping down the weeds, and reported those who went visiting and neglected their crops. When it was time to harvest, he helped run the horse-drawn thresher that went from farm to farm.

Things did not always go smoothly. The agent's word was law on the reservation, and Goodbird, one of the few who could communicate with him, sometimes found himself representing both sides of a controversy.

While some of the old warriors continued to live in the past, Goodbird was more interested in the future. He could see Indian ways were doomed; the game was gone, the old ones were dead or dying, the dances and ceremonies of their religion were forbidden -- one could be fined or jailed if caught worshiping. He married a girl from the Standing Rock Reservation -- a Sioux -- and worked to increase the size of his farm and develop his herd of cattle.

When the missionary came to Independence to preach, and asked him to serve as interpreter for the sermons, he was ready to turn his thoughts in a new direction. He still sought his god, and one Sunday morning in 1905 he stood to be baptised with his two small sons, Charley and Alfred. "Now I am traveling the new way," he thought.

Small Ankle, dead nearly 20 years, and Son of a Star, now bent and crippled, had always been reverent men. His new religion would be different, but his faith the same. "I think God made all people to help one another," he said. "I think each year I know God a little better. I am not afraid." In 1925 Edward Goodbird was ordained in the chapel at Independence as a minister in the Congregational church.

Epilogue

Waheenee entered the 20th century with the energy and stamina she had always shown. Her son Goodbird was not entirely right when he foresaw the end of Indian ways. The Hidatsa accommodated themselves to the white man's life style and changing times, but they preserved many of their own customs and values. When she was 72, Waheenee still rose at dawn to hoe her corn, still sang the corn songs to let it know that it was loved. She and Goodbird befriended scholar Gilbert L. Wilson in the early 1900s, and worked tirelessly to tell their family's story. Waheenee's incredible memory and Goodbird's artistic talent, combined with information from other family members, enabled them to honor their fathers and preserve their people's history.

Waheenee was proud that her son had grown up to be a good man, that he owned much land and many cattle, that he, like his father and grandfather, was a spiritual leader of his people. Yet *sometimes, she told Wilson, as she sat looking over the Missouri while dusk softened the contours of the hills, she remembered other times. "In the shadows I seem again to see our Indian village, with smoke curling upward from the earth lodges; and in the river's roar I hear the yells of the warriors, the laughter of little children as of old. It is but an old woman's dream. Again I see but shadows and hear only the roar of the river; and tears come into my eyes. Our Indian life, I know, is gone forever."*

Gone, too, before a great many years had passed was the river as she knew it. Chief Joseph was wise enough to look at white men in the 1870s and realize they "would change the rivers and mountains if they did not suit them." Few rivers have been as changed as the Missouri. The men the Nez Perce encountered in 1877 at the Cow Island crossing were there to remove rocks from the river channel; in 1906 Captain Grant Marsh was taking a load of cement up to build a dam on the Yellowstone. The river has been continuously "improved" ever since.

Teddy Roosevelt, who did so much to repay his debt to the West by creating national forests, parks and wildlife refuges, did not foresee that reclamation projects, while providing flood control and irrigation, would change forever the vital rivers which threaded the plains. Between 1944 and 1967 six massive dams were thrown across the Missouri in Montana and the Dakotas. Beneath the waters of the resulting reservoirs disappeared towns, homesteads, groves of cottonwoods, coulees, prairie wetlands, Waheenee's Like-a-Fishhook Village and all but the tip of Goodbird's Independence Hill. The Hidatsa were moved from the river valley to the harsh, dry hilltops.

Waheenee's life had spanned more than a half-century of conflict on the Missouri. Its waters had carried explorers, fur trappers, artists who sought to record its people, scientists who came to explore its mysteries, missionaries, miners, farmers, teachers, soldiers and vanquished warriors past her door. By the time she was an old woman, most of the issues that had set men against each other were resolved, for good or ill. Those who survived the conflicts, victor or vanquished, turned to learning to live with the results. The Hidatsa woman was right in the practical sense when she grieved for a vanished life, yet in a larger sense the essence of her life, and of all those who experienced trials and triumphs on the Missouri, remains. Known or unknown, their lives are threads in the fabric of our heritage, giving body, color and texture to our national character, connecting us with the past, it is true, but also providing the warp upon which we weave the future.

Bibliography

General Background

Athearn, Robert G. *Forts of the Upper Missouri*. University of Nebraska Press, 1967.
Monaghan, Jay, ed. *The Book of the American West*. Bonanza Books, 1963.
Nagel, Paul C. *Missouri*. W. W. Norton & Co. Inc., 1977.
Neihardt, John. *The River and I*. University of Nebraska Press, 1968.
Primm, James Neal. *Lion of the Valley: St. Louis, Missouri*. Pruett, 1981.
Ramsay, Robert L. *Our Storehouse of Missouri Place Names*. University of Missouri Press, 1973.
Vestal, Stanley. *The Missouri*. University of Nebraska Press, 1964 edition.

Chapter 1 -- Iron Eyes' Search for His Ideal

Chardon, Francis. *Chardon's Journal at Fort Clark, 1834-39*. Annie H. Abel, ed. South Dakota Department of History, 1932.
Fletcher, Alice C. and Francis La Flesche. *Omaha Tribe*, v. 1 & 2, University of Nebraska Press, 1972 edition.
Kurz, Rudolph Friederich. *Journal of Rudolph Friederich Kurz*. University of Nebraska Press, 1970 edition.

Chapter 2 -- At War with Life

Doty, James. *Journal of Operations of Governor Isaac I. Stevens of Washington Territory in 1855*. Ye Galleon Press, 1978 edition.
Goetzmann, William H. "The Grand Reconnaissance," *American Heritage*, v. 23, no. 6, 1972.
Hazard, Joseph T. *Companion of Adventure*. Binfords and Mort, Publishers, 1952.
Meinig, Donald S. "Isaac Stevens: Practical Geographer," *Geographical Review*, v. 45, 1955.
Richards, Kent D. *Young Man in a Hurry*. Brigham Young University Press, 1979.
Stevens, Hazard. *The Life of Isaac Ingalls Stevens*. Houghton, Mifflin & Co., 1900.
Stevens, Isaac I. *Report of Explorations and Surveys, 1853-55*, v. 12. Senate Executive Document. 36th Congress, 1st Session, 1860.

Chapter 3 -- What Manner of Work it Was

Boyer, Richard O. *The Legend of John Brown*. Alfred A Knopf, 1973.
Brown, Salmon. "Document: John Brown and Sons in Kansas Territory," *Indiana Magazine of History*, v. 31, 1935.
Monaghan, Jay. *Civil War of the Western Border, 1854-65*. University of Nebraska Press, 1955 edition.
Gates, Stephen B. *To Purge This Land With Blood*. Harper and Row, Publishers, 1970.
Warch, Richard and Jonathan Fanton, editors. *John Brown*. Prentice-Hall, Inc., 1973.

Chapter 4 -- A Name and a Brother

Adams, Alexander B. *Sitting Bull an Epic of the Plains*. G. P. Putnam's Sons, 1973.
Hill, Ruth Bebee. *Hanta Yo, An American Saga*. Doubleday and Co., Inc., 1979.
Mails, Thomas E. *The Mystic Warriors of the Plains*. Doubleday and Co., Inc., 1972.
Vestal, Stanley. *Sitting Bull, Champion of the Sioux*. University of Oklahoma Press, 1972 edition.

Chapter 5 -- The Girl with the Flag

Brashear, M. M. "Missouri Verse and Verse-Writers," *Missouri Historical Review*, v. 18, 1924.
Little, B. M. "A Century of Missouri Art," *Missouri Historical Review*, v. 16, n. 4, 1922.
-------------- "Lexington Church Records," *Missouri Historical Review*, v. 21, 1923.
McCausland, Susan Arnold. "The Battle of Lexington as Seen By a Woman," *Missouri Historical Review*, v. 6, n. 3, 1912.
Monaghan, Jay. *Civil War on the Western Border, 1864-65*. University of Nebraska Press, 1955 edition.
Synder, J. F. "The Capture of Lexington," *Missouri Historical Review*, v. 7, n. 1, 1912.
Wallace, John R. "Machpelah Cemetery," *Tombstone Inscriptions of Layfayette County, Missouri*. Marty Helen Brunetti, editor, v.3, 1977.
(no author) *History of Lafayette County, Missouri*. Missouri Historical Co. of St. Louis. 1881.
(no author) "Battle of Lexington" pamphlet. Division of Parks and Historic Preservation, Missouri Department of Natural Resources, n.d.

Chapter 6 -- To the Golden Hills

Adams, Alexander B. *Sitting Bull, an Epic of the Plains*. G. P. Putnam's Sons, 1973.
Kelly, Fanny. *Narrative of My Captivity Among the Sioux Indians*. Wilstach, Baldwin and Co. Printers, 1871.
Vestal, Stanley. *Sitting Bull, Champion of the Sioux*. University of Oklahoma Press, 1972 edition.

Chapter 7 -- Winter of the White Woman

Adams, Alexander B. *Sitting Bull, an Epic of the Plains*. G. P. Putnam's Sons, 1973.
Barsness, John and William Dickinson. "The Sully Campaign of 1864," *Montana Magazine*, v. 16, n. 3, 1966.
Judd, A. N. *Campaigning Against the Sioux*. Sol Lewis, 1973 edition.
Larned, William L. "Diary," *North Dakota History*, v.36, 1969.
Kelly, Fanny. *Narrative of My Captivity Among the Sioux Indians*. Wilstach, Baldwin and Co. Printers, 1871.
Pfaller, Louis. "Sully's Expedition of 1864," *North Dakota History*, v. 31, n. 1, 1964.
Robinson, Doane. "The Rescue of Frances Kelly," *South Dakota Historical Society Collections*, v. 4, 1908.
Sully, Langdon. *No Tears for the General*. American West Publishing Co., 1974.
Vestal, Stanley. *Sitting Bull, Champion of the Sioux*. University of Oklahoma Press, 1972 edition.
(no author) "Expeditions of Captain Jas. L. Fisk to the Gold Mines of Idaho and Montana, 1864-66," *North Dakota Historical Society Collections*, v. 2, 1908.

Chapter 8 -- Deprived of Glory

Geary, Daniel. "War Incidents at Kansas City," *Kansas State Historical Society Collections*, v. 11, 1909-10.
Hamilton, Chad. "A Colonel of Kansas," *Kansas State Historical Society Collections*, v. 12, 1911-12.
Jenkins, Paul B. *The Battle of Westport*. Franklin Hudson Publishing Co., 1906.
Lee, Fred J. *The Battle of Westport*. Westport Historical Society, 1982.
Monaghan, Jay. *Civil War on the Western Border, 1854-1865*. University of Nebraska Press, 1955 edition.
Monnett, Howard. *Action Before Westport*. Lowell Press, 1864.
Palmer, Henry E. "The Black-flag Character of War on the Border," *Kansas State Historical Society Transactions*, v. 9, 1906.

----------------"Company A, 11th Kansas Regiment, in the Price Raid," *Kansas State Historical Society Transactions*, v. 9, 1906.

----------------"The Lawrence Raid," *Kansas State Historical Society Collections*, v. 6, 1900.

Suderow, Bryce. "The Battle of Westport as Seen by an Federal Infantryman," *Westport Historical Quarterly*. Westport Historical Society, v. 10, n. 1, 1974.

(no author) "Henry E. Palmer," *Kansas State Historical Society Biennial Report*, v. 18, 1910-12.

Chapter 9 -- Up the Rainwater Creek

Athearn, Robert G. *Forts of the Upper Missouri*. University of Nebraska Press, 1972 edition.

Hanson, Joseph Mills. *The Conquest of the Missouri*. Murray Hill Books, Inc. 1946 edition.

Lass, William. *Steamboating on the Upper Missouri*. University of Nebraska Press, 1962.

Overholser, Joel F. *Fort Benton, World's Innermost Port!* River Press Publishing Co. Special edition, 1980.

Swift, James V. "Steamboating and Transshipment on the Missouri River," *Gone West!*. Jefferson National Expansion Historical Association, v. 1, n. 4, 1983.

Chapter 10 -- A Humble Niche

Athearn, Robert C. *In Search of Canaan*. The Regents Press of Kansas, 1978.

Bullock, Henry Allen, *A History of Negro Education in the South from 1619 to the Present*. Harvard University Press, 1967.

Christensen, Lawrence O. "J. Milton Turner: An Appraisal," *Missouri Historical Review*, v. 70, 1975.

Dictionary of American Negro Biography, W.W. Norton & Co., 1982.

Dillard, Irving. "James Milton Turner", *Dictionary of American Biography*. Charles Scribner's Son, 1964.

Dillard, Irving. "James Milton Turner: a Little Known Benefactor of His People," *Journal of Negro History*, v. 19, 1934.

Dillard, Irving. "Dred Scott Eulogized," *Journal of Negro History*, v. 26, 1941.

Moore, Webster N. "James Milton Turner, Diplomat, Educator and Defender of Rights," *Missouri Historical Society Bulletin*, v. 27, 1971.

Painter, Nell Irvin. *Exodusters*. University of Kansas Press, 1976.

Parker, T.A. *Report of the Superintendent of Public Schools of the State of Missouri to the General Assembly*, 1867, 1868, 1869 and 1870.

Parrish, William E. *A History of Missouri*, v. 3, 1860-75, University of Missouri Press, 1973.

(no author) Report of the Superintendent of Public Schools, 1871-72.

Newspapers: *Jefferson City Weekly Tribune*, April 13, 1870. *St. Louis Argus*, Nov. 5, Nov. 12, 1915. *St. Louis Post Dispatch*, July 9, 1911.

Chapter 11 -- On the Little Prickly Pear

Chapman, Berlin B. *The Otoes and Missourias, A Study of Indian Removal and the Legal Aftermath*. Times Journal Publishing Co., 1965.

Clárke, Helen P. Papers, 1872 - 1934. Montana Historical Society Archives, SC 1153.

---------------- "Sketch of Malcolm Clarke," *Montana Historical Society Contributions*, v. 2, 1896; v. 7, 1910.

Newspapers: *Montana Newspaper Association Inserts*, March 23, 1923 and Dec. 11, 1939.

Chapter 12 -- Goodbird's Mother

Gilman, Carolyn and Mary Jane Schneider. *The Way to Independence*. Minnesota Historical Society Press, 1987.

Wilson, Gilbert L. *Agriculture of the Hidatsa Indians, an Indian Interpretation.* University of Minnesota Bulletin, 1917.
-------------------- Gilbert L. Wilson Papers, v. 10 - 17, 1911-1915. Minnesota Historical Society.
-------------------- *Waheenee, An Indian Girl's Story told by Herself.* University of Nebraska Press, 1981.

Chapter 13 -- Die Auswanderer

Gering, John J. *After Fifty Years.* Pine Hill Printery, 1924.
Hofer, Arnold M., chr. *History of the Hutterite Mennonites.* Pine Hill Press, 1974.
Hostetler, John A. *Hutterite Society.* Johns Hopkins University Press, 1974.
Mendel, J. J. *History of the People of East Freeman, Silver Lake and West Freeman.* Freeman Courier, 1961.
Schmidt, John F., "The Immigrants and the Railroads," *Mennonite Life,* v. 29, n. 1 & 2, 1974.
Smith, C. Henry. *The Coming of the Russian Mennonites.* Mennonite Book Concern, 1927.
Stuckey, Harley J. *A Century of Russian Mennonite History in America.* Mennonite Press, Inc., 1973.
Unruh, John David, *The Mennonites in South Dakota.* Thesis, 1933.
Waltner, Emil J. *Banished for Faith.* Pine Hill Press, 1968.
Personal Interviews: Paul G. Tschetter, grandson of Paul J. Tschetter, provided written and oral information to the author on several occasions in 1987.

Chapter 14 -- A Sad and Terrible Blunder

Deatherage, C.P. *Steamboating on the Missouri River in the Sixties,* Ye Galleon Press, 1971.
Hanson, Joseph Mills. *The Conquest of the Missouri.* Murray Hill Books, Inc., 1946 edition.
Lass, William E. *Steamboating on the Upper Missouri.* University of Nebraska Press, 1962.
Marquis, Thomas B. *Custer on the Little Bighorn.* Dr. Marquis Custer Publishers, 1967.
Newspapers: *Bismarck Tribune,* August 12, 1874.

Chapter 15 -- The Whence, the Why and the Whither

Lanham, Url. *The Bone Hunters.* Columbia University Press, 1973.
Osborn, Henry F. *Cope: Master Naturalist.* Princeton University Press, 1931.
Plate, Robert. *The Dinosaur Hunters.* David McKay Co., 1964.
Sternberg, Charles H. *Life of a Fossil Hunter.* Jensen Printing Co., 1931.

Chapter 16 -- The Great Spirit Looks Some Other Way

Brown, Mark H. *The Flight of the Nez Perce.* G. P. Putnam's sons, 1967.
Chalmers, Harvey. *The Last Stand of the Nez Perce.* Twayne Publishers, 1962.
Howard, Helen Addison. *Saga of Chief Joseph.* University of Nebraska Press, 1978 edition.
Joseph. *Chief Joseph's Own Story.* Ye Galleon Press, 1984.
Josephy, Alvin M., Jr. *The Nez Perce Indians and the Opening of the Northwest.* Yale University Press, 1965.
---------------------- "The People of the Plateau," *Nez Perce Country.* National Park Service Division of Publications, 1983.
McWhorter, L. V. *Hear Me, My Chiefs!* Caxton Printers, Ltd., 1952.
---------------- *Yellow Wolf: His Own Story.* Caxton Printers, Inc., 1948.
Mueller, Oscar O. "Nez Perce at Cow Island," *Montana Magazine.* Montana Historical Society, v. 14, 1964.
Romeyn, Henry. "The Capture of Chief Joseph and the Nez Perce Indians," *Contributions.* Montana Historical Society, v. 2, 1896.

Chapter 17 -- Even an Indian

DiFrance, Charles O. "Some Recollections of Thomas H. Tibbles", *Nebraska History*, v. 13, n. 4, 1932.
Fletcher, Alice C. and Francis La Flesche. *The Omaha Tribe*. University of Nebraska Press, 1972 edition.
Green, Norma. *Iron Eyes' Family*. Nebraska State Historical Society Foundation, 1969.
Green, Norma Kidd. "Four Sisters: Daughters of Joseph La Flesche", *Nebraska History*. v. 45, n. 2, 1964.
Griffen, Fannie Reed. *Oo-ma-ha Ta-wa-tha*. published by author, 1898.
Harsha, William. *Ploughed Under*. Fords, Howard and Hulbert, 1881.
King, James T. "A Better Way: General George Crook and the Ponca Indians," *Nebraska History*, v. 50, n. 3, 1969.
Lake, James H., Sr. "Standing Bear! Who?" *Nebraska Law Review*. v. 60, n. 3, 1981.
Sheldon, Addison. *Nebraska: The Land and the People*. Lewis Publishing Co., v. 1, 1931.
Tibbles, Thomas Henry. *The Ponca Chiefs*. University of Nebraska Press, 1972.
Wilson, Dorothy Clarke. *Bright Eyes*. McGraw-Hill Book Co., 1974.
Newspapers: *Omaha Daily Herald*: May 3, 4, 6, 7, 13, 1879.

Chapter 18 -- Beyond the Stone Heaps

Adams, Alexander B. *Sitting Bull, an Epic of the Plains*. G. P. Putnam's Sons, 1973.
Finerty, John F. *War-Path and Bivouac*. Donohue Bros., 1890 edition: Lakeside Press, 1955 edition: University of Oklahoma Press, 1961 edition.
Miles, Nelson A. *Personal Recollections and Observations of General Nelson A. Miles*. Werner Co., 1896.
Pohanka, Brian C. *Nelson A. Miles, A Documentary Biography of His Military Career*. Arthur H. Clark Co., 1985.
Vestal, Stanley. *Sitting Bull, Champion of the Sioux*. University of Oklahoma Press, 1962 edition.

Chapter 19 -- Abode of Iron

Brooks, Chester L. and Ray H. Mattison. *Theodore Roosevelt and the Dakota Badlands*. National Park Service, 1983.
Cutright, Paul Russell, *Theodore Roosevelt, the Naturalist*. Harper & Bros., 1956.
Grantham, Dewey W. *Theodore Roosevelt*. Prentice-Hall, Inc., 1971.
Roosevelt, Theodore. *Ranch Life in the Far West*. Outbooks, 1981 edition.
------------------ *An Autobiography*. MacMillan Co., 1913.
------------------ *Ranch Life and the Hunting Trail*. Winchester Press, 1969 edition.
Harbaugh, William H. *The Life and Times of Theodore Roosevelt*. Oxford University Press, 1975 edition.
Hagedorn, Hermann. *Roosevelt in the Badlands*. Houghton Mifflin Co., 1921.
Putnam, Carleton. *Theodore Roosevelt, the Formative Years*. Charles Scribner's Sons, 1958.

Chapter 20 -- A Conqueror with a Coupling Pin

Briggs, Harold E. "The Great Dakota Boom, 1879 to 1886," *North Dakota Historical Quarterly*, v. 4, n. 2, 1930.
Hickcox, David H. "The Impact of the Great Northern Railroad on Settlement in Northern Montana, 1880-1920," *Railroad History*, Bulletin 48, 1983.
Jensen, Oliver. *The American Heritage History of Railroads in America*. Bonanza Books, 1981.
--------------- *Railroads in America*. American Heritage Publishing Co., Inc., 1975.
Holbrook, Stewart H. *James J. Hill, A Great Life in Brief*. Alfred A. Knopf, 1955.
--------------- *The Story of American Railroads*. American Legacy Press, 1981.
Martin, Albro. *James J. Hill and the Opening of the Northwest*. Oxford University Press, 1976.
O'Connor, Richard. *Iron Wheels and Broken Men*. G. P. Putnam's Sons, 1973.

Pyle, Joseph. *The Life of James J. Hill.* Peter Smith, 1936.
Rinehardt, Richard. *Workin' on the Railroad.* American West Publishing Co., 1970.
Sweetman, Luke D. "Laying the Iron Trail in the Northwest," *The Frontier*, v. 9, n. 4, 1929.
Wood, Charles R. *Lines West.* Superior Publishing Co., 1967.
Wood, Charles and Dorothy. *The Great Northern Railway.* Pacific Fast Mail, 1979.

Chapter 21 -- Chasing Crane's Story

Brown, Dee. *Bury My Heart at Wounded Knee.* Holt, Rinehart and Winston, 1970.
Eastman, Elaine Goodale. "All the Days of My Life", *South Dakota Historical Review*, v. 2, n. 4, 1937.
------------------------ "The Ghost Dance War and Wounded Knee Massacre," *Nebraska History*, v. 26, 1945.
------------------------ *Sister to the Sioux, the Memoirs of Elaine Goodale Eastman, 1885-91.* University of Nebraska Press, 1978.
Morgan, Thisba Huston. "Reminiscences of My Days in the Land of the Ogalalla," *South Dakota Historical Collections*, v. 29, 1958.
Smith, Rex Alan. *Moon of the Popping Trees.* University of Nebraska Press, 1975.
Wilson, Dorothy Clarke. *Bright Eyes.* McGraw Hill Book Co., 1974.

Chapter 22 Traveling the New Way

Gilman, Carolyn and Mary Jane Schneider. *The Way to Independence.* Minnesota Historical Society Press, 1987.
Goodbird, Edward. *Goodbird the Indian; His Story.* Minnesota Historical Society Press, 1985.
Wilson, Gilbert L. Gilbert L. Wilson papers, v. 10 - 17, 1911-15. Minnesota Historical Society.

Index

- A -

Alder Gulch, 43, 44, 68
American Fur Co., 4, 17, 68, 79
Anderson House, 40-41
Arapaho Indians, 7, 100
Arikara Indians, 5, 6, 7, 79, 104, 107, 157, 175, 176
Arkansas River, 63
Assiniboin Indians, 6, 7, 15, 16, 17, 32, 34, 140, 141, 143, 144

- B -

Bad River, 56
Bancroft, Nebraska, 136
Bannock Indians, 141, 144
Battle of Big Hole, 120-121
Battle of Black Jack, 26
Battle Camus Meadow, 120, 121
Battle of Canyon Creek, 121
Battle of Killdeer Mountain, 52-54
Battle of Lexington, 40-42
Battle of Mine Creek, 63
Battle of Pea Ridge, 42
Battle of Shiloh, 73-74
Battle of Slim Buttes, 117, 141
Battle of Westport, 61-64
Battle of Wilson's Creek, 39
Battle of Wounded Knee, 172-74
Bear Paw Mountains, 16, 112, 122, 123, 161
Beaver Creek, 141, 142
Bellevue, Nebraska, 4, 9
Belt Mountains, 17, 112
Benton, Sen. Thomas Hart, 17, 152
Big Blue River, 61, 62, 63
Big Foot, 169, 172-173
Big Horn Mountains, 77, 117
Big Muddy Creek, 16, 161
Big Sioux River, 84
Bighorn River, 100, 103, 107, 108
Billings, Montana, 121
Bismarck, North Dakota, 92, 102, 107, 146, 158
Bitteroot Mountains, 17, 119, 120
Black Bear, 80, 81, 82
Black Hills, 100, 109
Blackfoot Indians, 6, 7, 12, 15, 16, 17, 18, 77, 79, 87
Blood Indians, 16, 18
Blunt, Gen. James G., 59
Boonville, Missouri, 75
Box Elder Creek, North Dakota, 150
Box Elder Creek, Wyoming, 45
Bozeman, Montana, 102
Bozeman Trail, 43, 45, 49, 66
Bright Eyes (see Susette LaFlesche)
Brown, Ellen, 20, 21, 22, 25, 26, 27
Brown, Frederick, 20, 22, 23, 24, 25, 27
Brown, Jason, 20-28
Brown, John, Jr., 20-28
Brown, John, Sr., 21, 28, 37, 59, 60
Brown, Oliver, 22, 23, 24, 25, 28
Brown, Owen, 20, 22, 23, 24, 25, 26, 28
Brown, Salmon, 20, 22, 23, 24, 25, 26, 27
Brown, Wealthy, 20, 21, 25, 26, 27
Brush Creek, 62, 63
Bull Head, South Dakota, 56
Burnt District, 60
Butte, Montana, 160

- C -

Camp Jackson, 37, 38, 73
Canadian Pacific Railroad, 159, 160
Cannonball River, 47, 51
Cascade Range, 12, 162
Casper, Wyoming, 45
Chalk Buttes, 30, 32
Chamberlain, South Dakota, 166
Chasing Crane, 166-167, 169
Cherokee Indians, 76
Cheyenne Indians, 7, 83, 100, 117, 123, 124, 126, 138, 140, 141, 143, 144
Cheyenne River, 164, 169, 172
Chicago, Milwaukee and St. Paul Railway, 96
Chimney Butte, 149, 151
Chivington, Col. John M., 65
Cholera, 3, 4, 5, 20, 44, 57
Chouteau, Auguste, 2
Chouteau, Pierre, 2, 5
Chouteau, Pierre, Jr., 7
Citadel Rock, 17
Clark, William, 68
Clarke, Helen, 79-83
Clarke, Horace, 80-83
Clarke, Malcolm, 79, 83
Clarke, Nathan, 80, 83
Clearwater River, 120
Cody, William F., 164
Columbia River, 12, 18
Columbus, Nebraska, 95, 129, 131
Cope, Annie, 111, 112
Cope, Edward Drinker, 110-116, 117
Cothcocoma, 79, 80, 81, 82
Council Bluffs, Iowa, 4, 95
Cow Island, 113, 114, 115, 122, 182
Crazy Horse, 101, 138
Cree Indians, 6, 17, 18
Crook, Gen. George, 100, 101, 109, 111, 131, 132, 139
Crow Indians, 6, 7, 17, 30, 31, 32, 53, 105, 112, 119, 122, 140, 141, 144, 166
Crowfoot, 169, 172
Culbertson, Alexander, 12, 16, 17, 18
Curly, 105, 109
Curtis, Maj. Gen. Samuel, 61, 62, 63
Custer, Boston, 103, 105, 108
Custer, Col. George 100, 102-108, 111, 139
Custer, Libby, 102, 107-108
Custer, Tom, 103, 105, 108

- D -

Dakota Territory, 14, 50, 84, 92, 100, 132, 147, 156, 157, 159, 164
Dariusleut, 99
Dawes, Sen. Henry L., 136
Dearborn River, 18
Denig, Edwin, 6, 7
DeSmet, Father Pierre, 4, 15, 77
Devil's Lake, 156, 157, 159
Dickinson, North Dakota, 146, 154, 156
Dog Creek, 112, 113, 114, 122
Douglas, Sen. Stephen A., 19
Doyle, James, 21, 23, 26
Dundy, Judge Elmer, 132, 133, 134, 135

- E -

Eastman, Charles, 172-174
Elkhorn Ranch, 148, 149, 150, 151, 152, 156
Ellsworth, Kansas, 57
Ewing, Thomas, 60

- F -

Fargo, North Dakota, 95
Fighting Butte, 30
Finerty, John F., 139-145, 146
Finnegan, Mike "Red", 152-154
Fisk, Capt. James L., 55, 57
Five Villages, 86, 88
Flathead Indians, 16, 18, 119
Fort Abraham Lincoln, 102, 103, 107, 115
Fort Assiniboine, 161
Fort Benton, 16, 17, 18, 43, 66, 67-68, 77, 79, 80, 83, 110, 111, 114, 160, 161, 162
Fort Berthold, 5, 6, 9, 86, 157
Fort Buford, 69, 88, 102, 104, 107, 115, 146
Fort Clark, 5
Fort Ellis, 102, 105
Fort Kearny, 63
Fort Laramie, 2, 7, 43, 44, 49
Fort Leavenworth, 22, 39, 58, 60, 127
Fort Lewis, 17
Fort Peck, 115, 139, 140
Fort Pierre, 5
Fort Randall, 50, 66, 146
Fort Rice, 51, 66, 69, 77
Fort Riley, 63
Fort Scott, 60
Fort Snelling, 79
Fort Stevenson, 86, 107
Fort Sully, 50, 56, 57, 69

Fort Sumter, 37
Fort Union, 6, 7, 8, 12, 13, 15, 16, 17, 43, 66, 68, 69, 161
Fox Indians, 3
Franklin, Missouri, 68
Freedmen's Bureau, 74
Frenchman's Creek, 139
Fugitive Slave Law, 73

- G -

Gallatin River, 43
Geneva, Kansas, 44
Ghost Dance, 169-171
Gibbon, Col. John, 101, 102, 103, 104, 105, 107
Glacier National Park, 83, 162
Glenrock, Wyoming, 45
Goodale, Elaine, 166-174
Goodbird, Edward, 89, 90, 91, 175, 176-181, 182
Grand Forks, North Dakota, 95, 159
Grand River, 56, 117, 164, 169
Grant, Pres. Ulysses S., 95, 96, 97
Grasshopper Creek, 43
Gratz Bluff, 38
Great Falls, Montana, 160, 162
Great Northern Railway, 162-163
Gros Ventre Indians, 16, 18

- H -

Hampton Normal & Agricultural Institute, 166, 167
Harper's Ferry, Virginia, 28
Heart River, 47
Hebron, North Dakota, 180
Helena, Montana, 79, 83, 111, 157, 158, 160, 162, 163
Hidatsa Indians, 5, 6, 7, 85-91, 92, 175-181
Hill, James J., 157-163, 164
Hill, Mary, 159
Horsehoe Station, 45
Howard, Gen. O. O., 120, 121, 124, 126
Hutchinson County, South Dakota, 98
Hutterite religion, 93

- I -

Idaho Territory, 44
Independence, Missouri, 60, 61, 62, 68
Independence, North Dakota, 176, 180, 181, 182
Indian Territory, 3, 76, 83, 127, 128, 129, 130, 131, 133, 134, 135, 136
Inkpaduta, 50, 52
Iowa Indians, 3
Isaac, J. C., 110, 112, 113, 114

- J -

Jackson, Gen. Claibourne, 38
Jackson, Helen Hunt, 135

James River, 14, 96
Jefferson City, Missouri, 2, 38, 75
Joseph, Chief, 119-127, 128, 164, 182
Judith Badlands, 112-116
Judith River, 18, 67, 79, 110, 111, 112
Jumping Bull (brother of Sitting Bull), 52, 53, 54, 143, 172
Jumping Bull (father of Sitting Bull), 31, 34, 52, 56

- K -

Kanesville, Iowa (see Council Bluffs)
Kansas City, Missouri, 20, 58, 61, 62, 72, 75
Kansas River, 20, 21
Kansas Territory, 20, 21
Kansas-Nebraska Bill, 19
Kellogg, Mark, 103, 104, 105, 107
Kelly, Fanny, 44-49, 50, 51, 54-55, 56-57, 65
Kelly, Josiah, 44-47, 54, 57
Kickapoo Indians, 3
Killdeer Mountains, 49, 52, 153, 154
Knife River, 5, 86, 88
Kurz, Rudolph Friedrich 2-9, 10

- L -

LaClede, Pierre, 2
LaFlesche, Frank, 135-136
LaFlesche, Joseph, 4, 129, 130, 132
LaFlesche, Susette, 129-136, 172, 173
Lane, James Henry, 22, 60
Last Chance Gulch, 68
Lawrence, Kansas, 21, 22, 23, 24, 27, 60
Lean Elk, 121, 123, 124
Lecompton, Kansas, 26, 27
Lehrerleut, 99
Lewis and Clark Expedition, 15, 79, 160
Lexington, Missouri, 38-42, 58, 59-60
Lightning Lake, 13
Like-a-Fishhook Village, 85, 87, 90, 91, 175, 176, 178, 179, 182
Lincoln, Pres. Abraham, 18, 19, 37
Lincoln Institute, 75
Lisa, Manuel, 4
Little Bighorn River, 101, 103, 104, 108, 109, 117, 138, 141
Little Blue River, 60, 61, 63
Little Missouri River, 52, 53, 54, 55, 146, 147-148, 149, 150, 151-153, 154, 156, 179, 180
Little Missouri, South Dakota, 148, 156
Little Missouri Stockmen's Association, 149
Little Rocky Mountains, 122
Looking Glass, 119, 120, 121, 123, 124, 126

- M -

Maltese Cross Ranch, 148
Mandan Indians, 5, 85, 157, 175, 176
Marais des Cygnes River, 23

Marias River, 160, 162
Marmarth, North Dakota, 55
Marsh, Capt. Grant, 66-70, 71, 102-108, 182
Marsh, Othniel Charles, 111, 114, 116
McCausland, Susan Arnold, 38-42
McCausland, William, 38, 39, 42
McKinley, Pres. William, 154
McLean County, North Dakota, 85
Medicine Rocks, 30
Medora, South Dakota, 147, 148, 149, 152, 156
Miles, Gen. Nelson A., 115, 117, 124-125, 127, 139, 140, 141, 142, 143, 144
Milk River, 16, 17, 66, 117, 139, 140-142, 144, 160, 161, 163
Minneapolis, Minnesota, 159
Minot, North Dakota, 157, 160, 161, 164
Mississippi River, 2, 37, 66, 74
Missouri Compromise, 19
Missouri Equal Rights League, 74
Missouri Historical Society, 76
Missouri River, 19, 34, 43, 44, 50, 58, 62, 66, 86, 88, 90-91, 95, 101, 107, 109, 112, 113, 114, 115, 116, 122, 129, 139, 151, 152, 156, 160, 161, 168, 176, 177, 182-183
  Character: Introduction, 2, 19
  Steamboating: 66-70
Montana Central Railway, 160, 162
Montana Territory, 66, 109, 117, 146, 157, 162
Moreau River, 32
deMores, Marquis, 148
Mulligan, Col. James A. 39, 42
Mushroom Creek, 142, 144
Musselshell River, 67, 122

- N -

Nauvoo, Illinois, 4
Nebraska City, Nebraska, 27
Netuscheo, 80, 82
Neu Hutterthal, Russia, 93, 96, 97, 99
New England Emigrant Aid Society, 21
Nez Perce Indians, 18, 118, 119-127, 130, 140, 182
Niobrara River, 5, 83, 129, 130, 136, 167-168
North Middle Creek, 20, 21, 25
Northern Pacific Railway, 18, 94, 102, 146, 148, 158, 160, 162, 163

- O -

Oberlin College, 73
Ollokot, 120, 121, 124, 126, 127
Olympia, Washington, 18
Omaha Indians, 4, 129-131, 135-136
Omaha, Nebraska, 4, 63, 66, 131, 136, 148
Osawatomie, Kansas, 22, 23, 24, 25, 26, 27
Oto Indians, 3, 83
Ottawa Creek, 24

- P -

Palmer, Capt. Henry E., 59-64, 65
Pawnee Indians, 4, 83
Pend d'Oreille Indians, 18
Piegan Indians, 16, 17, 18, 77, 79-83, 84
Pierce, Pres. Franklin, 22
Pilot Knob, 58
Pine Ridge Indian Reservation, 169-174
Platte River, 4, 32, 45, 77, 167
Platte River Road, 43, 44
Plattsmouth, Nebraska, 63
Pleasanton, Gen. Alfred, 63
Ponca Indians, 83, 129-137
Poplar River, 16
Poppleton, Andrew J., 132, 133
Porcupine Creek, 31
Potawatomi Indians, 3
Potomac River, 28
Pottawatomie Creek, 21, 23, 24, 25, 26
Pottawatomie Rifles, 23-25
Powder River, 30, 100, 102
Prairie Flower, 130, 131
Prairieleut, 99
Price, Gen. Sterling, 38, 39, 42, 58, 59, 63, 73
Prickly Pear Canyon, 79, 83, 160
Puget Sound, 11, 12, 18, 162

- Q -

Quantrill, Charles, 60, 61

- R -

Raines, Gen. James E., 41
Rankin, Capt. W. G., 69
Red Blossom, 85, 88
Red Cloud, 100
Red River, 14, 95, 96, 156, 158, 159
Reed, Autie, 103, 104, 105, 108
Reno, Maj. Marcus, 103, 106, 107, 117
Reynolds, Charlie, 103, 104, 106, 108
Robidoux, Joseph, 3
Rocky Mountains, 11, 12, 19, 44, 83, 158, 160, 162
Roosevelt, Alice, 147
Roosevelt, Theodore, 147-155, 156, 163, 182
Rosebud River, 100, 101, 103, 104, 138, 140, 141
Royer, Daniel, 170
Rushville, Nebraska 171, 172, 173

- S -

St. Anthony's Falls, 159
St. Charles, Missouri, 2
St. Joseph, Missouri, 3, 4, 7, 8, 68
St. Louis, Missouri, 2, 3, 7, 9, 20, 37, 66, 67, 68, 70, 72, 73, 74, 75, 76
St. Paul and Pacific Railroad, 158
St. Paul, Minneapolis and Manitoba Railway, 157-162, 164
St. Paul, Minnesota, 12, 94, 157, 158, 159, 160, 162
Salt Lake City, Utah, 43, 44
Santa Fe Trail, 2, 24
Scarlet Woman, 33, 34
Schmiedeleut, 99
Scott, Dred, 73, 76
Scott's Bluff, 45
Shawnee Mission, Kansas, 21, 62
Shelby, Jo, 60, 64
Shell Creek, 87
Sheridan, Gen. Phillip, 58
Sherman, Henry, 21, 23
Sherman, William, 21, 26
Sherman, Gen. William Tecumseh, 58
Sheyenne River, 13, 14
Shoshoni Indians, 7, 18, 119, 140
Silver Lake, 99
Sioux Indians, 7, 13, 14, 15, 83, 86, 87, 92, 100, 104, 105, 106, 110, 111, 115, 116, 117, 125, 126, 129, 130, 138, 139, 140, 141, 142, 143, 153, 164-165, 166-174, 179
  Blackfoot Sioux, 52, 56, 100
  Brule Sioux, 32, 100, 166-168
  Hunkpapa Sioux, 30-35, 50, 51-54, 55, 65, 77, 83, 100, 117, 140, 142-44, 146
  Miniconjou Sioux, 52, 100, 143, 169, 172
  Oglala Sioux, 32, 45-49, 100, 117, 143
  Sans Arc Sioux, 52, 53, 100, 143
  Santee Sioux, 45, 50, 136, 172
  Two Kettle Sioux, 100
  Yanktonai Sioux, 52
Sitting Bull, 30-35, 50, 52-54, 55, 57, 58, 65, 69, 77, 100, 101, 111, 113, 115, 117, 125, 138, 139, 140, 141, 142, 143, 144, 146, 164, 169, 172
Small Ankle, 85-91, 175, 176, 177, 178, 180, 181
Snake River, 119, 120
Sni River, 59
Son of a Star, 85-90, 175, 177, 180, 181
Souris River, 14, 16
Spotted Tail, 100
Standing Bear, 129-137
Standing Rock Indian Reservation, 146, 164, 169, 181
Stanley, John Mix, 12, 16
Steamboat *Far West*, 102-108, 109
Steamboat *Josephine*, 115, 139
Steamboat *Louelle*, 66-70
Steamboat *Marion*, 68, 69
Steamboat *White Cloud*, 38, 39
Sternberg, Charles H., 110, 112, 113, 114, 115
Stevens, Isaac I., 11-18, 19, 29, 50, 77, 160, 162
Stevens, John F., 162
Strikes-Many Woman, 85, 88
Sully, Gen. Alfred, 50, 51, 66
Sumner, Sen. Charles, 24
Sun River, 18

- T -

Taylor, Muggins, 105
Terry, Gen. Alfred, 101, 102, 103, 104, 106, 108, 109
Teton River, 18
Thompson, Henry, 22, 23, 24, 25, 26, 27
Three Forks, Montana, 43, 44, 68
Tibbles, Thomas H., 131-132, 135-136, 192
Tileston, Laura, 166
Topeka, Kansas, 21, 22
Tschetter, Barbara, 97
Tschetter, Jacob, 96, 97
Tschetter, Joseph, 96, 97, 98
Tschetter, Lorenz, 93, 96, 98
Tschetter, Maria, 93, 95, 96, 97, 98, 99
Tschetter, Prediger Paul, 93-99
Tschetter, Susanne, 96, 97
Turner, Hannah, 72
Turner, James Milton, 72-76
Turner, John, 72
Turtle, 85, 86, 89

- U -

Underground Railroad, 20, 73, 74
Union Pacific Railroad, 95

- V -

Vigilance committees, 68, 148, 152
Virginia City, Montana, 44

- W -

Waheenee, 85-91, 175, 180-181, 182-183
Wakarusa River, 22, 23
Wakefield, Gardner, 44, 45, 46
Wallowa River, 119, 120, 127
Washington Territory, 11, 18
Waverly, Missouri, 20
Webster, John L., 132, 133
Weiner, Theodore, 24
Westport, Kansas, 60, 61, 62, 64
White Earth River, 69
White River, 164, 166
Whirling Hawk, 166-168
Wilkinson, Allen, 21, 23, 26
Williston, North Dakota, 161
Wilson, Gilbert L., 182
Winnipeg, Canada, 158
Winter Quarters, 4
Wolf Creek, 96
Wolf Point, 66, 161
Wood Mountains, 142

- Y -

Yankton, South Dakota, 96, 97, 98, 102, 114, 115
Yellowstone Park, 121
Yellowstone River, 6, 8, 15, 30, 31, 54, 55, 69, 83, 87, 100, 101, 102, 103, 104, 106, 107, 119, 158, 182
Young, Brigham, 4

Acknowledgments

Once again I find myself indebted to the dedicated librarians and reference specialists in libraries and historical societies around the country. My sincere gratitude goes to Laurel Boeckman of the Missouri State Historical Society, Betty Loudon of the Nebraska State Historical Society, Darrell D. Garwood of the Kansas Center for Historical Research, Peggy Smith of the Westport Historical Society, Dave Walter of the Montana Historical Society, Ruth Ellen Bauer of the Minnesota Historical Society, Rex Thrash of the Colorado Railroad Museum, and Ann B. Jenks, South Dakota State Historian. Teachers Gwendolyn H. Scott, Denver Public Schools, retired, and Helga Schmitz, Cherry Creek School District, were generous with their time and expertise.

I continue to mine the treasures of the Western History Department of the Denver Public Library, with the gracious assistance of Eleanor Gehres and her knowledgeable staff. Pat Johnson and the librarians at the Castlewood and Christensen branches of the Arapahoe Library District always cheerfully went that extra mile to find the references I needed. A special word of thanks to Paul G. Tschetter of Denver who was willing to open his home and library to me and share his family's records and memories of his grandfather, Prediger Paul. He provided me with insight I could have gained no other way.

A word on sources: all direct quotations in the text are quoted as they are found in a primary source. In the case of native Americans, one must acknowledge their words were necessarily filtered through the mind of an interpreter. Yet the persistent grace of their natural idiom -- whether the interpreter was a Harvard graduate or an illiterate trapper -- convinces me there is little misrepresentation. They were, after all, a people who relied solely on the oral tradition and who would naturally have drawn on their surroundings to give clarity and impact to their words.

ABOUT THE AUTHOR

NANCY MAYBORN PETERSON, currently of Littleton, Colorado, was raised along one of the major waterways of westward migration, the North Platte River in Scottsbluff, Nebraska. It was the Platte that served as the impetus for her first book, the very successful 1984 release ***PEOPLE OF THE MOONSHELL: A Western River Journal***.

Peterson's interest in the frontier era, particularly in the people who shaped the American West, has spawned numerous historical articles in regional publications. She has also published nature essays and light verse in the *Reader's Digest, Good Housekeeping,* and *The Wall Street Journal. Families, Catholic Digest,* and the magazine supplements of major daily newspapers have given voice to her humor pieces. Winner of numerous awards for both prose and poetry, she is past president of both the Denver Woman's Press Club and the Denver Branch of the National League of American Pen Women. She is also a member of the Western Writers of America and the Colorado Authors' League.

PEOPLE OF THE TROUBLED WATER (1988) is the first portion of Peterson's saga of the settlement of the Missouri River route, the years of discovery along the Missouri. The years of conflict, which followed as the concept of Manifest Destiny became reality, are covered in the second part of her Missouri River epic, ***PEOPLE OF THE OLD MISSURY***. As part of her research for these two books she has traveled the length of the Missouri on foot or by auto.

ABOUT THE ILLUSTRATOR

ASA BATTLES, also of Littleton, Colorado, specializes in the scratchboard art that graces the pages of ***PEOPLE OF THE OLD MISSURY*** and Peterson's 1988 book, ***PEOPLE OF THE TROUBLED WATER***. His American Indian (Choctaw) heritage and his extensive study of the Plains Indians culture brings incredibly authentic detail to his work. Battles' illustration and cover artwork for Peterson's earlier ***PEOPLE OF THE MOONSHELL*** brought high praise from a variety of critics. He previously illustrated ***Fodor's Guide to Indian America*** and ***Ritual of the Wind*** by Jamake Highwater, as well as several book articles for major publishers. He has exhibited at many shows throughout the western U.S. and received countless honors and awards.